Troubleshooting & Maintaining PCs

ALL-IN-ONE

4th Edition

by Dan Gookin

JUN - - 2021

for **dummies**®
A Wiley Brand

Troubleshooting & Maintaining PCs All-in-One For Dummies®, 4th Edition

Published by: **John Wiley & Sons, Inc.,** 111 River Street, Hoboken, NJ 07030-5774, www.wiley.com

Copyright © 2021 by John Wiley & Sons, Inc., Hoboken, New Jersey

Published simultaneously in Canada

No part of this publication may be reproduced, stored in a retrieval system or transmitted in any form or by any means, electronic, mechanical, photocopying, recording, scanning or otherwise, except as permitted under Sections 107 or 108 of the 1976 United States Copyright Act, without the prior written permission of the Publisher. Requests to the Publisher for permission should be addressed to the Permissions Department, John Wiley & Sons, Inc., 111 River Street, Hoboken, NJ 07030, (201) 748-6011, fax (201) 748-6008, or online at http://www.wiley.com/go/permissions.

Trademarks: Wiley, For Dummies, the Dummies Man logo, Dummies.com, Making Everything Easier, and related trade dress are trademarks or registered trademarks of John Wiley & Sons, Inc. and may not be used without written permission. All other trademarks are the property of their respective owners. John Wiley & Sons, Inc. is not associated with any product or vendor mentioned in this book.

LIMIT OF LIABILITY/DISCLAIMER OF WARRANTY: THE PUBLISHER AND THE AUTHOR MAKE NO REPRESENTATIONS OR WARRANTIES WITH RESPECT TO THE ACCURACY OR COMPLETENESS OF THE CONTENTS OF THIS WORK AND SPECIFICALLY DISCLAIM ALL WARRANTIES, INCLUDING WITHOUT LIMITATION WARRANTIES OF FITNESS FOR A PARTICULAR PURPOSE. NO WARRANTY MAY BE CREATED OR EXTENDED BY SALES OR PROMOTIONAL MATERIALS. THE ADVICE AND STRATEGIES CONTAINED HEREIN MAY NOT BE SUITABLE FOR EVERY SITUATION. THIS WORK IS SOLD WITH THE UNDERSTANDING THAT THE PUBLISHER IS NOT ENGAGED IN RENDERING LEGAL, ACCOUNTING, OR OTHER PROFESSIONAL SERVICES. IF PROFESSIONAL ASSISTANCE IS REQUIRED, THE SERVICES OF A COMPETENT PROFESSIONAL PERSON SHOULD BE SOUGHT. NEITHER THE PUBLISHER NOR THE AUTHOR SHALL BE LIABLE FOR DAMAGES ARISING HEREFROM. THE FACT THAT AN ORGANIZATION OR WEBSITE IS REFERRED TO IN THIS WORK AS A CITATION AND/OR A POTENTIAL SOURCE OF FURTHER INFORMATION DOES NOT MEAN THAT THE AUTHOR OR THE PUBLISHER ENDORSES THE INFORMATION THE ORGANIZATION OR WEBSITE MAY PROVIDE OR RECOMMENDATIONS IT MAY MAKE. FURTHER, READERS SHOULD BE AWARE THAT INTERNET WEBSITES LISTED IN THIS WORK MAY HAVE CHANGED OR DISAPPEARED BETWEEN WHEN THIS WORK WAS WRITTEN AND WHEN IT IS READ.

For general information on our other products and services, please contact our Customer Care Department within the U.S. at 877-762-2974, outside the U.S. at 317-572-3993, or fax 317-572-4002. For technical support, please visit https://hub.wiley.com/community/support/dummies.

Wiley publishes in a variety of print and electronic formats and by print-on-demand. Some material included with standard print versions of this book may not be included in e-books or in print-on-demand. If this book refers to media such as a CD or DVD that is not included in the version you purchased, you may download this material at http://booksupport.wiley.com. For more information about Wiley products, visit www.wiley.com.

Library of Congress Control Number: 2021930116

ISBN: 978-1-119-74030-8; 978-1-119-74031-5 (ebk); 978-1-119-74032-2 (ebk)

Manufactured in the United States of America

SKY10024569_012821

Contents at a Glance

Table of Contents

Introduction

If trouble were predictable, it wouldn't be a problem. That's because the problem with trouble is that it's unpredictable.

You hold in your hands a thrill-packed book that's all about solving computer problems. The topic is troubleshooting. It needs to be covered in so many pages here because a computer hasn't yet been invented that didn't have trouble following it like a shadow on a sunny day.

The computing experience should be a pleasant one. And it can be — if you're informed and able to deal with the troubles you encounter. This book helps you along that journey in an informative and entertaining way. Welcome to *Troubleshooting & Maintaining Your PC All-in-One For Dummies*.

About This Book

A byte of prevention is worth a gigabyte of cure.

This book's philosophy is that troubleshooting is easier to do when you understand how the computer works. This philosophy is the opposite of what most computer users expect, which is to look up a specific condition and find a specific cure for it. This approach has two glitches.

The first downfall with the look-it-up approach is that you don't learn anything. Because there's a method behind PC madness, often, the same solution can be applied to multiple problems. After you understand why things go wrong, it's not only easier to fix them — it's also possible to prevent them in the first place.

The second difficulty with the specific-solution approach is that it would make this book obnoxiously huge. With millions upon millions of potential hardware and software configurations available in all the PCs in the world, it would take several fat books to document every problem and its solution. Such a book would need to be delivered by forklift.

My approach is simple: Look up the problem, learn a bit about what might have caused it, and then arrive at a solution. The notion is that when trouble arises again later, you have the experience to deal with it in a practical manner. Because most PC troubles have a common origin, this solution works.

Before moving on, please be aware that there's a difference between trouble and an event that's merely annoying. For example, if the text you print from an email message is tiny, it's annoying, but it isn't a bug. Though specific annoying problems might not be covered in this book, you still can find a solution here. This is the beauty behind my philosophical approach to troubleshooting. After all, using Windows shouldn't be a frustrating experience.

How This Book Works

This book is composed of five *minibooks,* each of which addresses a computer troubleshooting topic. The minibooks are split into traditional chapters, all geared to a specific subject within the minibook topic. Then the chapters are split into sections consisting of paragraphs, words, letters, and — finally — tiny dots. So, if you understand tiny dots, you'll understand this book.

To run the special troubleshooting tools and utilities, you take advantage of the Windows Start menu. Tap the Windows key to pop up this menu, and then start typing the name of a tool or utility. The text explains what to type. You then choose the matching utility from the search results list. This method is much faster than hunting for tools on the Start menu's programs list.

Because this book approaches troubleshooting in a philosophical way, lots of material is cross-referenced. For example, startup issues are also related to disk disaster recovery. So, in both chapters, you'll find references to the other chapter's material.

This book covers all varieties of computers, from a traditional desktop to an all-in-one model, a laptop, a 2-in-1, or even a tablet. As long as the computer runs Windows 10, you're good.

Speaking of Windows 10, this book is specific to that operating system. When this book refers to "Windows," it means Windows 10.

Text that you type appears in **bold**. In the context of a step, where the text is normally bold anyway, the stuff you type appears in regular roman text.

Do not press the Enter key until you're directed to do so. And even then, I recommend that you review what you type before you press Enter, just to ensure that you get everything typed properly.

Do not press a period at the end of any text you type, unless I explain that the period is needed. Unlike sentences in English, computer commands don't end with a period.

Icons Used in This Book

TIP

I'd like to think that everything in this book is a tip, but for those special, worthy items, you'll find this icon lurking nearby.

WARNING

A reminder of something not to do, something to avoid, or something that can cause serious trouble is flagged by the Hazard icon.

REMEMBER

This icon flags text that is important enough to remember or that reminds you of something you may have forgotten that bears repeating.

TECHNICAL STUFF

When the urge to blurt out something nerdy overwhelms me, I succumb and use this icon to supply a warning sign. You're free not to read any technical text near this icon.

Beyond the Book

The publisher maintains a support page with updates or changes that have occurred since this book went to press. You'll also find bonus content, in the form of an online Cheat Sheet, which isn't really cheating and isn't a sheet.

To peruse the online content, visit `www.dummies.com` and search for *Troubleshooting & Maintaining Your PC All-in-One For Dummies* — the whole thing! Click the matching search result to view specific information about this book.

You can also visit my own web page for more information or as a diversion, `wambooli.com` — with specific information about this book found at `wambooli.com/help/troubleshooting`.

I provide frequent updates and posts on that page, offering bonus information, supplements to this book, tips, tricks, trivia, and fun. And there's only one little advertisement on the page and no pop-ups.

Where to Go from Here

Feel free to start reading this book in any minibook, chapter, or section. Everything is self-contained, so there isn't really a reason to read one section before another. For those rare times when it helps to know information located elsewhere in the book, I provide a cross-reference. But it's not necessary to read the book from front to back.

My email address is dgookin@wambooli.com. Yes, this is my real address. I reply to all email I receive, and you'll get a quick reply if you keep your question short and specific to this book. Although I enjoy saying "Hi," I cannot answer technical support questions or help you troubleshoot your computer. Thanks for understanding.

Please enjoy my book, and thank you for reading the Introduction.

Dan Gookin

1

Solve My Problem Now!

Contents at a Glance

Chapter **1**

Trouble Comes Hither

t's sudden, unexpected, and unwelcome. It's PC trouble, and it sneaks up like the dawn. Unlike the sun, however, technology issues hardly warm up your day with welcome sunshine. No, the dread-and-foreboding that comes with computer woe is a splash of cold water, a pebble in your shoe, and a long-term visit from an unwelcome guest all rolled into one.

You can't avoid computer woe, but you can prepare for its eventual arrival. You can also become familiar with the core cause of digital distress. The more you know about why things go wrong, the better you can prepare yourself for the inevitable.

The Root of All PC Trouble

The cause of nearly all PC trouble is rooted in one thing: change.

Computers foul up because something has changed. It could be something you did, such as modify a setting, uncover a software bug, run a malicious program, or experience any of several items that all qualify as "change." Even time itself is an agent of change, in that PC hardware gets old, eventually wears out, and fails.

The goal isn't to avoid change, but rather to be aware of its consequences. The process of troubleshooting becomes easier when you realize that something you just did, intentional or not, might have triggered a problem.

What's Changed?

No, it's not your fault that something changed. Computers are designed to be flexible. Rather than blame yourself when trouble arises, just recall what changed. When you do, you make it easier to troubleshoot and find the source of what's going wrong.

For example, you install a new keyboard and the mouse doesn't work. Perhaps you unplugged the mouse instead of the old keyboard? You update a graphics driver, but now all your computer games are reset to low resolution. The point is to be aware of what you've just done, to see how it relates to the current problem.

To help you discover what changed, or what might have caused recent issues, ask yourself, "What did I just do?" Specifically, did you recently or just now

>> Install new software?

>> Add new hardware?

>> Change a setting?

Think hard! That's because you do a lot with your computer and sometimes you do several things at once. For example, a dialog box may feature multiple settings but only one OK button. All the settings are applied instantly with a mouse-click. Undoing the change requires that you recall which changes you just made.

TIP

Windows keeps track of all system activities, including those that cause woe. See Book 3, Chapter 8 for information on the Event Viewer, which lets you peruse system logs for signs of trouble.

Installing software

Software covers the gamut, from the PC's operating system to programs you install. It also includes the software that controls specific pieces of hardware, which are referred to as *drivers*.

The best way to avoid issues caused by installing new software is to create a restore point. This way, should problems arise, you can uninstall the software and use the restore point to recover the system's previous configuration.

>> The good news: Windows automatically creates a restore point whenever you install new software.

>> The bad news: Some older programs may not prompt Windows to create a restore point. And, when you modify settings, a restore point isn't created.

>> Refer to Book 3, Chapter 5 for details on System Restore. That chapter explains how to manually set a restore point and how to use the System Restore utility to recover from software installation boo-boos.

Adding or removing hardware

Major hardware changes most definitely affect a computer system. Further, keep in mind that when you attach or remove a USB device, you're also adding and removing hardware. This process may trigger an issue that can occur right away or surface later, but the hardware change is probably the source.

>> Create a restore point before you make hardware changes. Unlike with software installation, you must manually create a restore point before installing new hardware. Refer to Book 3, Chapter 5.

>> The quick fix for bad hardware is to remove it. Sometimes, detaching the bum device fixes the problem, and sometimes not. If software (driver) was installed when you attached the hardware, the software must be uninstalled as well.

>> Ensure that you read the hardware installation directions (or flimsy pamphlet) before you install the device. The directions describe which to install first — the device or its special software. Sometimes, new hardware screws up because you omit that step.

>> If hardware is going to fail, it usually does so within 30 days of installation, which is why most hardware warranties are for 90 days or fewer. In my experience, hardware that fails generally does so within 72 hours.

>> A power supply (hardware) might fail when overloaded, which goes against the hardware-fails-quickly rule. See Book 2, Chapter 4 for details on the power supply.

>> Unlike software errors, which are consistent, hardware problems can be intermittent. See the later section "Hardware-versus-Software Problems."

Changing settings

If you're like me, you might change settings so often that you forget you do it. The settings can be subtle, from accessing a new Wi-Fi network to changing the screen resolution. Anytime you change a setting, you alter the computer's behavior, which can lead to something unusual or unexpected happening.

Most importantly, be on the lookout for User Account Control (UAC) warnings. Anytime you change a setting that can affect the entire system, you see such a warning, similar to the one shown in Figure 1-1.

As long as you're making the change, click the Yes button to proceed. If you're unaware of why the UAC warning appears, click No. And, if you have a standard-level user account, you must input an administrator password; a text box appears in the UAC warning (not shown in Figure 1-1).

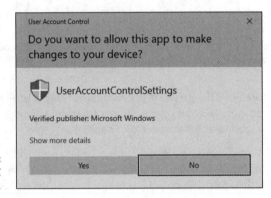

FIGURE 1-1:
A typical UAC warning.

Settings that affect the entire system feature the UAC Shield icon, shown in the margin. Choosing this type of setting prompts a UAC warning if your user account type is standard. Even then, administrator accounts get prompted with warnings as well. Regardless, the Shield icon serves as a reminder that the option you're changing can alter the system's behavior.

The point of the UAC is to pay attention! Changing settings can lead to PC trouble. For example, changing the text color to bright green and the text background color to bright green renders text unreadable. The solution is to undo the change.

REMEMBER

» A UAC warning appears whenever you change a system-wide setting. It's your clue that proceeding might portend problems.

» The best way to undo settings is to run System Restore, though a restore point may not be handy enough to affect the change. See Book 3, Chapter 5 for details.

>> By the way, green-on-green text is a horrid problem that's difficult to fix. You can select text to view it; selecting highlights the text and makes it readable. For a long-term solution, reboot into Safe mode to undo such a heinous text setting. See Book 3, Chapter 4 for details on Safe mode.

Hardware-versus-Software Problems

Because a computer system is a combination of hardware and software, problems fall into one category or the other. Determining the specific source, however, is an art form. People who troubleshoot computers for a living follow three general rules to diagnose such errors:

>> If the issue is consistent, it's probably software.

>> If the issue is inconsistent, it's probably hardware.

>> If the issue is with the PC's firmware — good luck!

You're probably used to such ambiguity when it comes to technology, though these three axioms are worthy to follow.

>> *Software* consists not only of the program you use, but also the operating system, control programs or drivers, and utilities. Software tells the hardware what to do. It's the computer's "brains."

>> *Hardware* is anything you can touch in a computer: the power supply, mass storage, keyboard, memory, and so on. By itself, hardware is dumb. It needs software to make the system useful.

>> *Firmware* is software that's encoded on a hardware chip. Firmware provides the smarts that gets the system started and controls specific hardware subsystems, including graphics, networking, power management, and other key parts of a computer.

Dealing with software issues

Software problems are predictable. If the Backup program won't run as scheduled, it's a consistent issue and the program itself (or the task scheduler) is to blame. If

Word always crashes when you try to print, it's a software issue not having anything to do with the printer.

REMEMBER

>> Software issues with a program — *bugs* — are fixed by the software developer. You can check the developer's web page for updates and support information, but you can't resolve the problem on your own, other than to avoid the feature that doesn't work.

>> Software drivers need updating from time to time, and even the update can be the problem. See Book 4, Chapter 2 for details.

>> Also refer to Book 2, Chapter 7 for various software solutions.

Solving hardware issues

The most obvious sign that hardware is to blame occurs when the device doesn't work. In that case, replace it. All hardware on a PC is component-replaceable, so if you need a new power supply, you buy a new one. You can even install it yourself, if you're handy with a screwdriver and don't mind risking death by opening the PC case.

For peripherals, you can troubleshoot by swapping out a suspect device with one that works. For example, if the keyboard is acting funky, attach another keyboard and see whether the problem persists. If not, the original keyboard is defective. Replace it.

The only time hardware swapping doesn't work is with a laptop. Because the laptop's hardware is integrated, you can't readily swap out a keyboard or replace a power supply. That's why I recommend a full warranty on a laptop, just in case the parts go bad.

>> Yes, you can replace any hardware on a PC, though at some point you must consider when to just buy a new computer. See the next section.

>> Even mass storage (a hard drive or SSD) can be replaced, though always ensure that you have a fresh backup handy and that you've created a system recovery disk.

>> Backup is covered in Book 4, Chapter 4.

>> Creating a system recovery disk is covered in Book 3, Chapter 1.

Addressing firmware issues

As with software, problems with the firmware must be addressed by the computer or motherboard manufacturer. Routinely, firmware updates are available.

You should install them when prompted, just as I recommend installing updates for Windows, Microsoft Office, and other software on your PC.

>> Firmware is software encoded on chips and integrated into the computer's motherboard. The chips are hard-wired, so you can't readily replace them.

>> Because the firmware controls so many aspects of the PC's basic hardware, a firmware bug would be near impossible to catch.

>> Some motherboard manufacturers sell diagnostic tools that let you check the firmware's status. Even then, if the firmware is suspect, you must choose between replacing the entire motherboard and buying a new PC. Neither option is inexpensive.

>> Updating firmware is part of updating software, including Windows. A firmware update may address bugs and other issues. See Book 4, Chapter 2.

When to Give Up

He's tried his best. He's written poems. He's showered her with gifts. The local florist beams whenever he walks in the door. Yet she refuses his overtures of affection. At some point, Stanley must give up and realize that Jessica Marie will never date him. Time to move on.

Yes, the same philosophy that applies to a teenage boy's dating strategy also applies to technology troubleshooting.

On the upside, I believe that you'll find your computer is far more attentive to your affections than your tenth grade crush. The computer *wants* to be liked. So, before you toss in the towel, consider some quick fixes, such as restarting the PC or using the System Restore utility.

If your tool chest of quick fixes doesn't work, turn to the Internet to pose questions and search for solutions. You might not be the only one who's ever had the same problem.

Computer repair places still exist in the real world. No, they're not cheap, but often they'll fix your problem faster and with less frustration than you'd experience working on your own.

And yes, this book offers plenty of suggestions and tips for fixing the most common PC problems, as well as advice on how to deal with just about any computer ailment.

Finally, at some point you must accept that you need a new computer. The typical PC has a life span of anywhere from four to six years — and more if you treat it well. After that time, however, and given the advances in technology, buying a new computer is a worthy investment.

>> Refer to Chapter 2 for additional help on how to fix common PC problems.

>> Also see Book 5, which presents techniques for breathing new life into an older PC.

Chapter **2**

Quick Fixes

Everyone knows some quick fixes, and most folks are eager to share them. These are home remedies for everything from stopping the hiccups to cleaning grout in the shower. Such solutions also exist for solving technology issues. After all, not everything needs to be difficult. And though the expert advice and specifics that you can find throughout this book are valued, sometimes a good ol' homespun trick fixes the problem.

Things to Try First

The very first thing you should do when something unexpected happens on your computer is to open both eyes and drop your mouth a bit. That's right: Look surprised. After years of using a computer, I've mastered this expression.

Once you survive the initial shock, consider a few quick fixes. In fact, add the items in this section to your list of ready-cures to remedy any digital distress.

Checking the Settings app

TIP

For a quick look into issues Windows already knows about, open the Settings app: Press the Windows+I keyboard shortcut. If any issues are pending, such as a Windows update, a security issue, or a similar problem, you see a notification atop the app's window. Choose the notification to take further action.

Restarting the PC

The old standby solution is to turn off the computer, wait a few seconds, and then turn it on again. This trick also applies to any technology, from cell phones to smart TVs to nuclear power plants.

TIP

A faster way to implement this solution is to sign out of Windows instead of restarting the PC. Signing out shuts down all running programs, which may solve the issue. Follow these steps in Windows 10:

1. **If you're able, close all open programs and windows.**

The purpose of this step is to ensure that you have no lingering unsaved data. If you do, the sign-out (or shutdown) process is interrupted.

2. **Tap the Windows key to summon the Start menu.**

3. **Click your Account icon on the left side of the menu.**

Use Figure 2-1 as your guide. You may see an image, as shown in the figure, or a generic humanoid icon.

4. **Choose Sign Out.**

Windows signs you out.

5. **If any stubborn programs remain open, click the Sign Out Anyway button.**

It's okay to force-close the stubborn programs because, after all, that's the point of signing out or, if this process fails, restarting the PC.

Eventually, the Windows 10 splash screen appears.

6. **Sign in to Windows.**

After you sign in again, check to ensure that the problem is gone.

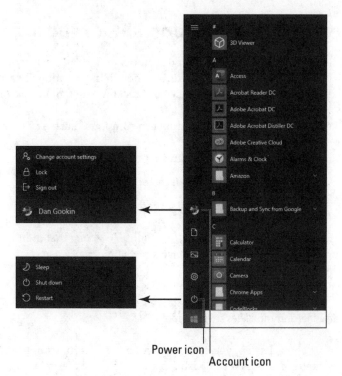

FIGURE 2-1:
Locating your
Account icon.

Power icon

Account icon

If the problem persists, you must restart the PC as the next possible solution:
From the Start menu, click the Power icon (refer to Figure 2-1) and choose Restart.
And, if the problem persists after that, you can try choosing Shut Down instead of
Restart, but at that point the solution most likely involves more troubleshooting
than just restarting the system.

>> The reason you wait a few seconds after turning off a computer (or any piece
of technology) is to avoid a rapid off–on cycle. Turning the power off and then
back on again immediately can damage the electronics.

>> The restart is also the most common solution to fix Internet issues: Restart the
modem, the router (or gateway), or both. See Book 2, Chapter 8 for details.

>> To restart a USB peripheral, unplug the USB cable and then reconnect it. For
USB-powered peripherals, disconnect both the power supply and USB cable,
and then reconnect them in any order.

**TECHNICAL
STUFF**

>> Restarting a computer to fix a problem has become such a common meta-
phor that the technique frequently appears in media as a general solution to
fix any problem. For example, "Turn off Congress and turn it on again." This
delightful development proves how worthy the simple trick can be.

Restarting a stubborn PC or laptop

If the computer doesn't obey your directions to sign out, restart, or shut down, you must resort to more drastic measures. Though it's emotionally satisfying to yank the device's power cord from the wall, I recommend a more reasoned approach.

Follow these steps to turn off a stubborn computer, such as a laptop:

1. **Press and hold the power button.**

2. **Keep holding the button until the device turns itself off.**

You might have to wait several seconds. Be patient.

These steps are reliable; I've yet to encounter a gizmo that didn't obey my forced-shutdown command. If so, you have a few choices.

If a desktop PC refuses to obey the press-and-hold technique, you can unplug the cord. Alternatively, you can use the secret power supply on-off switch, which is located behind most desktop-model PCs.

For a stubborn laptop, you can try evicting the battery from the case, though not every laptop features a removable battery. If your laptop lacks a removable battery, you can continue to press and hold the power button or set aside the laptop and wait for the battery to die.

REMEMBER

>> You don't need to press hard on the power button. The button isn't touch-sensitive, so the electronics aren't thinking, "Man! She's pressing down hard. She must really want me to turn off now!"

>> Normally, the press-and-hold technique fixes the problem. If not, you may want to check for an update to the computer's firmware. Specifically, you're looking for any issues with the power supply management driver, also called an Advanced Power Management (APM) driver. See Book4, Chapter 2 for details on upgrading the firmware.

>> See Book 2, Chapter 4 for more information on power management issues; PC shutdown snags are covered in Book 2, Chapter 9.

Running a troubleshooter

If Windows still has a pulse, you can get it to help you troubleshoot some common issues. And if Windows doesn't have a pulse, you can keep reading the rest of this book, which covers specific pulse-less Windows issues.

The key to getting Windows to help you is to locate one of several troubleshooters. These are software tools that help you discover problems and find solutions.

To view the gamut of troubleshooters offered by Windows, obey these steps:

1. **Tap the Windows key on the keyboard.**

   The Start menu pops up.

2. **Type** troubleshoot

3. **Choose the item labeled Troubleshoot Settings.**

   The Settings app opens, displaying the Troubleshoot topic.

4. **Choose the item Additional Troubleshooters.**

To proceed with troubleshooting, choose an item on the screen. For example, if your PC is having audio input issues, choose the item Playing Audio. Click the button Run the Troubleshooter and work through the steps presented in the trouble-shooting wizard.

>> If a troubleshooter fails, see Book 2 for information on troubleshooting specific hardware issues.

>> I confess that the troubleshooters are effective only a small number of times. The most successful one I've used is the Connect to the Internet trouble-shooter, which can reset the network adapter and often resolve some local network connection issues.

Repairing a program

Some programs, such as the applications in the Microsoft Office suite, offer a self-repair utility. So, whenever you have issues specific to a program, you can follow these steps to see whether the program has self-repair capabilities:

1. **Press Windows+I to bring up the Settings app.**

2. **Choose the Apps tile.**

3. **Select the app you want to repair.**

   Scroll through the list, and then click on an app to select it.

   After clicking on the app, you see the Uninstall button. If you're fortunate, you also see the Modify button. If it's enabled, you can continue:

4. **Click the Modify button.**

5. **Click the Yes button to proceed if you encounter a User Account Control warning.**

6. **If prompted, choose the Repair option.**

   Some programs display the Application Maintenance dialog box, like the one shown in Figure 2-2. If you see such a dialog box, click the Repair option, as illustrated in the figure.

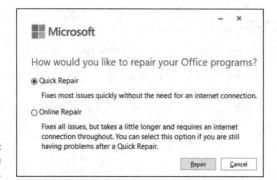

FIGURE 2-2:
Repairing a
program.

At this point, you continue running a version of the application's installation or setup program. What happens next depends on the program. Follow the steps on the screen as the repair utility does its job.

REMEMBER

» Not every program features a repair utility. If so, the Modify button (refer to Step 4) doesn't appear or is disabled.

» If you cancel out of a program repair (modify) operation, you might see confusing messages about canceling program installation. These are default messages that appear when you cancel program installation. My guess is that the installation program uses the same messages even when you're attempting to repair the program. Bottom line: Nothing is uninstalled.

» See Book 2, Chapter 7 for more information on solving software problems.

Fixing Windows

It's much better to fix Windows, or at least try, than to reinstall the entire operating system from scratch. The reinstall option is always available, but I strongly recommend fixing first.

Book 3 is stuffed with chapters that cover various tools you can use to address issues with the Windows operating system. Briefly, in order, I recommend the following fixes:

System Restore: For minor glitches, summon a restore point to address the problem. See Book 3, Chapter 5.

The System File Checker: This tool is the handiest utility for fixing Windows, yet it's too often overlooked. See Book 3, Chapter 4.

Windows Recovery: The Windows Recovery Environment boasts plenty of tools for fixing Windows, including reinstalling the operating system, should that task become necessary. See Book 3, Chapter 1.

Other tools are available as well, each of which is covered in each of which is covered in Book 3 of this minibook. Also, consider that the problem might not be with Windows; hardware issues can lead you to blame the operating system. Chapters in Book 2 cover various specific hardware problems.

Restoring the system

Many potential solutions are available to restore your computer system, but it helps to know exactly what "the system" is before you attempt one of these solutions.

For the most part, the *system* refers to software, or specifically, items stored on the primary mass storage device. This list includes the operating system, installed programs, and all your files. Various utilities are available to restore some or all of these items:

Backup and Restore: You can store anything from a single file to everything stored on the hard drive if you archive (back up) that data. The restore operation is how you get back the information. See Book 4, Chapter 4 for details.

System Recovery Disk: Use the data stored on the recovery disk (which is usually a thumb drive) to help fix or completely rebuild Windows. Further recovery is possible when you access the Windows Recovery Environment. Both topics are covered in Book 3, Chapter 1.

REMEMBER

Restoring the system is most successful when you use tools and run utilities that help you prepare for impending disaster. If you've not yet created a system repair disk, do so now. Also, configure the Windows 10 File History (the backup feature) if you've not yet done so.

Help!

Nothing beats having a local computer guru. It could be a relative — perhaps someone living with you — or someone in your office who knows computers well enough to help you resolve meddlesome issues.

When your local computer guru is stumped or — worse — *you* are the computer guru, you must turn elsewhere for help. Fortunately, you have plenty of resources on tap.

Locating Internet support

Back in the old days, support was provided by reading the product's manual. That type of support was despised, however, because the manual was poorly written, incorrect, or both.

If you were lucky, the hardware manufacturer or software developer provided a toll-free number to call. If you were lucky.

Today, free Internet support is available for nearly all major computer hardware manufacturers and software developers. The key is finding the correct website. That's because you don't want to risk visiting a site that purports to offer support but is instead designed to sell advertising or to infect your computer with malware.

To determine that you've reached the proper support site, ensure that the website domain matches the manufacturer or software developer. A major hint is the Padlock icon found on the web browser's address bar, similar to the one illustrated in Figure 2-3.

FIGURE 2-3:
The Padlock icon.

Microsoft Edge browser   Google Chrome browser

The Padlock icon appears on secure websites, and most manufacturers and developers have secure web pages. If not, it's okay, though you should ensure that the web page name matches the developer's name. This confirmation is very important! You want to get support directly from the source, not from a third-party site.

Once you've found the proper website, support comes in several areas. Yes, you must do some work to locate the answer you need. Support is available from these sources:

Software: For example, you can download a new driver for the PC's video card to help resolve compatibility issues. Or you can download a troubleshooter.

Forums: You're probably not the only one to experience a problem. Look for forums to browse for similar problems and find a solution.

Tech support: Most sites provide contact information for either phone or email support, or they may offer online chat.

More details on these resources are offered in the next several sections.

REMEMBER

» Find the official site for the support. Search for the manufacturer or software developer's name, and find the matching website.

» The support site may be listed with the flimsy documentation that came with the product.

TIP

» Sometimes, support information can be accessed from a Help menu within the program.

» Avoid product review websites or sites that are trying to sell you something. For example, many of the "what the heck is this file?" websites are fronts for outfits that sell antivirus or "PC cleaner" type of programs. Ensure that the site offers solutions other than obtaining their own program, which is a dubious choice, given that anyone can put anything on the Internet.

WARNING

» I'm not trying to condemn all third-party support sites. Though many of them offer legitimate support and software, some of them are devious. They may require a paid subscription or ask you to provide personal data to access the information you want. Worse, the software they provide features malware. You don't want that.

» Awhile back, you had to pay to obtain software driver updates. Today, these updates are provided for free. If you visit a site that claims you need to pay for an update, you're at the wrong site.

Quick Fixes

Downloading drivers

Perhaps the best aspect of online support is that you can obtain updated software instantly and at no charge. The primary reason to get this software is to address hardware issues; software drives the hardware, which is why this particular type of software is referred to as a *driver*.

As an example, you may find your PC's graphics incompatible with a new game. The game urges you to check for a driver update. To obtain the update, you must discover the make and model of the display adapter and then visit the manufacturer's website for a new driver.

To download a driver, follow these general steps:

1. **Save all your work and close all program windows, save for the web browser.**

   Installing a driver update may require that you restart your computer. By closing windows now, you save yourself this step later.

2. **Ensure that you've arrived at the proper website.**

   Refer to the preceding section for hints on how to confirm that you're at the developer's own website and not a bogus website.

3. **Locate the Software link or Drivers link.**

   Sometimes, this link is found under a general Support category.

4. **Click on the appropriate link to download the driver update.**

   Various links represent different hardware versions as well as different operating systems.

5. **Run the downloaded update.**

   Follow the directions on the screen.

After the update is installed, observe whether the problem is fixed. If not, more troubleshooting is necessary; but on the positive side, you've ruled out the driver as a potential source.

>> Various chapters in Book 2 describe how to obtain the proper hardware specifications you need in order to download a driver update. To determine which version of Windows you have, press the Win+Break key combination. In the System window, you see the Windows version as well as the system type, which is either 32-bit or 64-bit.

- » Don't freak out if you choose the wrong software. The installation program presents a warning if you don't have the proper operating system or hardware version.

- » For details on obtaining a new graphics driver, refer to Book 2, Chapter 3.

- » Other chapters in Book 2 cover obtaining drivers for specific PC hardware.

- » Sometimes, support software urges you to obtain a driver update or it obtains and installs the updates for you. The NVIDIA Control Panel program, installed with most NVIDIA display adapters, prompts automatically when a new driver or update is available.

- » Driver updates might also be installed automatically when you run the Windows Update program. See Book 4, Chapter 2.

- » You can also download diagnostics software from the Internet. For example, the Intel support page offers tools that can help address issues with the processor, firmware, and motherboard. The Crucial website provides a memory upgrade tool that analyzes which type of memory your PC uses and how best to install a memory upgrade. These tools are described in detail elsewhere in this book.

Perusing forums

I've found great success in perusing the support forms on the web. Manufacturers and developers are smart to let users post their own questions and puzzles and then let other users offer solutions. Tech support people also join the forums, which makes them a wonderful resource.

- » Not every manufacturer or developer's website offers forums. Even so, it's perfectly fine to use forums not located on the official site. Just be wary of clicking any links to so-called solutions.

- » To find forums, look for the Forums link. Find this link in a general Support category.

- » Use the forum's Search box to type in a query. You may have to phrase it several different ways to locate potential solutions. It's best to include the product name and version for accurate results.

- » Ensure that you check the date on various forum posts. The most recent dates are more likely to reflect your current problem.

TIP

- » It helps to include the word *solution* or *solved* in your search, because many of the forum topics may list the same problem but not offer any solutions.

Contacting tech support

The old toll-free phone numbers may still be around, but few manufacturers or developers cough up this information directly on their websites. No, you must hunt for the details.

Start looking under the Support category, though you may also find a separate Contact or Info category. The support that's offered comes in one or more types, including

>> Live chat

>> Phone

>> Callback

>> Email

>> Paid

I recommend trying live chat, if it's available. A window pops up on the screen and you get to type with "Linda" or "Bill" to explain your situation. They can walk you through some solutions or perhaps even offer to fix the problem remotely. See the next section, "Being wary of remote desktop access!"

Phone support is nice, but often the wait times are intolerably long. So be prepared to not only wait but also run the risk of chatting with someone who sports a heavy accent. This possibility is why I recommend live chat as your first choice.

If a callback option is offered, choose it. That way, the support people phone you up at a more convenient time to resolve the issue.

The email option works, but not quickly. It's also time-consuming to write back-and-forth.

A final option for tech support is to contact a professional tech support service. This is a paid service from a third party, sort of a for-hire online guru. The best services provide that you pay only when a solution is found. For example, you provide credit card information and then together you work on the phone or remotely to fix the issue. If the issue is resolved, you pay the agreed-upon fee; otherwise, you're not charged.

TIP

When dealing with any type of tech support, lower your expectations. Not everything that goes wrong with a PC can be fixed quickly or easily.

Being wary of remote desktop access!

WARNING

When remote tech support gets serious, you may be asked to surrender your PC to remote desktop access. This is a marvelous way for the other person to see your computer screen and control things, which greatly aids in troubleshooting. It also opens your PC to a certain risk, so my advice is to be careful!

No one can access your PC remotely without your permission. (That is, unless your PC has already been compromised by malware.) Ensure that you trust whoever is accessing the computer, which is a tall order. Be cautious of any tech support person eager to use remote desktop access, especially if they haven't yet directed you to perform a few basic tasks. Consider such a request a big red flag.

To ensure that remote desktop access is disabled in Windows, heed these directions:

1. **Press Win+Break to view the System window.**

2. **Choose the link Advanced System Settings.**

The link is found on the left side of the window. Upon success, you see the System Properties dialog box.

3. **Click the Remote tab in the System Properties dialog box.**

4. **Ensure that the first item is unchecked: Allow Remote Assistance Connections to This Computer.**

5. **Choose the option Don't Allow Remote Connections to This Computer.**

This item is located in the dialog box's Remote Desktop area.

6. **Click OK.**

You can also close the System window.

If you need remote assistance in the future, you can reenable this feature. Otherwise, by following the steps in this section, you ensure that remote desktop access isn't something that can automatically happen to your computer. Even then, a prompt first appears, where you must grant permission to the remote party for desktop access.

2

O, We Got Trouble!

Contents at a Glance

Chapter **1**

Startup Problems

f this book were about troubleshooting a computer that isn't turned on, it would be a pamphlet. Obviously, when a PC is turned off, it performs quite reliably. After power is supplied, however, trouble looms like a flatbed truck loaded with loosely packed logs on a bumpy road.

To best understand PC startup problems, this chapter walks you through the power-on process, from peaceful electronic slumber to full electron-invigorated operation. When you appreciate the computer's power-on sequence, though it may be technical, you can better pinpoint a startup problem and address specific issues.

The Onset of PC Heartbreak

Nothing beats that feeling when you arrive at your desk, set down a hot cup of delicious something, take your seat, and get ready to start a fresh, productive day. That feeling is destroyed when the PC forces you to take a detour from your planned route.

> » Initial computer woe is almost always a sign of hardware trouble. Replacing the bad part fixes the problem.

>> The change that causes computer startup trouble is time: Parts grow old and fail, most frequently when you turn on a computer. Even so, consider what you've changed or modified on your PC or added to it. Have you installed new hardware, modified a software setting, or updated Windows? One of these issues may have caused the problem.

>> If the problem isn't with the PC's mass storage system (hard drive or SSD), your data is probably safe. Replacing bad hardware, such as a video card or power supply, fixes the problem without losing your data. However:

WARNING

>> You risk losing your data by taking your PC into the shop for repair. The reason is that the technicians sometimes replace or erase the primary storage media. Of course, when the hard drive is the problem, it needs replacing anyway. This issue is why I recommend backing up your data; see Book 4, Chapter 4.

Phase I: Power On

During the initial power-on phase, the computer transforms itself from a chunk of quite useless expensive electronics into a chunk of quite useful expensive electronics.

What happens

You press the power button. When the computer is off, pressing the power button turns on the PC. It works this way whether the computer was properly shut down, was put into hibernation, or has met an inopportune demise.

The computer's *power supply* does its job: It starts converting alternating current into direct current. *Alternating current* comes from the wall socket. *Direct current* is used inside the computer to power its circuitry and motors.

What could go wrong

The computer fails to receive power. This issue could lie with the electrical supply, a defect in the building's wiring, a problem with the PC's power supply, or the old chestnut: The computer isn't plugged in.

Troubleshooting steps

The loud sound of nothing when you turn on a PC means that it has a power supply issue. Check the following items, in this order:

1. Does the PC have power?

You cannot compute when the power is off — unless you have a laptop, but more on this topic in a minute. Further, you cannot compute during a *dip,* commonly called a *brownout*. In this situation, the power is on but running at a low voltage. Lights work, but motors don't. If the lights are on (dimly) but your computer doesn't work, the electrical grid in your area may be experiencing a dip. Wait it out or check with the power company.

To ensure that a wall socket is properly supplying juice, try this test: Plug a lamp into the socket. If the lamp works, the problem lies with the computer's power supply. If the lamp doesn't work, buy a copy of *Troubleshooting Lamps For Dummies*, available at fine bookstores everywhere.

If the PC is connected to a power strip or an uninterruptible power supply (UPS), ensure that the gizmo is plugged into the wall and turned on.

2. Is the power supply on the computer operational?

When the wall socket is operating properly, the problem lies with the PC's power supply. Such issues are easy to detect. The power supply on every PC also contains a fan: If you can hear the fan spinning, the power supply is getting power. You may need to open the case to ensure that the power supply is properly connected to the computer's main circuitry, the *motherboard.*

If you don't hear the fan and the console lights are off, the PC's power supply may need replacing.

TIP

Many desktop PCs feature a rocker switch on the power supply. You access this switch from the rear of the PC's case. Ensure that it's in the On position, where a vertical bar is the international symbol for On.

3. Is the monitor on?

It's an obvious question, and even I have fallen prey to this maddening problem.

4. Is everything connected?

Both internally and externally, cables must be plugged in. Especially if you've just moved the computer, a cable can become unplugged easily.

Inside the PC is a different story: It doesn't happen often, but cables may wiggle loose — especially because of wide variations in the internal case temperature or if you drop the computer or kick it down the hall.

If you complete these steps and still cannot pinpoint the origin of the nothingness, the issue is most likely too large for you to resolve on your own. Before toting the computer into the shop, however, consider its age. Old computers die. They don't start. (Dead computers have a habit of not starting.) If your PC is more than eight years old, it might just have expired. To fix that problem, buy a new computer.

TIP

>> One way to confirm a dip is to check to see whether the refrigerator or furnace fan is running.

>> A laptop that fails to turn on when it's on battery power most likely has a problem with the battery: It's dead, it has a low charge, or it has grown so old that it no longer works. If you can, connect the laptop to a power outlet to either charge the battery or run the device from the building's power supply. If the battery is dead, replace it. If none of these steps works, it's time to take the laptop into the shop — or, if the laptop is quite old, it's time to buy a new laptop.

>> Some electrical circuits feature a residual-current device (RCD), also known as a ground fault interrupter (GFI) switch. This switch can trip for a variety of reasons, which cuts power to the circuit. Check for an RCD power receptacle and punch the reset button to reactivate the circuit.

>> If the RCD switch trips after you press the reset button, call an electrician.

WARNING

>> Avoid the temptation to run your PC from a UPS during a dip or power outage. Use the UPS power only to save your stuff and then properly shut down the computer.

>> Some UPSs beep during a dip. A few models feature digital displays that may graphically show that the incoming voltage level is below normal.

"DID MY PC SECRETLY RESTART?"

If you leave your computer on all the time, you may show up one morning and discover that Windows has automatically restarted itself; rather than see the desktop, you see the sign-on screen.

The main reason the computer has restarted itself is that the Windows Update utility has installed a mandatory update. See Book 4, Chapter 2 for more information on Windows Update.

If the computer restarted and no updates were installed, the power company might be to blame. The computer might also have a power glitch, though if that were true, you'd see other, random restarts at various times during the day.

Phase II: The POST

When abuzz with electricity, the computer's internal components spring to life. It might be a chaotic ballet of confusion, but one thing is in charge: the processor.

What happens

The processor, also known as the *central processing unit (CPU)*, is the computer's main chip. It's the boss. The main dude. *El Comandante Supremo*. After the power starts flowing in, the processor jumps (figuratively) to a specific code in memory, where it begins executing instructions. Those instructions place the computer in a *diagnostic*, or self-checking, mode. The computer inventories its various components.

A *POST*, or *Power-On Self Test*, is performed, in which the computer checks its own hardware. Memory is tested and its quantity determined. Control is passed to various subsystems (network, video, audio, and power management, for example), which also perform their own inventories and tests.

Information may be displayed on the screen as feedback during this stage. Most PCs, however, display a startup, or *splash*, screen. The screen may or may not divulge what's happening inside the computer. When it does, you may see a memory count or seemingly random numbers or a copyright notice. That diagnostic information is intended for troubleshooting (*very* nerdy troubleshooting, as in oscilloscope troubleshooting).

REMEMBER

>> One important message revealed at this point is which key or key combination to press to enter the computer's Setup program. See the section "Phase III: Startup Options," later in this chapter.

>> Just because hardware passes the POST doesn't mean that everything is well. Computer hardware also needs software to control it. If the software isn't working, a problem may still appear.

What could go wrong

Video problems present themselves by way of a series of beeps. The beep pattern reveals the problem, though if you hear beeps but see nothing displayed, the PC's power supply or display subsystem is at fault.

When the power supply and display subsystem are working, problems with other devices are indicated by messages appearing on the screen.

A common error you might see at this stage stems from the PC's motherboard battery failure. The battery maintains the system's internal clock as well as other information. The error message that's displayed may indicate a missing boot drive, a bad timestamp, or another inventory problem. Fortunately, this type of issue is limited to PCs older than seven or eight years because this is the lifespan for the motherboard battery.

Troubleshooting steps

Because hardware fails when the computer starts, the solution is to replace the defective hardware. The message on the screen indicates what the problem child is, such as the video system, the network adapter, or another subsystem. Make a note of whatever error message appears. Then deal with the issue by replacing the hardware. This step includes replacing the motherboard battery, should it fail.

>> If the motherboard or chipset is to blame for the problem, the best solution is to buy a new PC. You can replace the motherboard, but it's not cheap. Further, the motherboard may not be the problem.

>> Failed network firmware is fixed by installing a USB network adapter.

TIP

>> To discover which motherboard you use, pay close attention to your PC's splash screen. The motherboard (or chipset) manufacturer, as well as the version number, is often displayed. You can also run the UEFI program, as described in the next section.

>> Not every code you see on the splash screen is a POST error. Many computers display information during startup that is completely normal and expected.

REMEMBER

>> The computer may continue to start, even with defective hardware flagged by the POST. This condition is unacceptable, so don't use it as an excuse to avoid fixing the problem.

>> A common POST error is a missing input device, such as the keyboard or mouse. In fact, one of the most comical error messages from the early days of the PC went something like this:

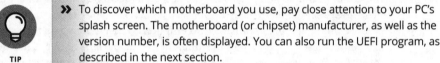

```
Keyboard missing, press any key to continue
```

WARNING

>> Another startup issue at the POST phase is the BIOS password. This isn't as big of an issue as it was years back, but my advice remains the same: *Do not use the BIOS password*.

Phase III: Startup Options

After the POST passes, you may see the system's startup keys displayed. These keys don't indicate any problems. On the contrary, the keys and their boot menu options are presented to help you troubleshoot the PC.

What happens

The boot menu may look like this:

```
F2 – Enter Setup
F7 – Update BIOS
F10 – Select Boot Device
```

The specific keys are different for each type of motherboard. Sometimes, they aren't displayed, but they're still available.

These keys control several actions that can take place after the POST and before an operating system is loaded. Here are what the keys might do:

Enter Setup Program (UEFI): The UEFI is the successor to the old BIOS Setup program. It provides a summary of installed features, basic hardware configuration, and other basic options.

Update the BIOS (Firmware): This option may be available, though most BIOS updates are performed from Windows.

Select Boot Device: If you desire to start the computer from removable media or the network, you choose this option. It allows a one-time change of the boot sequence.

This part of the PC boot process isn't prone to errors, but it's because of startup errors that these options are presented. See the next section for details.

>> UEFI stands for Unified Extensible Firmware Interface. Say "you fee."

>> BIOS is the Basic Input/Output System, which provided configuration and settings on PCs from the olden days. Though they're incorrect, people today still refer to the UEFI as the BIOS.

Startup Problems

>> The startup keys illustrated in this section probably won't be the same as any found on your PC. To know which are important, watch the splash screen as the PC starts. Write down the specific keys in the space provided in the nearby sidebar, "My PC's startup keys."

>> The F5 and F8 keys were used in older versions of Windows to access a startup menu or boot the computer into Safe mode, respectively. These keys are no longer used. The startup menu is now called the Windows Recovery Environment, which is discussed in Book 3, Chapter 1. Safe mode is covered in Book 3, Chapter 4.

What could go wrong

The only problem I've had is that the start key prompt appears too quickly. Even when I'm certain that I stabbed the proper key, Windows begins loading. To avoid this timing issue, you can restart the computer and have the Windows Recovery Environment appear automatically. From its menu, you can access features available from the startup options keys. See Book 3, Chapter 1.

Another issue is that the startup keys may not appear at all. In this case, enter the UEFI program and locate the option that determines whether the startup keys are displayed. See the next section.

MY PC'S STARTUP KEYS

To help you keep track of the startup keys on your computer and what they do, consider jotting them down here:

Key	Function
___	Setup program (UEFI)
___	Update BIOS/firmware
___	Enter Safe mode
___	Start Windows Recovery Environment
___	Select boot device

If a function isn't available, leave that item blank.

Troubleshooting steps

At this point, troubleshooting involves fixing problems; rarely does an issue crop up regarding the startup options.

The troubleshooting you can perform varies based on the startup option you choose.

Run the UEFI

Most commonly, you run the UEFI to do the following:

>> Confirm the PC's processor and motherboard names, model numbers, and so on. This process helps you gather information for additional troubleshooting, such as updating the BIOS.

>> Reset the firmware — for example, to roll back a recent update or undo a change that you may have made.

>> Activate the option to display the startup keys.

>> Update the BIOS, though this action is best initiated in Windows.

>> Reconfigure default PC settings, such as identifying the boot device, setting the date and time, and performing other, advanced configurations.

I'd like to be more specific with steps in the UEFI, but little consistency exists for the interface between the different manufacturers and even individual motherboard/firmware releases. Using the UEFI isn't complex, but locating the proper item can be tedious.

TIP

To exit the UEFI, you must inform the program whether you want to save changes. Typically, three commands are available:

```
Save Changes and Exit
Exit Without Saving Changes
Cancel
```

When you choose to exit without saving the changes, you may still be prompted to confirm whether you want to save. This situation is fine: It's perfectly all right to mess around in the UEFI and not change anything. Just remember to exit and *not* save, and then confirm your choice.

Update the firmware (BIOS)

A firmware update, once known as a BIOS update, can fix various issues with the motherboard and certain basic PC components, such as the network adapter and onboard graphics. It's popular these days to receive update notices through a helper program that always runs in the background in Windows. Otherwise, you must visit the manufacturer or dealer's website to download the update and install it yourself. Fortunately, this activity is rare.

As an example of a BIOS update, the popular Intel NUC line of mini-PCs runs a program called the Intel Driver & Support Assistant. It checks the Internet frequently for new drivers, including a firmware update. You see a notice in Windows 10 when an update is available: Choose the option to proceed and the update is performed automatically.

In many cases, a firmware update addresses problems with a computer's motherboard or other basic hardware. Most often, however, the updates address bugs or security issues. Always update when prompted.

WARNING

>> A firmware update requires you to restart the computer. Ensure that you save your work before you start the update process.

>> Of course, updating the firmware introduces the element of change into your computer. Run the UEFI program if you experience trouble with a firmware update; an option is available to roll back to a previous, stable firmware version.

Choose another boot device

One of the details stored in the PC's battery-backed-up CMOS is the PC's primary boot device. For nearly all PCs, that device is the main mass storage device, a hard drive or solid-state drive (SSD), from which the Windows operating system is loaded. This consistency is necessary, but it can be overridden.

To temporarily start the PC from another boot device, choose the Change Boot Device or Boot Drive command from the startup options. You see a list, such as this one:

```
1. SATA : PORT 3: HL-DT-ST DVDRAM GH24NSBO
2. SATA : PORT 6G 0 : WDC WD5000AAKX-08U PART 0 : Boot Drive
3. USB : SanDisk Ultra 1.26 : PART 0 : Boot Drive
```

```
4. UEFI : USB : SanDisk Ultra 1.26 : PART 0 : OS Boot Loader
5. LAN : IBA GE Slot 00C8 v1403
```

Granted, the list of boot devices can be intimidating. Devices are listed by their connection and type as read by the PC's firmware. A nerd could decipher the details, but what you're looking for is the word *boot*, which appears three times in the preceding list.

For example, if you want to start the computer from a USB thumb drive, you might choose Option 3, which contains the words *USB* and *SanDisk* (a thumb drive manufacturer) and *boot drive*. This choice assumes that you've connected the thumb drive and, further, that it's configured with an operating system or other bootable software.

>> After you choose the drive, the computer starts using that media. The next time you restart the PC, however, the original boot drive takes over again — that is, unless you press the startup option key to choose another device.

>> One reason to choose an alternative boot drive is to start a recovery disk for repair operations. See Book 3, Chapter 1 for details on creating a startup recovery disk.

>> If you plan to use the alternative boot device frequently (for example, to load Linux instead of Windows), alter the UEFI to choose that hard drive (or partition) as the PC's primary boot device.

>> The UEFI might also let you select the boot order — for example, first drive C, which contains Windows, or perhaps another drive formatted for Linux. A better solution is to obtain boot loader software that presents a menu every time the PC starts. You can then choose a startup device from the menu, or, after a delay, a default device is used to load an operating system.

TIP

Enter the Windows Recovery Environment

You might see a startup option to enter the *Windows Recovery Environment*. It's a centralized place to troubleshoot startup issues, solve problems with Windows, enter Safe mode, and access another boot device or enter the UEFI. Even so, I recommend starting the Windows Recovery Environment from within Windows. This topic is covered in Book 3, Chapter 1. Refer there for various methods to access the Windows Recovery Environment and to read about all the fun things you can do there.

"THE PC JUST KEEPS RESTARTING!"

A problem from years ago, which isn't that frequent today, was what I call the *restart loop:* On an error, the computer would automatically restart itself. Because no one thought this process through in any detail, the result was a PC that continually restarts itself, over and over.

PCs today are configured *not* to restart on an error — and it's about time! If your PC does experience this problem, you must enter the Windows Recovery Environment to fix it: Choose Troubleshoot and then Advanced Options and then, finally, Startup Settings. One of the settings (number 9) is Disable Automatic Restart After Failure. Choose that option to break the restart loop.

Disabling the automatic restart only fixes the automatic restart problem. You must still determine which piece of hardware is causing the trouble and then repair or replace this item.

Phase IV: The Search for an Operating System

The final task that the PC's hardware completes, after all the checking and test-ing, is to find and load an *operating system*, the main piece of software in the com-puter. This process is called *bootstrapping*, or, when you're in a real hurry, you can just use *boot*.

What happens

The PC's firmware loads the first chunk of data from the mass storage device identified as the boot drive. That chunk of data runs as a program, which loads the rest of the operating system into memory and begins processing its code.

>> The default boot drive is set in the PC's battery-backed-up memory. It can be changed in the UEFI, or another boot device can be selected temporarily. Refer to the earlier section "Phase III: Startup Options."

>> Some PCs can be configured to scan multiple boot devices in sequence. For example, the original PC scanned floppy drive A before jumping up to drive C (a hard drive). PCs with optical drives may first scan this storage for an operating system.

TECHNICAL STUFF

>> For PCs with multiple operating systems, a boot loader program may be loaded first. It displays a menu from which you can choose an operating system to load.

>> Technically, the PC hardware loads and executes the first portion of the hard drive into memory. That portion is the *master boot record,* or *MBR.* You find this term used quite a bit when diagnosing PC startup problems.

What could go wrong

Several startup error messages have similar, heart-stopping text. Each indicates that the computer is having difficulty finding the operating system:

```
Invalid Partition Table
Missing Operating System
Operating System Not Found
Non-System Disk or Disk Error
```

The worst error message is none at all; you see only a blinking cursor. Give it time, but eventually the lone, blinking cursor indicates some type of issue locating bootable media.

If the computer is equipped with an optical drive, you may see this message:

```
Press any key to boot from the CD or DVD
```

This message is *not* a sign of trouble. It merely means that you've stuck a bootable disc into the optical drive. Press Enter to boot from that disc, though the message disappears after a short timeout.

Troubleshooting steps

Many different solutions are available to a missing operating system error, from a damaged master boot record (MBR) to a kaput hard drive. The best way to troubleshoot the issue is to use the Windows Recovery Environment. Because Windows won't start, your option is limited to using a system repair disk, from which you can access the Windows Recovery Environment.

TIP

See Book 3, Chapter 1 for details on creating a system recovery disk. It's vital that you perform this step *before* disaster strikes the computer. Do it now!

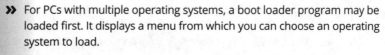

To troubleshoot the issue, follow these general steps:

1. **Use the Windows Recovery Environment to determine available storage on the computer.**

   Specifically, you're looking to see whether the primary boot drive is available. The drive's description varies, but you're looking for the words *boot drive* or *windows*.

2. **If the drive is available, run the Startup Repair option.**

   More details are offered in Book 3.

3. **If Startup Repair doesn't work, attempt to recover Windows.**

   The option you want is either System Image Recovery or Reset This PC. Again, these options are covered in detail in Book 3.

If hardware failure is to blame, you're not stuck. You can replace the primary storage device. After replacing the media, the next step is recovering your data. See Chapter 2 in this minibook for details, but be forewarned that primary storage media recovery works only when you've created a system image and have a fresh backup of your programs and data.

Phase V: Operating System Initialization

After the hardware locates an operating system, software takes over the computer. Windows continues to load itself, starting various processes and services that use the PC's hardware. Even at this stage, you can encounter problems.

What happens

Windows could be more thorough with its startup hardware investigation. Alas, due to the wide variety of PCs and components, the testing that Windows performs on the computer's hardware is intentionally sloppy. So, Windows may forgive a device that it knows might fail, which means that you may encounter the problem later.

Additional overhead is required when the system recovers from hibernation, also known as *hybrid sleep*. In this situation, information is loaded from the mass storage system into memory, and the computer picks up where you left off.

What could go wrong

Though Windows is forgiving, it might detect more problems than its capacity for mercy. When such problems arise, Windows automatically enters Safe mode.

At that point, it's your job to detect why Safe mode was activated. See Book 3, Chapter 4 for details.

If recovery from hibernation isn't possible, you see an error message displayed. You can attempt to recover the data, but my advice is to just keep working. The problem may be with the hibernation file, or something may have happened to the computer that prevents the hibernation file from being loaded properly.

Troubleshooting steps

If Windows flags the specific reason for failure, your first stop is the Event Viewer. Check the logs to see which part of the system failed, such as the video driver. You can also upgrade a driver. For example, an older network driver might be causing network conflicts or be unable to recognize a newer networking adapter.

Sometimes it's necessary to start Windows in Safe mode, to perform diagnostics or determine whether a problem lies with Windows itself or some other software.

For hibernation issues, it's best to remove the old hibernation file. This process happens automatically when hibernation fails. And, if you're prompted to remove the file, do so.

>> See Book 3, Chapter 8 for information on using the Event Viewer to track down system problems.

>> Various chapters in this book cover upgrading drivers, depending on which hardware needs fixing. Also see Book 4, Chapter 2 for information on Windows Update.

>> Using Safe mode is covered in Book 3, Chapter 4.

Phase VI: Sign In to Windows

After the Windows monsoon abates, you're presented with a sign-on screen. At this point, Windows is done loading, though when you sign in to your account, more activity takes place — and you can witness more opportunities for trouble.

What happens

You sign in. The traditional method is to select or type your account name and then type a password. You might also be prompted to type a PIN, scan your fingerprint, or look at the computer's camera for a face scan.

If multiple accounts are set up on the same computer, you must first choose your account from a list.

After you sign in, Windows loads other processes and starts numerous services. Any customization you've set is applied. Finally, startup programs you've chosen launch automatically.

Eventually, the dust settles and you start using the computer. Any chaos that ensues at that point is most definitely *not* caused by a startup problem.

What could go wrong

After you sign in, most problems are software related. This list includes buggy programs, improperly installed software, faulty updates, and issues arising from changes made to the computer's settings. These errors can occur at any time you use Windows.

Troubleshooting steps

Most problems that occur after you sign in can be addressed in Safe mode — for example, a bad driver or an improper Windows setting. See Book 3, Chapter 4 for information on Safe mode.

You can run the System Restore utility to undo any recent changes to the system. See Book 3, Chapter 5.

For general issues with software as well as with other hardware problems that can occur at any time, see the other chapters in this book.

The Last Thing You Do

After toiling (or playing or wasting time) with your computer, you eventually turn it off. As far as troubleshooting goes, turning off the computer again presents a spate of issues that may crop up. See Chapter 9 in this minibook.

TIP

The most important thing about any computer isn't its hardware or its software. No, it's the stuff you create — the *data*. No matter what happens to your PC, preserving this data must be your top priority. The best way to ensure that your data stays with you is to create a secondary, *backup*, copy of all your important creations, settings, savings, and stuff. Refer to Book 4, Chapter 4 for details.

Chapter **2**

Disk Disaster

L ong ago, permanent computer storage dwelled in the realm of the disk drive; spinning media was all the rage. With the advent of flash memory, however, mass storage devices no longer need to spin. Silicon storage, in the form of a solid-state drive (SSD) or a thumb drive, is available for mass storage. Still, the term *disk* remains — plus, it alliterates well with *disaster.*

The PC's mass storage system is perhaps the most vital part of the computer. That's because it houses the stuff you store and create. All your files, all programs, and various electronic tidbits of data are the reasons you use a computer in the first place. Therefore, I would argue that maintaining and troubleshooting your PC's storage devices is a top priority.

PC Storage Overview

It's easy to ignore the basic principles of computer science, so I will. Suffice it to say that mass storage is a key component of any computer system. Some mass storage devices come and go, yet the PC's primary storage remains vital to the entire computer operation.

Understanding computer storage

A computer features two types of storage: short term and long term. Both are required.

Short-term storage is the computer's memory, or RAM. It dwells inside the computer case, directly attached to the motherboard. This type of storage is where the action takes place. The processor directly manipulates memory, so RAM is required in order to get things done in a computer.

Long-term storage is often called *mass* storage. The function of a PC's hard drive (or SSD), thumb drives, and other removable storage is to house data for the long term.

Both short-term and long-term storage work together. Data is created or manipulated in memory. It's saved to long-term storage — specifically, the primary mass storage device. To work on the data again, it's transferred from long-term to short-term storage.

>> Just to confuse you, some sources refer to long-term storage as "memory," as in *permanent memory*. This term is accurate but confusing.

>> Long-term storage is necessary because RAM requires a constant flow of electricity to maintain its contents. When you transfer (save) information from memory to long-term storage, you create a permanent copy; unlike RAM, the contents of mass storage don't vanish when you turn off the computer's power.

Exploring mass storage devices

Mass storage can be classified in several ways, some of which overlap. In the big picture, I refer to storage by its location as well as by whether the device's media can be removed. The related terms are

>> Primary / secondary

>> Internal / external

>> Fixed / removable

A computer has only one primary mass storage device. All other devices are secondary, whether they're internal, external, fixed, or removable.

An internal storage device is located inside the PC case. This location is where the primary mass storage device dwells, plus other, secondary mass storage and perhaps an optical drive.

A *fixed* drive is one that cannot be removed or unplugged. Internal mass storage is considered fixed. (And it's *fixed* as in nonremovable; as opposed to *fixed*, meaning it was once broken.) A *removable* drive is any storage that can be unplugged or disconnected from the computer case. In the case of an optical drive, an internal optical drive is fixed, though its media is removable.

Mass storage devices also come in various types. These are the most common:

>> Hard drive

>> Solid-state drive (SSD)

>> Media card and thumb drive (flash storage)

>> Optical drive

The primary mass storage device on a Windows PC is a hard drive or SSD. It's internal and fixed. Any secondary mass storage devices can also be internal, if room is available inside the case. Internal mass storage is fixed, and external is removable.

Media cards and thumb drives are different formats for flash memory storage. A media card is inserted into a media card reader, usually part of the PC's console, but the reader can be external. Thumb drives attach directly to a USB port.

PCs started coming standard with optical drives in the mid–1990s. Because optical disc capacity hasn't kept pace with mass storage requirements, these drives are uncommon today. External (USB) optical drives remain available for compatibility with older media.

>> The *disk* is the media on which information is recorded. I prefer using the term *storage media* rather than *disk* because computers are moving away from spinning disk storage and toward solid-state storage. Solid-state storage doesn't spin, unless you accidentally leave a thumb drive in your pants pocket and put it through the wash.

>> The *drive* is the part of the device that reads the storage media. A hard *drive* contains a hard *disk*; you insert an optical disc into an optical drive; a media card is placed into a media drive or media card reader or is connected directly to a USB port.

>> Some mass storage devices offer a combination of sold-state electronics and traditional disk storage. These hybrid drives are a bit faster than traditional hard drives, but not as fast as pure SSDs.

>> As far as your experience using the computer is concerned, the SSD is slightly faster. A computer with an SSD primary mass storage device starts quite quickly.

>> Other differences between an SSD and a hard drive are noted throughout this chapter.

>> Media card readers are USB devices. Even a media card reader in the PC's case is connected by an internal USB cable.

Finding mass storage in Windows

Windows provides ready access to storage media in your computer via File Explorer. In Windows 10, you must choose This PC to view the mass storage devices, similar to what's shown in Figure 2-1.

Choose This PC

Choose This PC

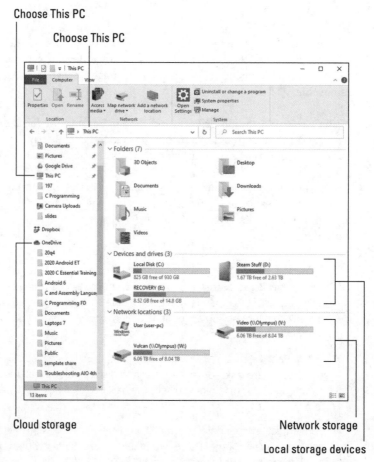

FIGURE 2-1: Storage devices in Windows 10.

Cloud storage

Network storage

Local storage devices

To summon a File Explorer window, follow these steps:

1. Press the Win+E keyboard shortcut.

A File Explorer window appears.

2. From the items on the left side of the window, choose This PC.

You can also choose This PC from the address bar, illustrated in Figure 2-1.

In the default view (refer to Figure 2-1), mass storage is categorized by location. Local storage is listed below favorite folders. The devices shown are internal or external; you can't tell by looking which is which, though drive C is always the primary storage device, internal, fixed.

Items in the Network Locations area might be network drives mapped to local storage, such as drive V in Figure 2-1, or media servers located on the network.

Cloud storage, when available, is mapped to locate storage, shown as the OneDrive item in Figure 2-1. It may not appear in the Devices and Drives category. See the nearby sidebar, "Where is cloud storage?"

REMEMBER

>> The number of storage devices available on your computer may be different from those shown in Figure 2-1, and from other computers.

>> In older versions of Windows, the window that displayed available storage was titled Computer. The title My Computer was also used.

>> When you add external storage to the PC, a new drive icon appears in the This PC window. Likewise, when the storage is removed, the icon disappears. See the later sections "Adding media" and "Removing media and mass storage."

WHERE IS CLOUD STORAGE?

The cheeky answer to the question of where cloud storage is located is, "In the sky." Or, if you're a nerd, you might answer, "On the Internet." Both answers are correct, but useless.

Cloud storage is best described as a mass storage device located somewhere on the Internet. You can use a web page to access the storage, or the storage can be available by way of a folder on your PC's hard drive. As such, cloud storage doesn't qualify as a device, like a hard drive or media card. Beyond checking the Internet connection, covered in Chapter 8 in this minibook, cloud storage is mostly integrated into the PC's mass storage device and treated like other files and folders.

Adding another mass storage device

Your two options for boosting PC mass storage are to add another drive internally or externally. The drive can be a traditional hard drive, an SSD, or a hybrid drive.

The internal drive might be a wee bit cheaper, but it requires the labor of opening the console, locating a spot for the drive, and connecting various cables and whatnot.

An external drive might not be as inexpensive as an internal drive, but it's far easier to add: Connect the power cord and USB cable. Plug in the drive. Ta-da.

Once Windows recognizes the drive, it's assigned a drive letter and you can begin using it in Windows.

>> Traditional hard drives are cheapest, but slower than the more expensive SSDs. A hybrid drive is a good compromise.

>> Ensure that you connect a USB 3.0 drive to a USB 3.0 port on the PC. This type of port is color-coded blue. You can use an older USB port, but the drive won't see the same data throughput as when a USB 3.0 port is used.

>> Internal drives might require more preparation. It's rare to do so, because most drives are sold preformatted for use in Windows. Even so, you may need to follow the steps in the later section "Creating a new volume in unallocated space" to set up the drive.

WARNING

>> Adding a new drive may shuffle drive letters for your PC's storage media. If you prefer consistent drive letters, see the later section "Assigning drive letters."

Adding media

Thumb drives and media cards aren't mass storage devices as much as they are media. You could argue that a thumb drive is both the drive and the media, but the device is attached and removed more frequently than a mass storage device, such as an external hard drive or SSD.

When you attach media or a thumb drive to the PC, a few things happen right away:

1. **Windows recognizes the new media and assigns it a drive letter.**

2. **If required, software drivers are installed.**

3. **If an AutoPlay action is set for the media, its action is triggered. Otherwise, the AutoPlay prompt appears.**

4. **The media is available for use.**

You can confirm that the storage is available by checking the This PC window, as described in the earlier section "Exploring mass storage devices." If the storage device is broken, unformatted, or formatted with an unknown file system, an error message may appear and the device won't be listed in the This PC window.

REMEMBER

>> When you attach a mobile device or digital camera to your PC, you're adding its storage to the PC.

>> The best tool you can use to diagnose storage problems is the Disk Management console. See the later section "Opening the Disk Management console."

>> When media isn't recognized, it's probably bad. You can try reformatting it — if possible. See the later section "Formatting media."

>> Most external storage uses a USB connection. If your PC features USB 3.0 ports (which are color-coded blue), use them to attach USB 3.0 thumb drives and other mass storage devices.

>> Another media port is the eSATA, though not all PCs feature this port. It's basically the port used inside the PC case to attach internal mass storage devices.

>> Also refer to the later section "Resolving AutoPlay issues" for information on how to handle newly mounted media in Windows.

REMEMBER

>> The drive letter doesn't change while media is inserted. For example, if the media card reader is known as drive G, all media you insert into the reader is accessed by using drive G. However:

>> A thumb drive is assigned a drive letter in the order the drive is attached. Just because the thumb drive was the letter *K* the last time you used it doesn't mean that it will be drive K the next time.

Replacing drive C

When the PC's primary storage device fails, it must be replaced. Other chapters in this book cover how to restore Windows and your programs and files, but the physical installation of the hard drive requires that you remove the original drive and replace it with a new one. Yes, you must open the PC console to perform this type of technological surgery.

>> After the drive is replaced, you use the Windows Recovery Environment to restore Windows. See Book 3, Chapter 1.

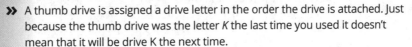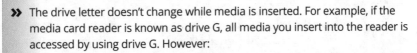
TIP

>> I recommend replacing the old drive C with a new one of a higher capacity. If you can afford an SSD instead of a hard drive, buy it.

» See Book 5, Chapter 2 for information on replacing your existing (and still working) drive C with a drive of a higher capacity. The process is called *cloning*, and it's how you can keep all your drive C data but swap in a larger storage device.

Assigning drive letters

Windows sees the various storage devices attached to a PC as unique. To organize the devices, each is assigned a drive letter. Further, a single hard drive can be split up, or *partitioned*, into multiple storage devices, each of which can be assigned a letter. The entire drive letter model can be quite confusing, especially given that other operating systems see all storage as one big container.

To start at the beginning, the primary storage device in Windows is known as drive C.

Why not drive A? Because, historically speaking, in 1981 drive A was the original IBM PC's boot device, and it was a floppy disk drive. Drive B was also a floppy disk drive. When the IBM PC XT appeared in 1983, it featured a hard drive, which was given the next letter of the alphabet, C. The PC has held on to this lettering scheme for compatibility purposes. In fact, even today, if you attach a floppy drive to your PC, it's assigned drive letter A.

After the primary storage device, drive C, additional internal mass storage devices are assigned drive letters D and up. This assignment is made during the computer's boot process and the drive letters increment alphabetically. These devices include internal storage, external hard drives, media cards, and thumb drives. In some cases, the letters are consistent, but they can change if you add or remove media or the media fails.

Network drives are assigned an available letter when they're connected. This process is covered later in this chapter, in the section "Changing drive letters," as well as in Chapter 8 in this minibook.

» Drive letters are followed by a colon, as in C: or D:.

» A single physical hard drive can be divided into multiple *logical* hard drives. Each logical drive is then assigned a letter. For example, if the primary mass storage device has two partitions, they might show up in the This PC window as drives C and D. See the section "Fun with Partitions," later in this chapter, for more information.

» Icons shown for drives can be either generic, such as those used in Figure 2-1, or specific, sometimes even looking like the drive itself or the media read by the drive.

TIP

**TECHNICAL
STUFF**

>> The boot drive shows the Windows logo. Refer to Figure 2-1.

>> The name associated with a drive is called the *volume label*. You can change the name, just as you can rename any file. Especially for removable media, the name may help you recognize the device's contents. The name is not, however, used by Windows to identify the drive; the drive letter is used instead.

>> When optical drives were popular, they typically landed drive letter D. If additional hard drive storage was available inside the PC, the optical drive was christened with the next available drive letter. Many PC users were confused by this inconsistency. Even in computer documentation, the claim was often made that the optical drive was D:, which was never a guarantee.

Resolving AutoPlay issues

Adding storage to a PC can conjure forth the AutoPlay notification, similar to the one shown in Figure 2-2. Click or tap the notification to see a summary of actions you can perform on the media, as illustrated in the figure.

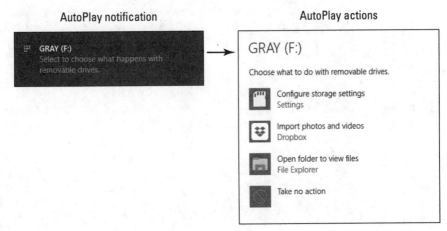

FIGURE 2-2:
The AutoPlay
notification and
options.

The list of actions depends on the media. For example, when Windows believes that the media contains mostly digital images, you see actions to import the images. For media containing music, you see options to listen to or import the songs.

Your choice is recorded, so the next time that media is inserted, the same action takes place. Still, you may want to change that action. If so, follow these steps to adjust the AutoPlay feature:

1. **Press Win+I to open the Settings app.**

2. **Choose Devices.**

3. **On the left side of the window, choose AutoPlay.**

   You see various types of media and options for that media, as shown in Figure 2-3.

AutoPlay master control   Default actions

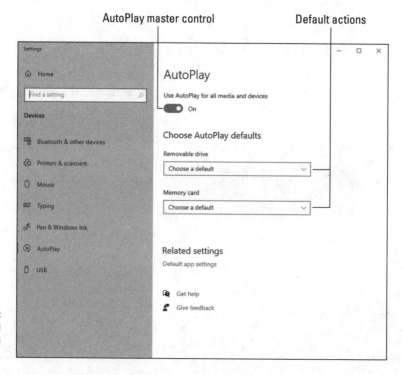

FIGURE 2-3:
AutoPlay control
in the
Settings app.

If AutoPlay bugs you, slide the master control, illustrated in Figure 2-3, to the Off position to disable the feature. Otherwise, you can click the menu below each type of storage to select a default action. The action you chose takes place automatically when the storage device is attached.

To be prompted every time, select the option Ask Me Every Time.

To not be bothered when a specific device is inserted, choose Take No Action from the menu.

TIP

Your goal is convenience: If you always import photos from your camera's media card, choosing that AutoPlay option to import photos and movies saves you time.

TECHNICAL STUFF

Some media may contain a file named autorun.inf. This file contains instructions on what to do when the media is inserted, such as run a setup or install program. Even if the program doesn't run automatically, you can right-click the media's icon and choose the AutoRun command from the menu to automatically do whatever it is that the media's developer prefers you do with the media.

Removing media and mass storage

Windows has no problem recognizing new drives or media; you can add storage at any time. When you desire to remove the storage, you can't just yank out media or disconnect a drive. If you do, Windows gets angry and you run the risk of losing files or permanently damaging the media.

For media cards, thumb drives, and optical discs, follow these steps to remove the media:

1. Open the This PC window.

Press Win+E to summon a File Explorer window, and then choose This PC from the locations on the left side of the window. Refer to the earlier section "Exploring mass storage devices."

2. Right-click the drive icon.

3. Choose Eject.

The Eject command appears only on media that can be ejected, not on fixed internal drives.

You can also find an Eject button on the File Explorer window's Ribbon interface: After selecting the drive, click the Drive Tools Manager tab.

External mass storage devices, hard drives, and SSDs must be dismounted before you can detach their cables or turn off the storage. Follow these steps:

1. Locate the Safely Remove and Eject Media notification on the taskbar.

The icon is shown in the margin, though you may have to click the notification triangle on the left end of the taskbar's notification area to see this icon.

2. **Choose the device to remove from the list.**

   Two names are used to reference the device — a technical name and the drive label — as illustrated in Figure 2-4.

3. **When you see the notification appear, informing you that it's safe to remove the device, remove the device.**

FIGURE 2-4:
Properly ejecting
a storage device.

This operation can also be completed in the Settings app, though this approach is more difficult because only the device name and not the drive label is displayed.

To use the Settings app to eject media or remove a storage device, follow these steps:

1. **Press Win+I to open the Settings app.**

2. **Choose Devices.**

3. **Locate the Connected Devices heading.**

   Ensure that Bluetooth & Other Devices is chosen on the left side of the window.

4. **Select the drive from the list.**

   Refer to Figure 2-5.

5. **Click the Remove Device button.**

6. **Disconnect the device when you're informed that it's safe to do so.**

External mass storage device   Properly eject/remove

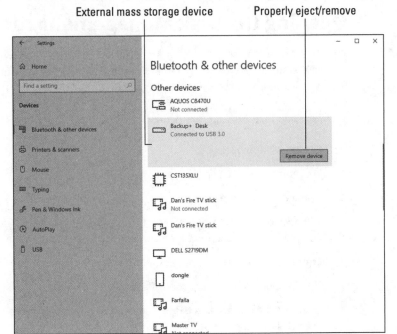

FIGURE 2-5:
Using the Settings
app to remove
storage.

If you compare Figures 2-4 and 2-5, you see that the Backup+ Desk item in the
Settings app is referenced as drive D from the Safely Remove icon's menu. Unless
you know this detail, it makes more sense to use the Safely Remove icon to eject
media and remove drives than to use the Settings app.

TIP

>> When you have trouble removing media, close all open windows. Then try
ejecting the media again. If your attempt fails, sign out of Windows and then
sign back in again. At this point, you can try removing the media again.

>> It's always safe to remove any media when the computer is turned off.

Mass Storage Tools and Utilities

To help keep your PC's mass storage system healthy and happy, and to customize
it beyond your nerdliest dreams, Windows provides a spate of interesting and useful tools. Chief among them are the Disk Management console, which is technical,
and the Tools tab in a drive's Properties dialog box, which isn't as technical.

Disk Disaster

Opening the Disk Management console

The Disk Management console is a special location in Windows where you can view the state of the PC's available storage devices, plus perform some special feats that cannot be accomplished elsewhere.

To access the Disk Management console, heed these directions:

1. Tap the Windows key.

The Start menu pops up, but you're going to use a shortcut.

2. Type Computer Management

You need only type the first part of the text. What you're looking for is the Computer Management desktop app, which appears atop the search list.

3. Choose the Computer Management desktop app.

The Computer Management console opens.

4. From the list of items on the left side of the window, choose Storage and then Disk Management.

The Disk Management console appears, as shown in Figure 2-6.

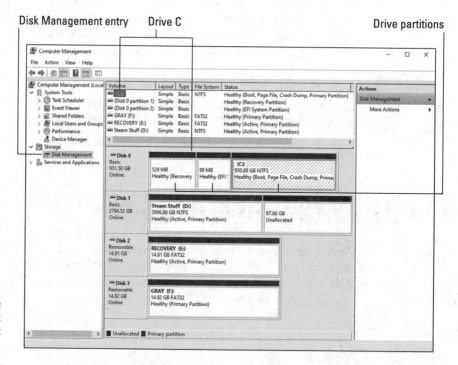

FIGURE 2-6:
The Disk Management console.

It may take a few moments for the Disk Management console to populate with your PC's available storage devices. You see them listed in the center part of the window, as illustrated in Figure 2-6.

Various sections later in this chapter describe what you can do with the Disk Management console.

A shortcut to access the Computer Management console is to press the Windows+X keyboard shortcut. From the supersecret menu that appears, choose Computer Management. This trick quickly works through Steps 1 through 3 in this section.

The Computer Management window is a console. This type of window features various parts, each of which controls a different aspect of Windows. Each part plugs into the basic console frame, which includes a center window with details and then a list of actions in the rightmost panel.

Finding mere mortal storage media tools

For less complicated and routine storage media maintenance, you can visit a storage device's Properties dialog box. There you see not only detailed information about the device, such as its capacity and available storage, but also a fine collection of tools.

Figure 2-7 illustrates the General and Tools tabs of a PC's primary storage device, drive C. The tools available are referenced in the figure.

To view a storage device's Properties dialog box, obey these steps:

1. **Press Win+E.**

   A File Explorer window appears.

2. **Choose This PC from the list of locations on the left side of the window.**

3. **Right-click a storage device icon.**

   In Figure 2-7, I clicked on the PC's primary mass storage device, drive C.

Later sections in this chapter cover using the tools on the Tools tab. Disk storage issues are covered in Book 5, Chapter 2.

Disk Disaster

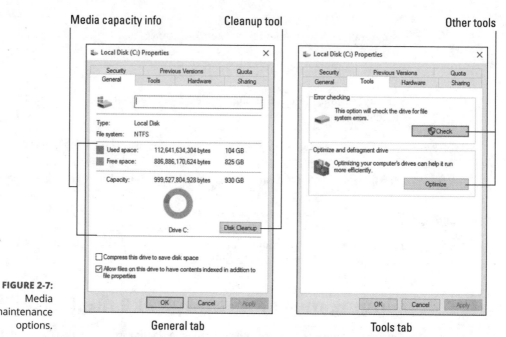

Media capacity info   Cleanup tool   Other tools

General tab   Tools tab

FIGURE 2-7:
Media
maintenance
options.

Drive Management and Maintenance

The good news is that routine maintenance for your PC's mass storage devices is a process that occurs automatically. In fact, many of the management and maintenance chores are no longer necessary on some devices, such as media cards and SSDs. Even so, the tools linger, just in case. It also helps to become familiar with what can go wrong and why regularly using storage tools was once considered mandatory.

Understanding fragmentation

It sounds evil, but file fragmentation occurs naturally as you use storage media. The problem is that fragmentation can impede file access, which makes it appear that drive access has slowed incredibly.

To understand how files become fragmented, think of a typical hard drive as a stadium parking lot, illustrated in Figure 2-8. As cars arrive, they fill in the spaces in an orderly fashion as employees guide the cars into adjoining spaces, illustrated as Lot A in the figure.

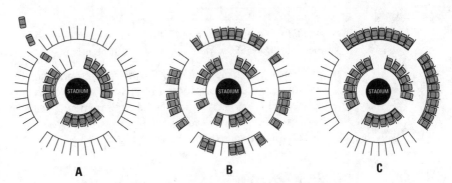

FIGURE 2-8:
A stadium
parking lot.

A   **B**   **C**

Because the game is boring, people start to leave. As they do, vacant spaces appear in the parking lot, illustrated as Lot B in Figure 2-8. A similar process takes place on a PC's mass storage device as you delete files.

File fragmentation happens when new files are saved. When a chunk of storage isn't large enough for the entire file, the operating system splits the file into chunks or fragments. The file remains whole as far as you're concerned; it's reassembled when it's opened, but doing so slows down access.

To carry this concept over to the parking lot, suppose that in Figure 2-8, in Lot B, a clutch of seven cars has arrived. They'd have to locate spaces all over the lot and wouldn't be able to tailgate together.

The defragment process physically moves the file chunks on the storage media. It reassembles files whole; plus, it locates frequently used files at the start of the media to make access quicker.

After a drive is defragmented, it might look like Lot C in Figure 2-8. The cars around the stadium are organized into adjoining stalls. New cars arriving have no trouble finding space.

>> Disk defragmentation utilities first appeared back in the early 1990s. Their effect was drastic because hard drives had been so badly fragmented. These utilities became overnight bestsellers.

>> A file defragmentation utility ships with Windows 10. It's called Microsoft Drive Optimizer, though the window is titled Optimize Drives.

>> The original Microsoft disk defragmentation utility was called *defrag*. That term is still used today by ancient and grizzled nerds.

>> A *defragmentation* utility reorganizes media in two steps: First, files are reassembled into single chunks. Second, the files are moved so that they lie on the media with no spaces between them.

Disk Disaster

WARNING

TECHNICAL STUFF

» One type of media you do not defragment is flash memory. This type of media includes SSDs, media cards, and thumb drives.

» One reason not to defragment SSDs, media cards, and thumb drives is that current technology allows for the information stored on the media to be accessed only a given number of times. This number is huge, so the device will be useable for years and years. Yet, by defragmenting a media drive, you decrease its life span dramatically.

Defragmenting a hard drive

In Windows 10, the defragmenting process is automatic; you don't need to do a thing. The Microsoft Drive Optimizer (the defrag utility) runs automatically. You can still perform a manual defragmentation or just check on the status of local storage. Follow these steps:

1. **Tap the Windows key.**

2. **Type** defrag

3. **From the Best Match list, choose the item Defragment and Optimize Drives.**

   The Optimize Drives program window appears, as shown in Figure 2-9.

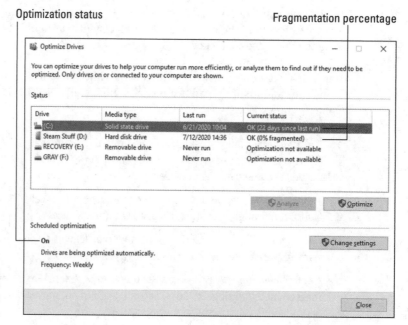

FIGURE 2-9: Drive fragmentation info.

These steps merely summon the program window. In most cases, these steps are sufficient because once the window is open, you most likely see that nothing needs to be done. As shown in Figure 2-9, the fragmentation status is OK and if the percentage fragmentation is shown, it's probably zero.

The old rule was that you must defragment a hard drive when 5 percent or more of the drive was fragmented. In Windows 10, this condition should never happen.

WARNING

>> The title of this section refers to a "hard drive." Other types of storage media are listed in the Optimize Drives window, but only hard drives benefit from optimization or defragmentation.

>> Do not attempt to defragment an SSD. Even if the drive is shown in the Optimize Drives window and the text *Optimization not available* doesn't appear, do not optimize the drive.

>> You cannot defragment a network drive.

>> If you truly want to defrag a hard drive, choose it from the list (refer to Figure 2-9) and click the Analyze button. Then click Optimize if you really, *really* want to defragment the drive. The Analyze button is available only when the highlighted storage device can be optimized.

>> It's possible to disable automatic optimization. If you don't see On listed as the current status (refer to Figure 2-9), click the Change Settings button to reactivate this useful utility.

>> You can also access the Optimize Drives window from the Tools tab in any storage device's Properties dialog box. Refer to Figure 2-7.

>> Even when a drive is badly fragmented, you may not notice any drastic improvement in performance after optimization. That's because today's hard drives are relatively fast. Further, Windows optimizes storage access, which helps improve overall drive performance.

>> Also see Book 5, Chapter 3 for information on speeding up a slow PC.

Checking storage media for errors

As with disk optimization (refer to the preceding section), the process of addressing disk errors takes place automatically. Every so often, Windows performs a disk check, and when errors are found, they're fixed.

To perform a manual disk check, follow these steps:

1. **Press Win+E.**

2. **Choose This PC from the list of locations on the left side of the File Explorer window.**

3. **Right-click the icon for the media storage gizmo you want to check.**

For example, drive C.

4. **Choose Properties.**

5. **In the Properties dialog box, click the Tools tab.**

6. **Click the Check button.**

If you see a User Account Control, type the administrator's password or click the Continue button.

Eventually, you see a window that says, basically, give up. Figure 2-10 shows such a window.

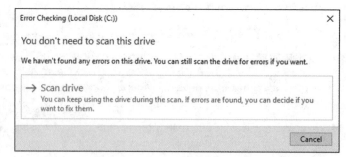

Error Checking (Local Disk (C:))   ✕

You don't need to scan this drive

We haven't found any errors on this drive. You can still scan the drive for errors if you want.

→ Scan drive
You can keep using the drive during the scan. If errors are found, you can decide if you want to fix them.

Cancel

FIGURE 2-10: It's not impressive, but it's useful.

The message informs you that Windows regularly scans the media for errors. If you're insistent (when, for example, you experience problems and want to confirm that the drive is okay), click the Scan Drive button. (Refer to Figure 2-10.)

After the scan is complete, you see a summary. Most of the time, no errors are found; click the Close button. If errors are found, they're fixed and you see that information in the summary.

TIP

» The best thing you can do about storage media errors is to back up your computer! See Book 4, Chapter 4. Having a fresh backup doesn't prevent errors, but it helps you recover from them.

» Windows may check storage when it first starts. For example, if the PC was improperly shut down, a media check takes place automatically the next time you turn on the system. That's because:

» The number-one cause of storage woe is an improper shutdown. In fact, the reason you must properly remove media is to prevent storage errors and other issues. Refer to the earlier section "Removing media and mass storage."

WHAT'S THE POINT OF A FILE SYSTEM?

A file system provides the methods for storing and retrieving files on storage media. The process can be quite complex, but it's all handled by the operating system. So it's nothing to worry about, aside from compatibility when you select a file system while formatting media.

In the old days, PCs used a simple file system called FAT or FAT16. Its limitations prevented PCs from storing files over a certain size and from accessing high-capacity media. This limitation was the reason that early PCs had to partition large hard drives. Otherwise, only a portion of mass storage could be used. Thanks to today's file systems, which can store massive files on huge hard drives, such restrictions no longer apply.

TECHNICAL STUFF

>> The original name of the disk checking utility was Check Disk, or chkdsk (the program's filename). Later, the name was changed to ScanDisk. Back in the old days, computer nerds would run Check Disk or ScanDisk as a type of witch doctor fix for all sorts of computer ailments. The display was interesting, and the final message, "No errors found," made people feel better about using their computers.

Formatting media

Long ago, formatting computer media was part of your daily computer duties. Back then, floppy disks were all the rage, and they arrived unformatted in the box. Today's mass storage devices, media cards, and thumb drives come preformatted. Still, the option is available to format the media — typically, for one of two reasons:

>> To completely erase the media, removing all previous contents

>> To reset the media's file system to a compatible one

Yes, it's true: The format process erases the media's current contents. That aspect wreaked havoc back in the early days, though many "unformat" utilities were available. Still, today you can completely zap the contents of a thumb drive or media card by applying a quick format.

The second reason for formatting media is to reset the media's file system. The format process is what lays down a specific file system type on the media. The operating system uses this file system to store information, and not all operating systems read every available format.

Table 2-1 lists media formats available to the Windows Format command. This list doesn't include all current media formats, such as those used by Apple's Macintosh line of computers.

Disk Disaster

TABLE 2-1   **File Systems and Formats**

File System	Meaning	Description
exFAT	Extended File Allocation Table	Also known as FAT64, designed by Microsoft for use with media cards and flash drives.
FAT32	File Access Table, 32-bit	An updated version of the FAT that allowed access to larger hard drives. Still popular because the FAT32 is recognized by many operating systems; not as useful as NTFS, however.
NTFS	File System for Windows NT	The current and best mass storage media format; used primarily on hard drives and SSDs.
FAT	File Access Table	The ancient file system used by the original PC. You may find this format on older media. Use this format only if compatibility is required for an antique computer.

To format media, to either erase it or change the file system for a thumb drive or media card, follow these steps:

1. **Press Win+E to bring up a File Explorer window.**

2. **Choose This PC from the left side of the window.**

3. **Right-click the media you want to format.**

   For example, a thumb drive.

4. **Choose Format from the shortcut menu.**

   The Format command is dimmed for media you cannot format, such as an optical disc or any removable media with its write-protect tab in the locked position. (Refer to the nearby sidebar, "Write-protecting media cards.") Neither can you format the media that's running Windows, such as drive C.

5. **Choose a file system for the drive.**

   This step is required only if your purpose is to apply a new file system to the media. For example, you must reformat a thumb drive to exFAT so that it's compatible with a Macintosh.

   If you don't choose a new file system, the default that's shown is used.

6. **Ensure that Quick Format is selected.**

   You don't need to fully format media that already has a format. And, if security is your concern, refer to the nearby sidebar, "Wipe out your data."

   The rest of the options in the Format dialog box don't need to be adjusted, unless you're directed to do so by a higher authority or you're drunk and just want to experiment.

7. **Click the Start button.**

A suitable warning appears, reminding you that formatting media is a drastic step and erases any data stored on the media.

8. **Click the OK button to begin the formatting process.**

9. **If Windows detects that the volume is being used, click the No button to cancel.**

Media is used when files are open, folder windows are open, or programs are accessing the drive or media card. If you're certain that nothing is accessing the card, click the Yes button to proceed with the format.

10. **Click the OK button to acknowledge that formatting is complete.**

You can now use the media.

WRITE-PROTECTING MEDIA CARDS

Media cards, such as the SD card and Memory Stick, feature a write-protect mechanism. It's located on the left side of the card, illustrated nearby. Slide the tab to the LOCK position to prevent information from being added to, erased from, or altered on the media. To unlock, slide the tab away from the LOCK position.

Write-protecting media dates back to floppy disks, which featured a write-protect slot. This feature offers protection for the media, though the lock is easily picked. Still, it's a trick you probably didn't know about. Now you do.

The Format dialog box appears, as shown in Figure 2-11. The media's current format is shown on the File System menu, such as FAT32 (Default), shown in the figure.

The freshly formatted (or reformatted) media is empty, though Windows creates the root folder. At this point, you can use the storage device as you see fit.

REMEMBER

>> You cannot unformat a drive.

>> Formatting erases the media! If your purpose is to apply another format to the media, the process erases the media's current contents. Format first, and then copy to the freshly formatted media the information you want to share.

>> If you're in the habit of applying volume labels to media, you can do so in the Format dialog box. Refer to Figure 2-11.

>> You can also format media when using the Disk Management console: Right-click on a partition to choose the Format command.

>> The Quick Format option is best for erasing media and applying a new file system. The only time you use a full format (uncheck the Quick Format box) is to prepare new media.

>> Information stored on the media isn't destroyed when you apply a format. Computer experts can recover information from media that's been reformatted. See the nearby sidebar, "Wipe out your data."

Select file system

| Format GRAY (F:) | × |

Capacity:

14.9 GB

File system

FAT32 (Default) → FAT32 (Default)
NTFS
FAT32 (Default)
exFAT

Allocation unit size

8192 bytes

Restore device defaults

Volume label

GRAY

Format options

☑ Quick Format

Start   Close

FIGURE 2-11: The Format dialog box.

Keep this item checked

Add a volume label

WIPE OUT YOUR DATA

It's true that reformatting media, specifically using the full format and not the quick format, does erase all the media's data. But when you must ensure that all the information is gone, reformatting isn't your best choice.

For example, when you sell a computer, you don't want your personal, financial, and questionable info to remain on the device. Or, say you're a politician — but I digress. The point is how to remove the information from the media, to "wipe" the drive.

Software tools are available to scrub data from any media. This process involves repeatedly writing information until any trace of the original data is gone. Still, files can be recovered using the software approach.

To fully render media useless, the drive hardware must be damaged. The best way to destroy a hard drive is to drill holes into it; typically, three holes at least ¼-inch in diameter at different locations in the physical disk. Because you probably don't have a drill press in your office, consider using a data destruction company. They'll either incinerate or shred the drive.

Changing drive letters

The stars may be fixed in the heavens, but your PC's drive letters aren't fixed in the computer's universe. It's possible to change the letter assigned to a storage device. The question is this: Why would you want to?

As an example, I prefer to keep external drive letters consistent. So the USB optical drive always uses drive letter R. That way, when I add the drive, it's not assigned the next available letter. It's consistent.

To reassign drive letters, heed these steps:

1. **Ensure that you're not using the drive.**

No files on the drive are open, and no programs from the drive are active. This admonition includes folder windows. If any of these conditions isn't met, the procedure won't go smoothly.

2. **Open the Disk Management console.**

Press the Windows+X keyboard shortcut and choose Computer Management from the supersecret menu. In the Computer Management console, choose Disk Management from the list of items on the left side of the window.

3. **Right-click the storage media you want to modify.**

   Storage media are listed by drive letter in the upper center part of the window.

   I do not recommend that you change drive C, the Windows boot drive.

WARNING

4. **Choose the Change Drive Letter and Paths command.**

   The Change Drive Letter and Paths dialog box appears, as shown on the left in Figure 2-12. It sports the icon and letter for the drive you selected and lists any associated drive letters and pathnames.

Currently assigned drive letter

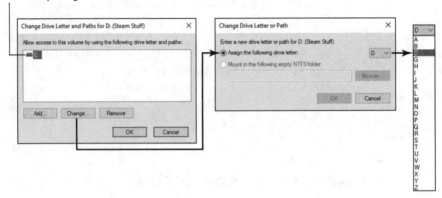

FIGURE 2-12:
Reassigning a
drive letter.

5. **Click the Change button.**

   The Change Drive Letter or Path dialog box appears (in the center in Figure 2-12).

6. **Choose a new drive letter from the drop-down list.**

7. **Click OK.**

   An important warning appears. Windows and various programs rely on consistent drive letters. Files become "lost" when you change the drive letter. When this happens, you must help Windows or specific programs relocate the files.

8. **If you want to proceed, click Yes to confirm that you've read the warning.**

   The drive is instantly assigned a new letter. An AutoPlay notification may appear.

9. **Close any windows that remain opened.**

I don't recommend merely changing a drive letter "just because." Have a good reason, such as the thumb drive keeps using a different letter. Following the steps in this section fixes that issue.

To reset the drive letter, simply repeat these steps. You can assign and reassign drive letters all the doo-dah day.

Joining storage media to a folder

The whole drive-letter thing is particular to Windows. Other operating systems integrate multiple storage devices into a single folder tree. For example, in Unix operating systems, you use a pathname (folders) to access removable storage. This approach makes sense because pathnames are easier to deal with than random letters of the alphabet.

In Windows, you can map a drive to a specific folder. This process doesn't eliminate the drive letter, but it makes accessing the files easier. For example, rather than remember that your projects are on external drive E, you can map drive E to your Documents\Projects folder and access the files from there.

To map a storage device to a folder, follow these steps:

1. Create an empty folder in your user account area.

Press Win+E to open a File Explorer window. Choose your account name from the address bar's menu. Within your account's folders, create a new folder: On File Explorer's Home tab, in the New group, click the New Folder button. This folder is the location where the storage media is mounted.

For example, create a folder named Projects in the Documents folder. The folder must be empty; it cannot contain any files or subfolders.

2. Open the Disk Management console.

Specific steps are provided in the section "Opening the Disk Management console," earlier in this chapter.

3. Right-click on the storage media's icon and choose the Change Drive Letter or Path command.

4. Click the Add button.

The Add Drive Letter or Path dialog box appears.

5. Click the Browse button.

6. Use the Browse for Drive Path dialog box to locate the empty folder you created in Step 1.

The empty folder becomes the media's mounting point.

Your account folder is found on drive C in the Users folder.

TIP

7. Click OK to set the folder you selected.

Back in the Add Drive Letter or Paths dialog box, you see the full pathname to the folder that's listed.

8. Click OK.

The storage media is now linked (or joined) to the folder you specified. When you open the folder, you see the contents of the storage media's root folder displayed, but the pathname on the address bar reflects the new folder you created. Plus, the media is still available in the This PC window, and it's still assigned the same drive letter.

>> You can add multiple mounting points for a single drive letter. To do so, repeat the steps in this section and choose another folder. A single drive can be mapped into several locations.

>> To disassociate a drive from a folder, repeat Steps 1 through 3. In the Change Drive Letter and Paths dialog box, select a pathname and click the Remove button. Click the Yes button to confirm.

>> Removing a drive's mounting point from a folder doesn't delete the folder. In fact, you can use that empty folder again to reattach the media, or to attach other media.

>> If the removable storage is unavailable, the folder appears empty.

Fun with Partitions

Back in the old days, the FAT file system limited the operating system from accessing a hard drive's full capacity. The solution was to split a single physical drive's storage into multiple *logical* drives. That way, the disk's entire capacity could be used: Each partition was assigned its own drive letter, and everyone was happy.

Today's file systems can access massive storage media, so partitioning isn't needed, because of disk size constraints. Storage is still partitioned, however: The PC's primary boot drive is often partitioned to help with the PC recovery-and-boot process. Also, some users partition humongous drives into logical drives for organization or improved speed purposes.

>> Partitioning applies only to hard disk drives and SSDs. You cannot partition media cards or thumb drives.

>> All drives are partitioned. A single hard drive has at least one partition.

» The whole drive doesn't need to be partitioned. Any unused space is considered unallocated.

» The initialization process for a mass storage media involves partitioning first. After this step, the partitions are formatted. The partitions are then assigned drive letters. The term for such a partition created in this manner is *logical drive.*

» For the Windows operating system, partitions are either primary or extended. Only one *primary* partition is required, which is the Windows boot drive. *Extended* partitions become other drives in the system, also known as *logical* drives.

» Non-Windows partitions can also exist on a mass storage device — for example, for other operating systems or data recovery partitions. These non-extended partitions aren't mounted in the Windows operating system as logical drives.

Examining disk partitions

The best place to examine any partitions on your PC's mass storage system is the Disk Management console. Follow these steps to open the console:

1. **Press the Windows+X keyboard shortcut.**

The supersecret menu appears.

2. **Choose Computer Management.**

The Computer Management window appears.

3. **From the list of consoles on the left side of the window, choose Disk Management.**

The center of the window is populated with available mass storage devices.

The bottom center part of the Disk Management console, shown in Figure 2-13, lists physical storage devices connected to your PC. Disk 0 in the figure is divided into three partitions. Disk 1, an external hard drive, has only one partition. Disks 2 and 3 are thumb drives.

In most cases, a physical disk has only one partition, such as Disk 1 in Figure 2-13. The device shown in the figure is an external hard drive, drive D, as shown in the Disk Management console.

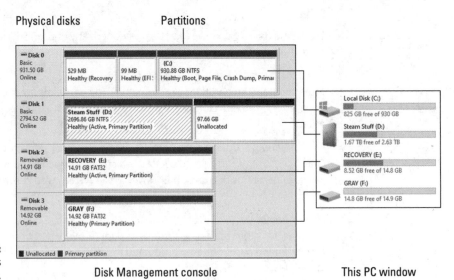

FIGURE 2-13:
Physical drives
and partitions.

Disk Management console   This PC window

The primary mass storage device, shown in Figure 2-13 as Disk 0, has three partitions: a Recovery partition, which contains the Windows Recovery Environment; one for the UEFI, or system configuration utility; and another for drive C, the PC's boot drive.

Of the three partitions on Disk 0, only one is mapped to a logical disk drive in Windows. It's the primary partition. You see the word *Boot* in the description. The other two partitions are boot partitions, but used for specific purposes.

What's *not* shown in Figure 2-13 is any unallocated storage space. This space would appear as an empty spot on the drive. You can use unallocated space to create a new partition, or you can expand an existing partition into that space. You can also shrink a volume to create unallocated space.

>> Internally, Windows labels mass storage devices starting with Disk 0 (zero).

>> See Book 3, Chapter 1 for information on the Windows Recovery Environment.

>> Disk 0 is the first physical hard drive inside your computer. Any additional hard drives, internal or external, are numbered Disk 1, Disk 2, and so on.

>> Each partition has a format type or method, such as NTFS or FAT32, as shown in Figure 2-13.

>> Another name for a partition, or logical drive, is *volume*. It isn't a loudness thing; instead, think of a volume in a book.

Shrinking a volume

Shrinking a volume takes advantage of a hard drive that isn't using all its space. For example, you can have a 3TB (terabyte) hard drive and use only 1TB of that storage. It's possible to shrink the volume to 2TB, which allows 1TB to be allocated as a second hard drive or for use as a boot drive for another operating system, such as Linux.

To shrink a volume, follow these steps:

1. **First, clean up some of the crap.**

   To get the most space available, consider removing some unused files from the drive. Empty the Recycle Bin. And, perform other actions to ensure that you're not wasting space on the drive. See Book 5, Chapter 2 for more tips and suggestions on cleaning up storage.

2. **Open the Disk Management console.**

   Directions are found earlier in this chapter, in the section aptly titled "Opening the Disk Management console."

3. **Right-click a volume.**

   It cannot be the system volume, such as drive C, or a media card, a flash drive, or an optical drive. It must be a hard drive or SSD.

REMEMBER

4. **Choose the Shrink Volume command.**

   Windows examines the media to see how well it can be shrunk. Then it displays the Shrink dialog box, shown in Figure 2-14, where you can set the size of the new partition. (And I wish they'd update the dialog box to use gigabytes instead of megabytes.)

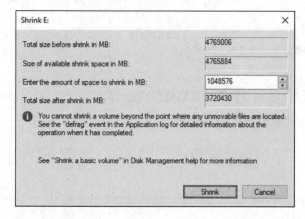

FIGURE 2-14:
Shrinking a volume.

Shrink E: ✕

Total size before shrink in MB: 4769006

Size of available shrink space in MB: 4765884

Enter the amount of space to shrink in MB: 1048576

Total size after shrink in MB: 3720430

ⓘ You cannot shrink a volume beyond the point where any unmovable files are located. See the "defrag" event in the Application log for detailed information about the operation when it has completed.

See "Shrink a basic volume" in Disk Management help for more information

[Shrink]   [Cancel]

5. **Set the amount of disk space to release.**

   Use the text box by the item Enter the Amount of Space to Shrink in MB to set the new volume size. In Figure 2-14, the amount listed is 1048576MB, or 1TB of storage.

   Set the size to whatever amount you need. Don't restrict the existing volume too much; otherwise, it may fill up and cause other problems.

   TIP

6. **Click the Shrink button to reduce the drive's size.**

   The computer busies itself with shrinking the volume. When the operation is complete, you see the new, unallocated volume appear in the same slot as the current drive in the Disk Management console. Figure 2-15 shows a before-and-after comparison of my test drive E, which I shrunk by 1TB (or 1,000GB).

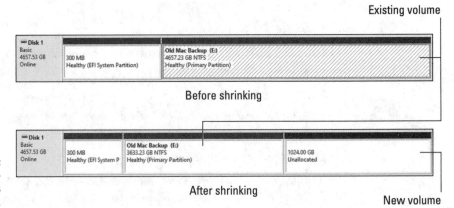

FIGURE 2-15: The before-and-after effects of drive-shrinking.

The effect of shrinking a volume is to create unallocated space on the drive, as shown on the bottom right in Figure 2-15. That space is unallocated, meaning that it's not a volume at all. See the later sections "Creating a new volume in unallocated space" and "Extending a partition" to discover what you can do with such a chunk of disk storage.

Creating a new volume in unallocated space

To make the unallocated portion of a hard drive useful, you must create a new volume, one that's recognized by Windows. You can create five types of volumes:

Simple: This typical hard drive is the type that most PC users have in Windows. If you're shrinking a volume to create a new logical drive, this option is the one you want.

Spanned: A spanned volume combines two or more unallocated volumes, even on separate physical hard drives, creating a new drive. The new drive combines all the space of the various unallocated areas into a single volume.

Striped: Striped volumes are used to improve disk performance by spreading information between multiple disks. The net result is that several drives are used to quickly access information, which makes all disk operations faster. You need two or more unallocated chunks of disk space to set up a striped volume.

Mirrored: A mirrored volume is a duplicate; information is written to and read from two disks. Mirroring is done primarily to avoid errors. It requires two disks to work.

RAID-5: A RAID-5 volume is used in conjunction with at least two other volumes to create a redundant storage system. This option works best when separate physical hard drives are part of the RAID-5 system.

Of all these options, the one you want is a Simple volume. Follow these steps to create a Simple volume in unallocated space on a hard drive or SSD:

1. **Right-click the unallocated space in the Disk Management console.**

2. **Choose New Simple Volume.**

   The New Simple Volume Wizard appears. If this item is dimmed, you've maxed out the number of partitions allowed by Windows. See the nearby sidebar, "No more partitions!"

3. **Click the Next button.**

4. **Set the size of the new volume in the MB text box.**

   The size is already preset to equal the available media capacity. I recommend using this preset size, unless you have some master scheme for partitioning the media and you don't fall over the partition limit, described in the nearby sidebar, "No more partitions!"

5. **Click the Next button.**

   Windows lets you assign the drive a letter, or you can use the suggested letter. The suggested letter is the one Windows would assign to the drive when the PC first starts.

TIP

   If a thumb drive or media card is bogarting the drive letter you want, open a File Explorer window, browse to This PC, and eject the media. Then you can use the media card's former drive letter for the new mass storage device.

6. **Click the Next button.**

   A partition requires a file system. The new partition must be formatted so that Windows can access the media.

7. **Ensure that NTFS is chosen as the file system.**

8. **Type a new volume label for the drive (optional).**

9. **Ensure that the Perform a Quick Format option is chosen.**

WARNING

And, while you're at it, leave the option Enable File and Folder Compression unchecked. I do not recommend compressing media. See Book 5, Chapter 2 for my reasons.

10. **Click the Next button.**

A summary screen appears. Looks good. If not, click the Back button to fix stuff.

11. **Click the Finish button to create the new volume.**

Windows prepares the disk partition, formats the media, and assigns the drive letter.

The partition appears ready for action in the Disk Management console. You see the label, the drive letter, and the drive's capacity and file system. The drive also shows up in the This PC window. Its contents are empty. The storage media is available for use.

>> Refer to the earlier sections "Changing drive letters" and "Joining storage media to a folder" for information on changing drive letters or mounting a drive as a folder.

TECHNICAL STUFF

>> Don't be disappointed if the new volume shows up with less capacity than you wanted. The missing bytes are overhead, used by the formatting process.

NO MORE PARTITIONS!

Don't be surprised if none of the new volume commands is available. The reason is that Windows places a limit on the number of partitions the computer system can access. The official limit is four primary partitions, or three primary partitions and one extended partition.

Because Disk 0 C is typically partitioned into three primary partitions (the UEFI, drive C, and Recovery), you can have one more partition on the media — and that's it!

The partition limitation doesn't apply to multiple mass storage devices: You can keep adding hard drives to the system, providing you don't split any of them into multiple partitions.

All hope isn't lost, however. Third-party utilities let you create additional partitions. For example, if it's your intent to install Linux as a second operating system on the PC, the Linux setup utility creates the necessary partitions for you. Other third-party utilities help you create additional partitions. And, if it's your intent to run multiple operating systems, get a boot loader manager program, which usually comes with tools for creating and managing partitions.

Extending a partition

Another way to put unallocated storage to work is to extend an existing volume. For example, in Figure 2-15, on the bottom you see a 1024.00GB chunk of empty space. You can create a new volume, as described in the preceding section, or extend an existing partition, which makes that drive larger.

To extend a partition, heed these directions:

1. **Open the Disk Management console.**

2. **Right-click the volume you want to extend.**

   The volume can be extended only when it dwells on a storage device with unallocated space and the volume is not in use. (Refer to the bottom of Figure 2-15.)

3. **Choose the Extend Volume command.**

   The Extend Volume Wizard opens.

4. **Click the Next button.**

   The next screen of the wizard allows you to select chunks of unallocated space on your PC's mass storage system.

5. **Choose the chunk(s) of unallocated space to add to the existing drive.**

   Any unallocated space on the current drive (the one you're extending) already shows up in the Selected column (on the right side of the window). Any additional unallocated space on other drives shows up in the Available column. Use the Add or Remove buttons to choose which unallocated volumes to use.

   If the Next button isn't available, the value specified by Select the Amount of Space in MB is too high. Set it to a lower value.

   TIP

6. **Click the Next button.**

7. **Click the Finish button.**

   As if by magic, the size of the drive instantly increases, by grabbing up all unallocated portions.

8. **Close the Disk Management Console window.**

The drive is now living large and ready for use.

TECHNICAL
STUFF

If the operation fails, it might be due to a size restriction set in the media's master boot record (MBR). The FAT32 file system cannot access devices larger than 2TB. Further, if the media was initialized using the MBR scheme, it cannot extend partitions beyond the 2TB mark. The solution is to convert the boot record to the GUID Partition Table (GPT) format. To perform this operation, you need a third-party disk partition manager that can make the change without destroying the media's data.

THE DISKPART UTILITY

The command prompt window features a text mode tool that provides a less visual way to manage your PC's storage system. The DISKPART utility is preferred by nerds who find the Disk Management console too friendly. In fact, I see no advantage to using DISKPART, other than a few advanced commands that it offers.

To run DISKPART, start an administrator command prompt. Type **DISKPART** and you start the program, which is command-line-driven. You can type HELP to see a list of commands, but otherwise you're on your own.

The nerds and IT specialists prefer DISKPART because it can be automated. You can run scripts in DISKPART that help configure a PC's storage system. This operation works faster than trying to use the Disk Management console to individually configure multiple PCs.

Deleting a partition

Another way to create room for a partition is to delete an existing partition. The effect is brutal: All the data on that partition is obliterated. You can use forensic disk utilities to recover the data, but that's not my point: Deleting a partition is a drastic move that should be handled with care. This warning is especially true because other operating systems' disk partitions aren't fully visible to Windows. Proceed with caution.

To delete a partition, gingerly proceed with these steps:

1. **Open the Disk Management console window.**

2. **Right-click the volume you want to annihilate.**

The volume cannot be the system volume, from which Windows was started, or any volume that's in use.

3. **Choose the Delete Volume command.**

The Delete Volume command removes the partition's reference from the media's master boot record (MBR). The media's data isn't wiped clean, but it cannot be easily recovered, which is why a warning appears.

4. **Click the Yes button in the warning dialog box.**

Another warning may appear if Windows believes the volume to still be in use. Otherwise, after a few tense moments, the partition is banished.

With the partition gone, its location in the Disk Management console is shown as unallocated. You can do three things with this chunk of storage: Reallocate the space, extend an existing volume, or use the space to install another operating system. Other sections in this chapter describe the details of reallocating and extending partitions.

Chapter **3**

Monitor Mayhem

I t was common a few years back for new computer users to believe that the monitor is the computer. This was a time before the all-in-one PCs, where the console and monitor are stored in the same unit. Even so, it's easy to understand why a newbie would think that the monitor is the computer: You see the monitor. The computer case, where all the action happens, just sits there. Even so, the monitor is not the computer; it's the PC's primary output device. As such, it's important that you understand the PC's monitor and know how to address its visual issues.

The PC Graphics System

The PC graphics system is composed of two parts. The part you see is the monitor. The part you don't see is the display adapter. They work together to create the image on the screen.

Using the proper monitor terms

It's *tres gauche* to refer to the computer monitor as a TV set. It's not. It's a monitor. And though monitors can be used for watching TV, that's not the point of owning a computer.

Here are the terms used to describe a computer monitor and how to apply them:

Monitor: A monitor is a chunk of computer hardware. It's the gizmo that displays images created by the computer's display adapter, which is located inside the computer case.

Screen: The screen is the part of the monitor that displays an image: text, graphics, Windows desktop, games. All this information shows up on the screen part of the monitor.

Display: The display is the image you see on the screen. For example, the display may show you the Windows desktop, some icons, and a window with a picture of a cat wearing a banana as a hat.

Here are some additional points that may help clarify the differences:

>> When you clean the monitor, you're cleaning the entire thing: base, back, top, and screen — unless you're a teenage boy, in which case you clean only the top part.

>> Cleaning the screen doesn't clean the display. Nope — the screen cleaning process removes dust, fingerprints, and sneeze globs.

WARNING

>> Ensure that you use a screen cleaner designed for flat-screen or touchscreen monitors. Avoid using abrasive chemicals, such as ammonia or alcohol.

Exploring the PC's graphics system

To best troubleshoot computer graphics, it helps to understand the PC's graphics system. The two parts are the monitor and the display adapter. The monitor is the visual part; the display adapter is found inside the computer case. Figure 3-1 illustrates a typical PC graphics system.

Also shown in Figure 3-1 is a USB cable. This option is required for monitors that double as a USB hub but also for touchscreen monitors.

>> All the graphical action takes place on the display adapter. It generates an image, which travels over a cable to the monitor and appears on the screen. The same configuration works in an all-in-one PC, but without the cable.

>> Display adapter circuitry is located on the PC's motherboard. It can also be found on an expansion card, which plugs into one of the expansion slots on the motherboard.

>> Display adapter cards offer more graphics horsepower than the motherboard's display adapter circuitry.

TECHNICAL STUFF

>> The illustration in Figure 3-1 shows an uninstalled display adapter. For the adapter to work, it must be installed inside a computer. You can try to run your PC's graphics system as shown in the figure, but response time is horrifically slow.

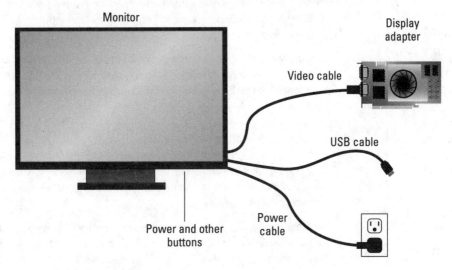

Monitor

Display adapter

Video cable

USB cable

Power and other buttons

Power cable

FIGURE 3-1: The PC graphics system.

Connecting the display adapter and monitor

A monitor requires two cables: a power cable and a data cable. The *power* cable plugs into the wall or, better, into a UPS so that it can work during a power outage. (Though the only "work" you should do in in a power outage is to shut down the computer.)

The *data* cable connects the monitor to the PC's display adapter hardware. Several types of connectors are available, as illustrated in Figure 3-2.

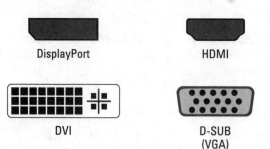

FIGURE 3-2:
Common
display adapter
connectors.

DisplayPort

HDMI

DVI

D-SUB
(VGA)

Of the lot, the two most common are HDMI and DisplayPort:

HDMI: The High-Definition Multimedia Interface is one of two popular connectors used today. Not only is it found on computer monitors, but most video equipment also uses this standard.

DisplayPort (DP): This port was designed to replace the DVI and older adapters. Along with HDMI, this format is the other common display connector. The connector shape illustrated in Figure 3-2 is the most common, though variations such as Mini-DisplayPort (common on laptops) exist.

Older formats still available include

DVI: The Digital Visual Interface, or just "digital," connector is color-coded white. It was once the most popular connector type, though today's monitors rarely come with this type of adapter.

D-SUB: Once known as the VGA connector, the D-SUB is found on some monitors for compatibility with older PC graphics systems. VGA stands for Video Gate Array. This connector might also be known as the *analog* video connector.

Legacy connectors: On some older PCs, you may find S-Video output as well as composite output.

Display adapters come with at least one connector, though it's common to find an adapter with several connectors — usually, both DisplayPort and HDMI. Likewise, monitors may sport several connectors, including DisplayPort, HDMI, and legacy connectors. The PC's graphic system needs to use only one connector. For example, use a DisplayPort cable to connect the DisplayPort output on the display adapter to the DisplayPort input on the monitor.

>> HDMI and DisplayPort can also carry an audio signal, a feature missing on the older standards.

>> If the monitor contains a USB hub or requires a USB cable to enable the touchscreen, a USB cable must be connected as well. The connection has nothing to do with the PC's graphics system.

> » Adapters and dongles are available to interconnect the various types of ports. I recommend strongly that you avoid such jerry-rigging. Buy the proper cables and use the proper hardware.

Discovering your PC's display adapter

Video performance is controlled by the display adapter. It's based on two factors: the graphics processor and video memory.

The graphics processor is called the graphics processing unit, or GPU. As with the CPU inside the PC, the GPU has varying degrees of horsepower and a myriad of names, numbers, and brands.

Video memory is the same type of memory as the PC's primary memory, but dedicated to assisting the GPU in its graphical duties. The more graphics memory available, the better the display adapter's performance.

The motherboard's display adapter is perhaps the weakest hardware you can choose. The GPU is rather simple, and video memory is shared with the PC's primary memory.

A display adapter card comes with one or more GPUs, plus onboard video memory. Some display adapters come with gigabytes of memory, with perhaps the upgrade potential for more.

To discover which type of display adapter lurks in your PC's bosom, follow these steps:

1. **Right-click the desktop and choose Display Settings.**

   The Settings app starts, but it's only a stepping stone in your journey.

2. **Click the link Advanced Display Settings.**

3. **Click the link Display Adapter Properties.**

   The word *Properties* is followed by a display number. If your PC sports multiple display adapters, choose the link for Display 1.

A dialog box appears, revealing details about the display adapter installed in your PC. Figure 3-3 shows two such dialog boxes.

On the left in Figure 3-3, you see the manufacturer's name and details about a display adapter expansion card. The GPU is a GeForce RTX 2070. The card features 8GB of RAM, which is supplemented by 16GB of system memory.

Display adapter card   Display adapter on the motherboard

FIGURE 3-3:
Display adapter
information.

On the right in Figure 3-3 is a small-footprint PC's display adapter information. The adapter is integrated into the motherboard, yet it uses an AMD Radeon Graphic Processor chip. The adapter has 4GB of dedicated memory, which is supplemented by 4GB of main memory.

>> Your PC's display adapter Properties dialog box offers more details and information than you can get from just looking at the card.

>> Graphics memory is also known as VRAM, for Video RAM. Or, to unravel that term further: Video Random Access Memory.

>> In addition to the GPU, high-end display adapters offer a 3D physics engine. This technology is vital for playing high-end computer games.

>> Display adapter cards come with a specific amount of memory installed. Some cards allow you to add memory.

>> The memory on the display adapter is bolstered by adding system memory, as illustrated in Figure 3-3. No direct method is available to adjust the quantity of shared system memory.

>> The more video memory, the better the graphics performance on a PC. Dedicated memory is better than shared memory.

TIP

>> The best way to ensure that you're properly using your PC's display adapter is to keep its software (the device driver) up-to-date. See the section "Updating the video driver," later in this chapter.

Exploring the monitor

The less sophisticated yet more visual part of the PC's graphics system is the monitor. As hardware goes, it's kind of dumb; the monitor does what the display adapter tells it to do. The device has some adjustments, but for the most part the display adapter drives the monitor and everyone is happy.

Today's monitors use liquid crystal display (LCD) technology. They're thin, light-weight, and easy on the eyes, unlike the bulky, glass monitors of yore.

The monitor's main contribution to your PC's graphics system is its screen size, which is measured on the diagonal. Along with the screen size is the monitor's aspect ratio, or the relationship between the screen's horizontal and vertical sides. Figure 3-4 helps you understand a monitor's size and aspect ratio values.

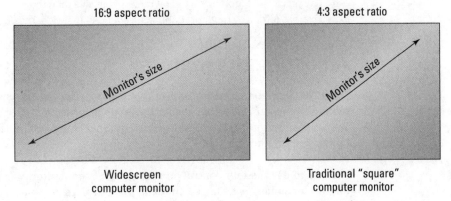

FIGURE 3-4: Measuring a monitor.

The monitor has both a power connector and a data input connector.

The power cable connects to a power supply or a UPS (uninterruptible power supply).

The input connector matches the graphics output connector on the PC, with many monitors supporting multiple inputs, such as both HDMI, DisplayPort, and even legacy ports. Be aware that some monitors don't come with graphics cables.

Multiple inputs allow the monitor to serve multiple devices. For example, you can use one monitor for both a computer and gaming console. Controls on the monitor determine which input source to use; refer to the next section.

Both touchscreen monitors and monitors with a USB hub feature a USB cable. The USB cable is required for a touchscreen monitor so that the computer can read touch input.

TIP

One key issue with monitors is *glare,* or the reflection of light off the screen and into your eyeballs. The best way to reduce glare is to position the monitor so that bright lights aren't reflected on the screen. Don't compute with your back to a bright window. When you can't move the monitor, buy an antiglare screen cover.

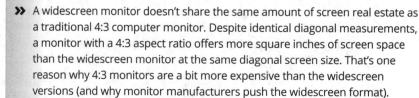

>> Those older, bulky, glass monitors are called CRT monitors. CRT stands for cathode ray tube. These monitors are still available today, specifically for graphic design; the analog nature of the CRT monitor better reproduces colors that match the real world.

>> An HDTV can also double as a monitor, though these monitors aren't specifically designed for computer output.

TECHNICAL STUFF

>> A widescreen monitor doesn't share the same amount of screen real estate as a traditional 4:3 computer monitor. Despite identical diagonal measurements, a monitor with a 4:3 aspect ratio offers more square inches of screen space than the widescreen monitor at the same diagonal screen size. That's one reason why 4:3 monitors are a bit more expensive than the widescreen versions (and why monitor manufacturers push the widescreen format).

Adjusting the monitor

A typical computer monitors sports five buttons. One is for power, turning the monitor on or off. The other four provide input for the monitor's control menu. One of two button types is used: the traditional press-and-release button or a touch-sensitive button.

It's rare to use the four control buttons to adjust a monitor. When you must, the four buttons manage an onscreen menu system. Here are typical functions:

Menu: This button activates the menu, but may also exit from the choices displayed.

Up: This button moves a menu selection bar up.

Down: This button moves the menu selection bar down.

OK: This button selects an item.

Pressing the Menu button summons the monitor's menu, such as the one illustrated in Figure 3-5. The menu highlights the button's functions, as shown in the figure. Use the buttons to manipulate the menu and make hardware monitor adjustments. For example, choose Input Source to select which HDMI or Display-Port to use.

>> Rarely do you need to adjust the monitor.

>> Touch-sensitive buttons can be difficult to see, though some illuminate when touched.

TIP

>> If it's available, use the Auto item on the onscreen menu to adjust the monitor. This item may be titled Auto Tune or Auto Adjust. Its function is to quickly adjust the monitor to use the best settings available.

>> The color temperature item sets the overall tone of the image displayed. When adjusting this setting, try to have something white displayed on the screen. Then you can see the effects: Warm tones (9600 degrees) show up as yellow; cold tones (2400 degrees) show up bluish.

>> Some monitors feature an ambient light sensor. This feature can be used to automatically adjust the monitor's brightness. The setting is found on the onscreen menu, where it can be enabled or you can set brightness manually.

>> Laptops have keyboard function keys that adjust the monitor's brightness and contrast. Beyond that, laptop monitors lack the specific adjustments that desktop monitors have, mostly because the laptop's monitor is dedicated to the laptop and therefore requires no additional configuration.

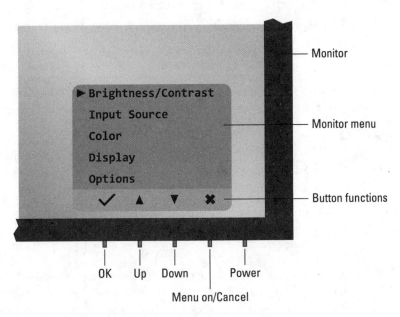

FIGURE 3-5:
A typical monitor menu.

Saving your eyeballs

Those old CRT monitors caused an ailment I referred to as "eyeball frazzle." More properly, it's called *dry eye*, and it was the bane of computer users back in the day.

Today's LCD monitors are kinder to human vision. Two features you may consider activating to help your eyeballs further are Dark mode and night light. These monitor adjustments are made in Windows in the Settings app:

1. **Press the Windows+I keyboard shortcut to summon the Settings app.**

   First, determine whether to activate Dark mode. In this mode, some apps use a dark background as opposed to light or white. This mode can be easier on the eyes and better for computing in low-light situations, such as inside an old nuclear reactor.

2. **Choose the Personalization tile.**

3. **Select the Colors item from the left side of the window.**

4. **Choose Dark for the settings Choose Your Default Windows Mode and Choose Your Default App Mode.**

   As you select the Light or Dark buttons, the screen updates to reflect the changes. When you're good to go, continue with Step 5.

5. **Click the Home button in the Settings app's upper left corner.**

6. **Choose the System tile.**

   The night light feature presents itself in the Display category; a master control switch lets you set the night light on or off. This feature activates warm colors, specifically at night, to help better transition a human with late-night computer habits into sleep.

7. **Click the Night Light Settings link.**

8. **Set a night light schedule or choose to have the computer set a schedule based on sundown/sunup times for your location.**

   If you opt to have the computer set the schedule, you must activate location settings for the computer. See Book 4, Chapter 1 for more information on the location privacy setting.

The Dark mode feature is activated all the time in Windows. Night light can be activated at any time, but it's best to set a schedule; this feature is most useful at night.

TIP

In addition to Windows, many popular application programs also feature a dark mode. Refer to the program's settings or preferences command to see whether a Dark mode option is available.

Orienting a monitor vertically

Many widescreen monitors can be mounted horizontally, which is traditional, or vertically, which is surprising the first time you see it. I think I was in my accountant's office when I saw that he used his monitor vertically. (And he had two of them mounted that way; see the next section.)

TIP

Reorienting a monitor from horizontal to vertical is a fun exercise. I recommend that you perform the software steps first and then physically orient the monitor. Obey these directions in Windows:

1. **Right-click the desktop.**

2. **Choose Display Settings.**

   You see the Display Settings window.

3. **If your PC has more than one monitor attached, click to select the monitor you want to adjust.**

4. **Choose an item from the Orientation menu.**

   Your four choices are

   Landscape: This is the standard presentation for a widescreen monitor.

   Portrait: This is the vertical presentation, which effectively rotates the display 90 degrees to the left.

   Landscape (flipped): This horizontal presentation rotates the standard Landscape option 180 degrees (upside down).

   Portrait (flipped): In this vertical presentation, the screen is rotated 90 degrees to the right.

   Choosing the flipped option or not depends on how the monitor is mounted relative to its original position.

5. **Carefully click the Apply button.**

   The display changes, reflecting your choice. If you goofed, click the Revert button or — if this operation proves too awkward — just wait, and after 15 seconds the display is restored.

6. **To confirm the change, click the Keep Changes button.**

   Yes, clicking the button is an exercise because the mouse hasn't changed its orientation. Have fun.

After the display is adjusted, you can orient the monitor properly. At that point, using the mouse works as you would expect.

You must repeat these steps for a second monitor, if your PC is so blessed.

Connecting a second monitor

Most display adapters can support a second monitor. For example, when you see two HDMI connectors on a single display adapter expansion card, adding a second monitor is as easy as plugging it in. Well, and buying the monitor and the rest of the setup. In most professional settings, a second monitor is considered routine.

To connect the second monitor, plug it in. It doesn't matter which connector you use when two or more are present on the PC or the display adapter card. Windows instantly recognizes both monitors, and it chooses one as the primary monitor and the other as the secondary monitor.

TECHNICAL STUFF

You may be able to attach a third or fourth monitor (or even more!) to your PC. The only limitation is the display adapter and how many ports it has. If you need more monitors, add another display adapter card, or the smart thing is to purchase a multimonitor display adapter card in the first place.

Configuring the second monitor

Beyond the physical connection, you must direct Windows to deal with its new graphical real estate. The operating system's disposition is to echo the display on both monitors. To control this setting, press the Windows+P keyboard shortcut. Choose one of four options to set how Windows treats the second monitor:

PC Screen Only: This option uses only the primary monitor.

Duplicate: Choose this option to echo the display to both monitors.

Extend: This is the option you want, which extends the Windows desktop and workspace across both monitors.

Second Screen Only: This option uses only the secondary monitor.

The most effective use of a second monitor on a desktop PC is to extend the desktop across both monitors (the second option in this list). After setting up the monitor in this manner, your next job is to configure how the two monitors interact. Obey these steps:

1. **Right-click the desktop.**

2. **Choose Display Settings.**

    You see the Display Settings screen, which shows the second monitor connected, as illustrated in Figure 3-6. If you don't see this exact screen, use the Windows+P keyboard shortcut to set up the monitors to extend the desktop across both screens.

Primary monitor   Secondary monitor

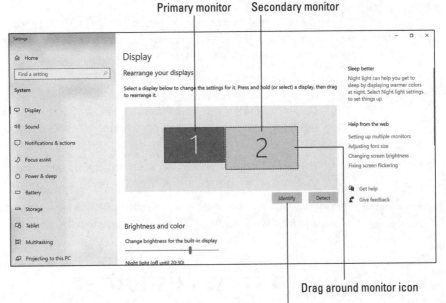

Drag around monitor icon

Display monitor numbers on the screen

FIGURE 3-6:
Adjusting the
second monitor.

3. **Click the Identify button.**

   Numbers appear on the monitors to match the numbers shown on the Display Settings screen. Now you can tell which monitor is which, according to Windows.

4. **Drag the monitor preview icons to match their physical monitor layout.**

   For example, though Figure 3-6 shows Monitor 2 on the right, on my desk Monitor 2 is on the left.

   When the preview matches the monitors' physical layout, drag to straddle a window between the displays. Use the overlapping window as a guide to make further adjustments. You may never get the relationship perfect, especially if the monitors are of different sizes and resolutions, but you can get close.

TIP

5. **Click the Apply button.**

   If the positions need adjustments, repeat Steps 4 and 5.

The taskbar appears on both monitors, though Monitor 1 is considered the primary monitor.

» The *P* in the Windows+P keyboard shortcut most likely stands for *p*rojector. The Windows+P key combination is used to quickly configure a laptop for projecting a presentation — for those who remember this handy keyboard shortcut.

REMEMBER

>> Windows sets each monitor's options individually, such as resolution and orientation. To change these settings, first click to select the monitor and then set its resolution, colors, and other options.

>> When you change a monitor's resolution, you may also need to adjust the monitor's positions. In Figure 3-6, Monitor 2 has a higher resolution than Monitor 1, which is why its preview is larger. If I reset the resolution to a lower setting, the preview changes, as does the monitors' relationship with each other.

>> The second monitor settings work with laptops, though in most cases a laptop uses a projector as a second monitor. The options are the same.

WARNING

>> Do not unplug a monitor while the computer is in hibernation. Doing so can prevent the logon screen from showing up when the computer restarts.

Captain Video Troubleshooter

Sometime in the future, digital superheroes will swoop down from distant mountaintops, ably assisting computer users with their PC's video system troubles. From diagnosing a nonresponsive monitor to surrendering your troubleshooting expertise to Windows, Captain Video Troubleshooter can help you.

Seeing nothing

When you see nothing, the first thing you should try is opening your eyes. That often solves the problem right away.

Ha-ha.

When you see nothing on the monitor's screen, check the basic hardware first: Is the monitor turned on? Is it plugged in? Is the monitor properly connected to the display adapter? If the monitor has multiple inputs, is the proper one selected?

A computer or monitor in Sleep (low-power) mode shows its power-on LED in an amber color rather than in the normal color (green, white, or blue). Wiggle the mouse. If you still don't see anything, the problem is with the video signal not reaching the monitor.

Press the monitor's menu button, as described in the earlier section "Adjusting the monitor." If the monitor's menu appears, the monitor is fine and the problem lies with the display adapter.

REMEMBER

>> When a monitor has multiple inputs, ensure that the proper input is selected. Use the monitor's onscreen menu to cycle through the inputs until the active one is found. Be aware that most monitors automatically detect and switch to the active input. Refer to the earlier section "Adjusting the monitor" for details.

>> Sometimes it helps to unplug the monitor cable and then plug it back in. When the issue is a power-supply issue, such as when the monitor's power light doesn't come on, unplug the power cord and plug it in again.

WARNING

>> Never try to fix a monitor on your own. Never open a monitor's case.

>> When a monitor is dead, throw it out. Do so properly, in accordance with whatever rules govern the disposal of computer equipment in your locale.

Seeing only the mouse pointer

I've encountered this problem a few times: After the computer awakens from Sleep mode, you see only the mouse pointer and not the Windows desktop. You can move the mouse pointer but not see anything to click.

Two solutions work for the mouse-pointer-only screen. The first is to press Ctrl+Alt+Delete, which summons a special lock screen. If this solution works, click the Cancel button to return to your Windows session.

The second solution, unfortunately, is to turn off the computer: Press and hold the power button until the PC turns off. When the computer powers up again, start Windows normally.

TIP

You might consider updating the display adapter driver. See the later section "Updating the video driver."

Swapping monitors

Because the PC's video system contains two parts, you must check two hardware items for the source of visual trouble: the monitor and the display adapter. To do forensic troubleshooting, it helps to swap out the parts to determine specifically where the trouble lies.

Obviously, you cannot swap out a monitor and a display adapter unless you have spares lounging about. But when you have a spare monitor or display adapter, you can use them to help troubleshoot.

Start with the monitor:

1. **Turn off the computer and monitor.**

2. **Unplug the monitor and disconnect it from the console.**

3. **Attach the replacement monitor.**

4. **Turn on the computer.**

If the computer displays an image on the replacement monitor's screen, the problem lies with the original monitor.

You can use similar steps to troubleshoot a display adapter. If the computer features motherboard display adapter circuitry, attach the monitor's cable to this output instead of the display adapter card's output. (These outputs are located in different locations on the back of the PC.) If you're fortunate enough to have a spare display adapter, you can swap it with the current one. To accomplish this task, you must venture inside the PC's case. If this task is beyond your skill set, you must find or hire someone else to complete the job.

REMEMBER

>> The replacements you use for swapping must be working for the swap to be an effective troubleshooting tool.

>> You don't have to remove the display adapter card to disable it. Run the PC's setup program or UEFI and see whether an option exists to switch to motherboard graphics only. This step is impossible, of course, when you can't see the screen.

Saving the screen

The intended purpose of a screen saver program was to prevent the perils of phosphor burn-in. Back in the CRT monitor days, a computer was often used for a single task, especially in an office setting. Because the same image was displayed pretty much all the time on the screen, the image burned the CRT's phosphor; the image was visible even when the monitor was turned off.

To help "save" the screen, screen saver software was born.

At first, screen savers merely blanked the display after a period of inactivity. Later screen savers added graphical images. Today, screen savers are mostly toys, though they can also serve a security function by locking the computer after a period of inactivity. Phosphor burn-in is no longer considered a serious computer maintenance issue.

To configure the screen saver, follow these steps:

1. **Right-click the desktop and choose Personalize.**

The Settings app appears.

2. **From the items listed on the left side of the window, choose Lock Screen.**

3. **On the right side of the window, click the Screen Saver Settings link.**

If necessary, scroll down to find the link.

The Screen Saver Settings dialog box appears, as shown in Figure 3-7.

4. **Choose a screen saver type.**

This step is the fun part. Also, click the Settings button, if available, to customize the screen saver.

5. **Set the Wait time.**

Ensure that the wait timeout is less than the monitor timeout set in the Power settings; see the next section.

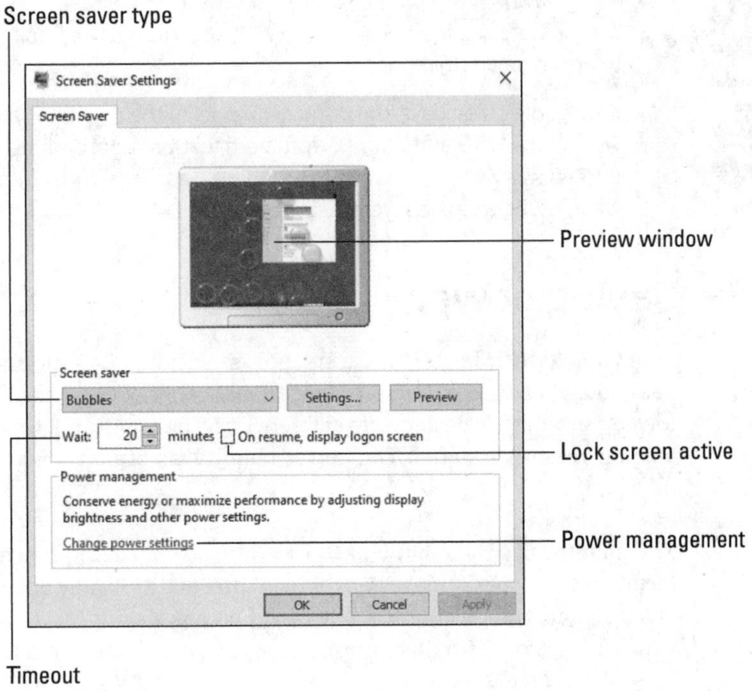

Screen saver type

FIGURE 3-7: Screen saver settings.

6. **Activate the option to display the logon screen.**

   When this option is active, only a user with an account or knowledge of your password can gain access after the screen saver kicks in.

7. **Click the OK button.**

The screen saver doesn't activate until the timeout duration has passed. Press any key or wiggle the mouse to reset the timer.

To disrupt the screen saver, press any key or wiggle the mouse. At this point, choose your account to sign in to Windows.

>> If you set the screen saver timeout to a value greater than the power savings timeout, you never see the screen saver.

>> You can instantly lock the screen in Windows: Press Win+L, where the *L* must stand for *l*ock. You must sign in to regain access to the computer.

>> A blank screen saver may present a puzzle in that the monitor is on (its power lamp is properly colored) but nothing appears on the screen.

WARNING

>> Avoid downloading screen savers from the Internet. Many "free" screen savers are malware or blast your desktop with advertising. See Book 4 for more information on malware.

TECHNICAL STUFF

>> Back in the olden days, the primary culprits of the phosphor burn-in peril were Lotus 1-2-3 and WordPerfect, both text-based programs. Phosphor burn-in was noticeable when the monitor was turned off, but more noticeable when other programs were run.

Saving power

Compared to their heat-generating, power-sucking, CRT monster monitors of the past, today's LCD monitors are marvelously energy efficient. Further, each has a lower-power mode designed to save energy. The monitor detects when the display adapter ceases its signal. The power lamp turns orange or yellow, and everyone hugs a tree.

The monitor is only a dumb partner in the power saving scheme. The true mastermind is the operating system, which directs the display adapter to suspend the video signal. This setting is made based on a period of inactivity — a timeout — which is controlled by using a setting in the PC's power management system. Follow these steps:

1. **Tap the Windows key to pop up the Start menu.**

2. **Type the word** power **and choose the matching result Power & Sleep Settings from the search results list.**

   The Settings app opens, displaying the Power & Sleep screen, as illustrated in Figure 3-8. The Screen item controls the monitor's timeout.

3. **Select a timeout value from the menu.**

   Two menus control the monitor's power timeout — one for battery-powered and the other for running the computer from a powered outlet.

Monitor timeout settings

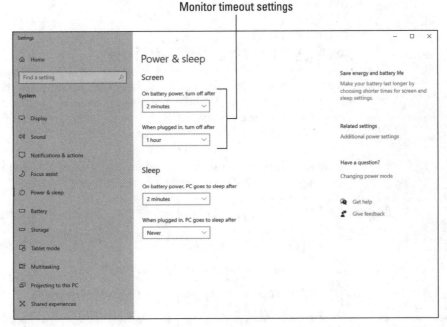

FIGURE 3-8:
Monitor power
options.

I set the screen saver to a 45-minute timeout, and then the power timeout takes place at one hour, or 15 minutes later.

>> The On Battery Power item (refer to Figure 3-8) appears for laptops as well as for desktop PCs connected to a UPS, or uninterruptable power supply. A desktop PC must be connected not only to the UPS for power but also via USB cable for the computer to read which power source is used.

>> If you're using a screen saver, ensure that its timeout is *less* than the power saver timeout. Otherwise, you never see the screen saver. Refer to the preceding section.

REMEMBER

>> When it enters power-saving mode, the monitor may display an onscreen message, such as "No input" or "Signal lost." Technically, these are error messages, but they're to be expected when the monitor goes to sleep.

>> The onscreen error messages also appear when the display adapter malfunctions. In that case, an unexpected "No input" message is truly an error message.

>> The monitor also goes into power-saving mode when the computer is turned off, though for true power savings, I recommend that you turn off the monitor as well as the computer.

>> See Chapter 4 in this minibook for more details on the PC's power management software.

Adjusting the resolution

The term *resolution* measures different things in the computer realm. For a digital picture, it may refer to the amount of detail in an image. For a computer's graphics system, resolution measures the number of pixels, horizontally and vertically.

A display adapter has a range of resolutions it can generate. More importantly, a monitor has a preferred set of resolutions that look good on the screen. Your goal is to match the two settings to produce the optimum image.

To check or set the current display resolution, heed these directions:

1. **Right-click on the desktop.**

2. **Choose Display Settings.**

3. **Click the Display Resolution menu to view your options.**

Figure 3-9 illustrates the menu as it appears in the Settings app. One or more settings can be flagged as Recommended. This resolution is considered optimum for the monitor.

4. **Set a new resolution, if desired.**

Windows previews the new resolution.

5. **If you set a new resolution, click the Keep Changes button to lock it in.**

If the new resolution displeases you, click the Revert button or wait for the original resolution to be restored.

To set the resolution for a second monitor, choose that monitor from the Settings app screen (not shown in Figure 3-9), and then repeat Steps 3 through 5.

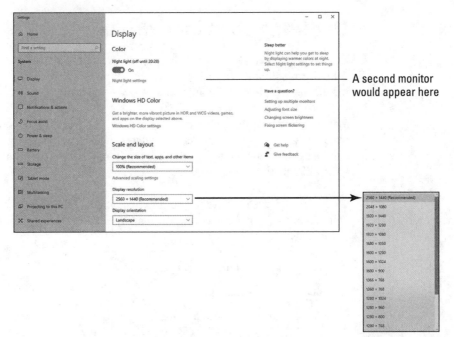

A second monitor would appear here

FIGURE 3-9:
Setting monitor resolution.

The advantage of a higher resolution is that the monitor displays more details. Items look crisper, and more information can be displayed.

The advantage of lower resolution is that items appear larger on the screen. If you have difficulty viewing the screen, choose a lower resolution.

>> A *pixel* is a single dot of color on a computer monitor or display. It's a portmanteau of *pic*ture *el*ement.

>> When the resolution seemingly and without explanation switches to very low (items look comically large on the screen), the problem is most likely a lost or improperly installed video driver. Reinstall the current driver to remedy the situation. See the later section "Updating the video driver."

>> Safe mode uses a low-resolution setting because only a basic video driver is loaded. The resolution returns to normal when you exit Safe mode. See Book 3, Chapter 4.

TECHNICAL STUFF

>> Choosing a nonrecommended resolution won't harm the monitor, though the image may look improper, fill the screen, or feature other unwanted visual artifacts.

Updating the video driver

Not every problem with the PC's graphics system is hardware. Some problems come from software. In fact, when that computer game crashes, it could be that the display adapter's software — its *driver* — needs an update.

Many display adapters come with companion software, such as the NVIDIA Control Panel. The software checks for updates, which can be configured to download and install automatically. I strongly recommend that you configure such software to install automatic updates.

When updates aren't installed automatically, you can perform a manual update. Your adventure starts by visiting the display adapter's Properties dialog box. Obey these steps:

1. **Press Win+X to summon the supersecret menu.**

2. **Choose Device Manager.**

   The Device Manager window appears, listing your PC's hardware by category.

   When Windows has detected hardware problems, a warning icon appears by an entry in the Device Manager window.

   TIP

3. **Expand the Display Adapters item.**

   Click the right-pointing chevron. You see all display adapters installed in the PC.

4. **Double-click your PC's display adapter.**

   The display adapter's Properties dialog box appears.

5. **Click the Driver tab.**

   Five important buttons appear on the Driver tab, as illustrated in Figure 3-10. Also important is the driver date. When this date is old, it indicates that a driver update check is in order.

6. **Click the Update Driver button.**

   It doesn't hurt to click the button. Consider it practice for when you need to update the driver — for example, when the PC is having graphical difficulties or compatibility issues.

7. **Choose the option Search Automatically for Updated Driver Software.**

   It may take some time for the driver to be found and downloaded from the Internet. When no updates are available (meaning that the current or best driver is installed), the message says so. Otherwise, a software update is downloaded and installed.

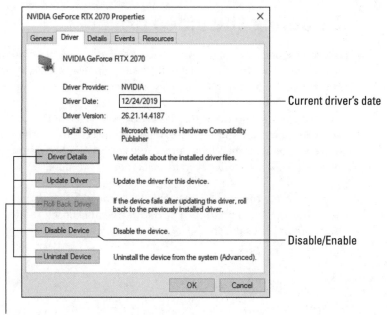

Current driver's date

Disable/Enable

Driver controls

FIGURE 3-10:
Controlling the
display adapter's
driver.

The computer doesn't need to be restarted when an update is installed, but the screen may flicker or go dark. If a restart is needed, a message appears, prompting you to do so.

TIP

REMEMBER

» If you experience problems with the update, click the Roll Back Driver button. You might have to perform this task in Safe mode. See Book 3, Chapter 4.

» You can also use the System Restore utility to roll back a driver update. See Book 3, Chapter 5 for information on System Restore.

» If for some reason the old driver is broken and an update isn't available, click the Uninstall Device button. (Refer to Figure 3-10.) This might happen if the current (or best) driver is installed but corrupted. After you click the Uninstall Device button, check the box that deletes the driver and then click OK. Restart the computer. At that point, a new driver is automatically downloaded from the Internet.

» See Book 3, Chapter 2 for more information on the Device Manager.

» You can also check for a driver by visiting the developer's website and looking for the Support link or Drivers link. Confirm which display adapter you have by following the directions outlined earlier in this chapter, in the section "Discovering your PC's display adapter."

» Don't forget to check for updated software for a second display adapter if your PC sports this hardware.

Disabling the video driver

A troubleshooting trick that may help recover a malfunctioning display adapter is to disable it and then reenable it. This solution uses software as opposed to uninstalling and reinstalling the display adapter card.

In the display adapter's Properties dialog box (refer to Figure 3-10), click the Disable Device button and then OK. Obey the directions on the screen, and be prepared for the display to look quite primitive. That's because disabling the adapter reverts the PC's graphics system to its most basic state.

After disabling the adapter, reenable it: In the display adapter's Properties dialog box, click the Enable button. The hardware comes back to life, and the graphical issue might be resolved.

Chapter **4**

Internal Issues

W *ho knows what evil lurks within a computer box!*

I prefer to call the computer box the *console*, which is the operating term for the device. The term *console* is also used to describe a dedicated gaming computer, so it's no longer as descriptive as it once was. Still, whether it's a gaming system or a PC, a lot goes on inside that box. Some of the stuff, you can fix — if you're brave enough to venture inside and face the evil!

Deep Inside the Case

The original success of the IBM PC, and the billions of computers that followed its design, was that the internal components are readily accessible and replaceable. Venturing inside the case isn't something you do every day, but it's often necessary to fix hardware problems or upgrade components.

Opening the PC case

Here are some things you don't need in order to open a PC case safely:

>> Goggles

>> Welding gloves

>> Hazmat suit

No, you don't need those things. Instead, you need this item:

>> Screwdriver

You might not even need the screwdriver, because some computer cases have easier internal access than others. Regardless, the process of opening the PC case goes like this:

1. **Ensure that you have a recent backup available, and create a restore point.**

   This precaution allows you to undo anything that might cause a software issue after you close the case. See Book 3, Chapter 5 for more information on System Restore; information on backing up is found in Book 4, Chapter 4.

2. **Shut down Windows and turn off the PC.**

   Sweet mercy, you don't want to open a PC case when the power is on!

3. **Unplug the PC.**

   Disconnect the power cord. Do not skip this step!

WARNING

4. **Remove the console case cover.**

   Computer cases are screwed shut; you find several screws on the rear of the case. For a desktop tower or minitower PC, remove the two screws that anchor the left side of the case (as you're facing the front of the console). Some consoles may feature a case-release mechanism instead of the two screws.

   Not every case opens. All-in-one PCs may feature an access panel for upgrading. Small-footprint desktop PCs open at the top. And mini-PCs, laptops, and two-in-one models don't open at all.

REMEMBER

5. **Behold the computer's guts!**

   Ew.

GROUNDING YOURSELF

Electrostatic discharge can be a shocking experience. What happens is that the electrical potential between you and whatever you touch is great enough that a spark jumps out. The spark is the electrostatic discharge, and it can damage delicate electronic components. It's a bad thing. To help prevent electrostatic discharge, you must ground yourself.

In addition to having strong moral beliefs and a hardy stalk of ethics, you need to neutralize the electrical potential between yourself, the computer case, and any components you're working with. To easily accomplish this task, always keep one hand touching the computer's metal casing while you're working. By touching both the casing and whatever doodad you're installing or removing, you reduce the chance of an electrical-component-killing electrostatic discharge.

If the console is dirty inside, clean it! Use a small vacuum to suck out the dust bunnies. You can use an air can to blast clean the components, but doing so creates a blizzard of dust. I use an air can in combination with the vacuum. Don't touch anything as you clean.

TIP

>> Unplug the power cord from the computer, not from the wall. If you unplug from the wall, some dutiful person may plug it back in "to help you out." Nope. Unplug the cord from the computer.

>> The console is designed to keep the scary electronics away from your fingers, spilled beverages, and pets. When you remove the case, you expose those dangers but also increase the potential of damaging static discharge. See the nearby sidebar, "Grounding yourself."

>> When you're done, close the case. See the section "Closing the PC case," elsewhere in this chapter.

Exploring the motherboard

Not every computer looks identical inside, though all PCs have similar components. Before you rummage around inside the console, get to know the territory. Figure 4-1 shows a typical PC's innards the way you might behold them after opening the PC's case.

Power supply   Power cables   Drive bay

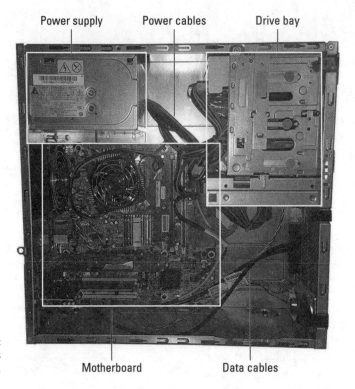

FIGURE 4-1:
A typical PC's
guts.

Motherboard   Data cables

Figure 4-1 serves as a guide. The major items listed may not be in the same spot on every PC, though each item is present. Here are some important components to find in the PC case:

Power supply: The power supply converts the alternating current (AC) from the wall into direct current (DC) inside the computer. Further, the power supply's fan helps keep the system cool. See the later sidebar "The computer's biggest fans."

Drive bay: Also known as the *disk drive cage,* the drive bay holds the primary storage device, and it may have room for other drives as well, including an optical drive.

Motherboard: The motherboard is the PC's main circuitry board. It's difficult to see because it's obscured by expansion cards, cables, the drive bay, or other mystery electronics. Figure 4-2 illustrates a motherboard that has been freed from the confines of its computer box prison.

Cables: Two types of cables coil through the confines of the console. Power cables originate at the power supply and provide juice to the motherboard. Data cables sprout from the motherboard and connect to vital computer components. The smaller the computer case, the more the cables obstruct your view of the items inside.

I/O connectors   Processor/Fan   Memory slots

Main power connector

SATA connectors

Clock battery

Expansion slots

PCI slots (x2)

PCIe slots (x2)

FIGURE 4-2:
A typical
motherboard.

The motherboard is a busy place. It's home to locations involving some important upgrades and fixes. Figure 4-2 illustrates what a motherboard can look like.

Here are the important items to find:

Processor: The PC's primary chip, the processor roosts on the motherboard — but you can't see it! That's because the processor wears a large cooling fan as a hat.

Memory: A PC has two or four (or more) memory card slots, into which plug memory cards. See the later section "Expanding memory." The slots shown in Figure 4-2 lack memory cards.

Expansion slots: To help customize your computer, expansion slots allow you to connect bonus circuitry in the form of expansion cards. The most common card is the display adapter card, though a variety of cards are available. See the later section "Adding an expansion card."

Clock battery: The clock battery helps the PC keep track of time when the computer is unplugged. It lurks somewhere on the motherboard, so it's difficult to see but looks like a large coin.

Firmware: Not illustrated in Figure 4-2 or obvious on any motherboard are the chips that give the PC its personality. Once known as the BIOS, these chips provide basic computer services, such as graphics, networking, and other items.

Connectors: To communicate with the rest of the computer, the motherboard is dotted with connectors. Into these connectors plug cables, such as the power cable or the SATA cable that connects the console's mass storage devices.

Even when you can see all these items on the motherboard, their identity may remain a mystery. For example, I don't recommend that you remove the processor's cooling fan hat just to determine the chip's make and model number. A software solution is available that precludes the need to open the PC case.

To view information about your PC's innards, press the Windows+Break key combination. (The Break key is labeled Pause, or Break/Pause on some keyboards.) Upon success, you see the System window, similar to what's illustrated in Figure 4-3.

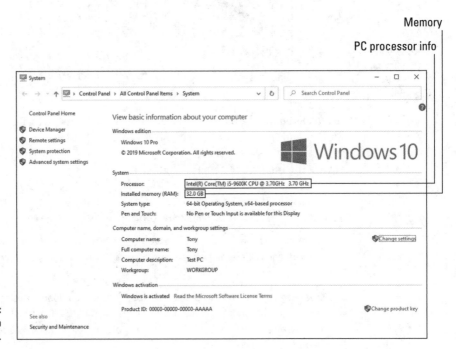

FIGURE 4-3:
The System window.

If your PC's keyboard lacks a Break key, in any File Explorer window's address bar, type the following:

```
Control Panel All Control Panel Items System
```

As you type each word, search matches appear, confirming that you're on the proper path.

The System window divulges information you can't discern by looking at the motherboard directly. (Well, if you're a true nerd, you could, but that's not my point.) As an example, in Figure 4-3, the processor is an Intel(R) Core(TM) i5-9600K CPU running at 3.7GHz. The PC has 32GB of RAM installed.

>> It's not necessary to remove the motherboard from your PC. I don't recommend it. I don't even recommend replacing a motherboard. Unfortunately:

>> Replacing the motherboard is necessary when it's defective. This replacement is covered under the manufacturer's warranty. Beyond that period, I would recommend getting a new PC as a better option than replacing a motherboard.

TECHNICAL STUFF

>> Some nerds enthusiastically support a motherboard replacement. Doing so really depends on the entire system: If the power supply, memory, display adapter, and other components are current and working well, consider a motherboard replacement if it's cheaper or improves system performance. Such an upgrade however, ranks high on the difficulty scale.

>> Figure 4-2 is rather generous in that cables, expansion cards, and even the drive bay normally obscure the view of the motherboard. When you're installing expansion cards or storage, some items need to be removed to access various features.

>> Firmware can't be replaced, but it can be updated. Also known as "updating the BIOS," refer to Book 4, Chapter 2 for additional details.

>> Another term for the processor is *CPU*, or *central processing unit*. Too many people confuse the CPU with the computer case, which is inaccurate. The computer box is the console. The CPU is the processor.

TECHNICAL STUFF

>> The PC and motherboard shown in Figure 4-1 and 4-2 are from an older system. Newer PCs are even more compact and lack some of the legacy connectors shown.

THE COMPUTER'S BIGGEST FANS

Beyond providing power, the power supply's other job is to keep the console cool. It's such a big job that the power supply's fan isn't the only fan inside the case. Another important fan is located atop the processor. High-end display adapters sometimes sport two fans. Additional fans can be found inside the case.

Keeping cool is a big deal inside a PC. That's because heat causes most internal hardware problems. When the temperature gets too high, electronics fail. The computer could restart. Cables could pop loose. A constant temperature is preferred, and the fans inside the console help to maintain that constant temperature.

Closing the PC case

After meddling with your computer's delicate innards, you need to close the case and turn the system back on, the whole time praying to your favorite deity that not only will the sucker work but also the problem will be fixed.

After installing or replacing or checking whatever prompted you to open the case, follow these general steps to close 'er up:

1. **Ensure that your job is complete.**

   Check for any spare parts, screws, wrappers, eyeglasses, or electronic detritus remaining from whatever operation you performed.

   Check any cables that might have loosened.

   Ensure that every latch, screw, and cover you removed is properly replaced.

   Double-check to confirm that the installation was done properly.

2. **Plug in the console.**

3. **Turn on the computer.**

   Yes, I recommend that you perform these two steps *before* you reattach the side of the computer case. The reason is to test; it's a pain to reopen the case when something doesn't work right. Trust me — but be careful when you run the computer with its case open.

4. **Confirm that the upgrade or fix worked.**

   For the most part, when you see the manufacturer's splash screen, you're good. For other upgrades, wait until Windows starts and displays the sign-on screen.

5. **Reattach the console side.**

   Ensure that the case is fully closed. Some of the cases require a certain finesse before you get everything lined up. Locate the screws you removed when you opened the console, and screw them back into place.

6. **You're done.**

WARNING

A computer's case must be properly shut for the system to meet radio frequency interference (RFI) standards. These standards, monitored by the FCC in the United States, help keep the electronic noise generated by a computer inside the case from messing with other radio signals. So, as much as you would think it's neat-o, do not run the PC with the cover off.

Things to Upgrade, Fix, or Repair Inside the Case

For a hardware issue, one solution is to swap out the malfunctioning device with one that works. This process works well for peripherals, but when it comes to items internal to the PC's case, a more common approach is to replace the item. The process can be scary, but quick and satisfying — especially when you're comfortable rummaging around inside several hundred dollars' worth of electronics.

Upgrading the power supply

Your PC's power supply can die, which is good news; the device is designed to sacrifice itself to save the rest of the PC's electronics. Replacing the dead power supply helps you recover from the disaster nicely.

When choosing a replacement power supply, you must know its form factor and its wattage.

» The *form factor* is the power supply's dimensions. The most common is the ATX standard, which most home- and small-office computers use. ATX stands for Advanced Technology eXtended.

» The power supply's output is measured in watts. More watts are better. In fact, if the power supply failed because you added more internal components to the PC, definitely get a new unit that provides more watts, such as a 750W power supply to replace a 500W model.

Look on the back of the PC's case to determine the power supply's make or model. If this information isn't obvious, you must open the case and look for a sticker on the power supply that details its information. Your goal is to purchase a compatible or better replacement.

When you have the replacement power supply handy, follow these steps to perform power supply surgery:

1. Open the PC's case.

Directions are offered earlier in this chapter.

2. Disconnect all power supply connectors inside the console.

This step is tricky. Some PC power supplies have more cables than an octopus has legs. These cables can be stiff and difficult to manage, but they lack suction cups. Instead, specific connectors appear at the cable's ends or along the cable's length. These cables provide power to the motherboard, display adapter, mass storage, and other locations. See the nearby sidebar, "Power connections from beyond," for more information.

TIP

To help you reconnect the power cables, place colored sticky dots on each cable and connector. Match the colors.

3. Remove the screws that anchor the power supply to the case.

An ATX power supply has four screws on the back.

4. Liberate the old power supply!

Wiggle the power supply free from the case. It might not be easy; you may have to remove a hard drive or an expansion card. Otherwise, the typical ATX power supply rests on a tiny shelf and is easily removed from the case.

5. Insert the replacement.

Shove it into the case, resting the gizmo on its tiny shelf. Ensure that the four screw holes on the power supply line up with the holes on the case.

6. Insert and tighten the power supply's anchor screws.

7. Reconnect the power supply cables.

Don't worry about messing up this step. The cables cannot be plugged in backward. If you miss a connection, the device doesn't work, though double-check the motherboard connections and the power connections on the display adapter.

8. Turn on the PC.

Yes, keep the case open. You want to ensure that the system starts and you see the initial splash screen on the monitor. When Windows starts, shut down the PC again.

Do not touch anything inside the console while the power is on and the case is open.

WARNING

9. **When you're sure that everything is working, close the PC case.**

   See the earlier section "Closing the PC case."

POWER CONNECTIONS FROM BEYOND

Just as your house features different types of electrical sockets and plugs, the power supply in a PC offers different sockets and plugs. Here are the most common types:

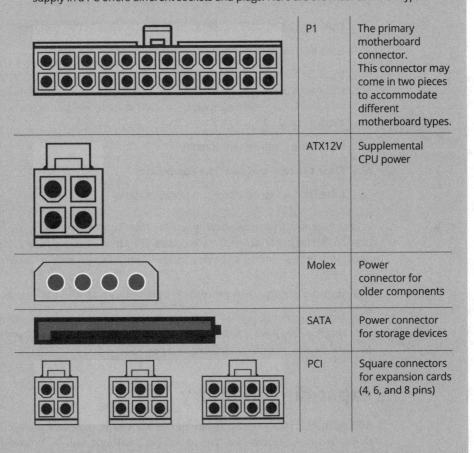

P1	The primary motherboard connector. This connector may come in two pieces to accommodate different motherboard types.
ATX12V	Supplemental CPU power
Molex	Power connector for older components
SATA	Power connector for storage devices
PCI	Square connectors for expansion cards (4, 6, and 8 pins)

In addition to these connectors, the power supply also uses splitters to provide for more connectors and adapters to switch from one connector type to another.

Replacing the clock battery

The computer's internal clock is kept accurate by a connection to an Internet time server and a constant flow of electricity. Without the time server, the clock would be off every day because computer clocks are notoriously inaccurate. But without electricity, the computer believes the time to be midnight on January 1, 1980.

A battery affixed to the motherboard keeps the clock running while the PC is turned off. The battery also backs up other information about the PC. When the battery dies, not only is the time and date inaccurate but the PC may also believe it has lost some vital components. To remedy this situation, the clock battery must be replaced. Follow these steps:

1. **Open the computer's case, as described earlier in this chapter.**

2. **Remove the battery from the motherboard.**

It's often a lithium battery, one of those coin-size jobs you can buy anywhere that watch or hearing aid batteries are sold. Figure 4-2 illustrates what it may look like, but it could be anywhere — even mounted perpendicular to the motherboard.

3. **Install the replacement battery.**

4. **Close the case and start the computer.**

Directions are found elsewhere in this chapter.

When you restart the computer, you may have to run some setup or basic configuration, including setting the proper date and time. Nothing inside the PC is damaged, so after you complete basic configuration, the system should work normally.

TIP

» Ensure that you match the replacement battery type with the original.

» Motherboard batteries last for years. When the battery goes, it's often a sign that the computer is ancient and needs to be replaced. Rather than replace the battery, consider upgrading to a new PC.

Expanding memory

Adding memory to your PC is one of the least expensive and most effective ways to improve its performance. The ordeal isn't without a hitch, however: A memory upgrade involves understanding two items: memory card slots on the motherboard and the memory cards that insert into those slots.

A typical PC features two or four memory card slots on the motherboard.

Into the memory card slots you install memory cards. These are known by the acronyms SIMM and DIMM, which stand for Single Inline Memory Module and Dual Inline Memory Module, respectively. The difference is whether the card features chips on one (single) or both (dual) sides.

Memory cards are installed into one, two, or all four of the motherboard's memory card slots. Further, the memory cards you install must match in some manner. You can't willy-nilly mix memory card capacities.

Figure 4-4 illustrates how two different memory capacities can be installed on a motherboard with four memory card slots. Each row shows a different total capacity created by using sets of four memory cards, two memory cards, and one memory card.

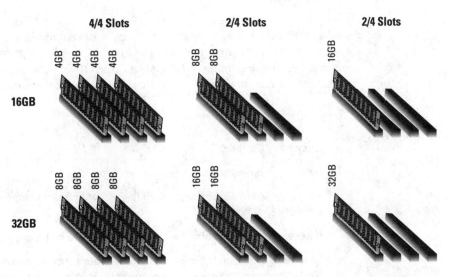

FIGURE 4-4:
Memory module
allocation.

The primary reason for using all four slots instead of two or one is cost: A single 16GB memory card is far more expensive than four 4GB cards. To save money, manufacturers and dealers fill all the slots as opposed to using fewer memory cards to keep slots open for expansion. The problem with this arrangement is that it makes upgrading more difficult.

When upgrading memory, you must maximize the slots in a most efficient manner.

Suppose that your PC has 8GB of RAM total. The memory is installed on two 4GB memory cards, leaving two slots open. You want to install 32GB total RAM in the PC. Here are your upgrade choices:

>> Remove the two 4GB memory cards. Replace them with four 8GB cards, which is the least expensive option. (Using a single 32GB card would be very expensive.)

>> Remove the two 4GB memory cards and replace them with two 16GB cards. This option isn't as cheap as using four 8GB cards, but it leaves two memory slots open for future expansion.

>> If the motherboard allows you to mix memory card capacities, add two 8GB cards in the empty slots. This choice lets you keep the original cards, but add 16GB for a total of 24GB of RAM. It's not quite 32GB, but it doesn't waste the existing cards.

TIP

Perhaps the easiest way to upgrade memory is to visit an online site that offers a memory scanner program. For example, crucial.com lets you download a memory scanner that determines which type of chips the motherboard prefers, examines installed memory, and offers various solutions for memory upgrades.

To perform the physical upgrade, follow these steps:

1. **Open the PC's case.**

Refer to the earlier section "Opening the PC case."

You may need to shove cables out of the way or uninstall items so that you can access the memory slots.

2. **If necessary, remove any memory cards that are no longer needed.**

To remove a card, press down on the clips located at either end of the memory slot, as illustrated in Figure 4-5. A gentle press is all you need, which lifts the card from the slot.

3. **Install the new or replacement memory cards.**

The card features a notch, which lines up with a key on the open memory slot, as illustrated in Figure 4-5. Orient the card, and then press it firmly into the slot. When you do, the clips on both ends of the slot clamp down, though I recommend ensuring that they are fully closed.

4. **Start the PC to test the memory.**

If the system doesn't start, well, you did something wrong or the memory is bad. Consider reinstalling the original memory.

5. **Close the PC.**

Refer to the directions in the earlier section "Closing the PC case."

Open memory slot   Memory card   Key   Closed clip   Open clip

FIGURE 4-5:
Memory slot
clips.

TIP

The way to avoid damaging memory cards is to handle them carefully. Avoid touching the metal edge, the part that's inserted into the slot. Touch the PC's metal case before picking up a chip, to help neutralize static electricity. Treat the cards gingerly.

>> Memory banks are organized in pairs, often color-coded on the motherboard. Each pair must have the same memory card size. You cannot mix and match memory cards between different-colored slots.

>> Some motherboards insist that all memory cards be of the same capacity. If so, the slots all use the same color.

**TECHNICAL
STUFF**

>> Beyond SIMM and DIMM, memory cards have a boatload of acronyms and technical descriptions. I could once read the numbers on the chips to determine the memory capacity and type. Today it's not as easy, which is why using an online memory-buying website with a companion diagnostic program is the best way to obtain a memory upgrade for your PC.

BUYING REPLACEMENT PARTS

Gone are the days when most major cities featured computer parts stores. Cavernous retail, big-box stores like Circuit City and Fry's are rare these days. Instead, you must turn to the Internet to locate internal computer parts, especially highly specialized parts like power supplies and memory.

The variety of online stores is rich and the selection wide, but unlike at the brick-and-mortar stores, you must either pay for overnight shipping or wait until the part arrives.

Ensure that you review the website's refund-and-return policy. Some items, such as memory, might not be returnable.

The warranty is also something you must check. A 90-day warranty is okay for electronics; if they fail, it happens quickly, so even a 30-day warranty is okay in some situations.

Tech support for replacement parts is limited to non-existent. Most of these places assume that you know what you're doing when you buy a loose hard drive or an expansion card. Refer to Book 1, Chapter 2 for tips on finding helpful information on the Internet.

Adding an expansion card

Because most of the formerly optional PC hardware is now included in the firmware, the need for adding expansion cards to a PC isn't as great as it once was. Beyond a display adapter, few people bother opening the PC case and expanding the system's potential by plugging in a few neat-o expansion cards.

Back in the day, expansion cards added more memory, more ports, mouse support, a modem, networking capabilities, sound hardware, and other options all considered basic today. Even display electronics are on the motherboard, though that video system isn't powerful enough to run popular games, so display adapter cards are common.

Expansion cards plug into expansion slots. The current standard is called PCIe, which stands for Peripheral Component Interconnect Express. An older standard, PCI, wasn't as fast. Both slot types are shown earlier, in Figure 4-2, which depicts a typical PC motherboard.

Most expansion cards sold today are PCIe, so you need only worry about older expansion slot standards for compatibility with ancient expansion cards.

To install an expansion slot into your PC, obey these directions:

1. **Study the instructions that came with the expansion card.**

Check the directions for specifics, such as which type of slot is needed, whether one or two slots are needed, and whether the card needs supplemental power.

2. **Open the computer case.**

Directions are found earlier in this chapter. Pay heed to my admonition for backing up data and setting a restore point.

3. **Locate an available expansion slot.**

4. **Remove the slot cover associated with the expansion slot.**

The slot cover is part of the console, on the back of the PC. It not only anchors the back half of the card but also provides access for any connectors the card surrenders to the outside world.

Some slot covers are anchored with a single screw; unscrew it and remove the slot cover. (You don't need to keep the slot cover, but I do.) Some fancy PC cases may have a special locking mechanism that keeps the slot covers snug without the need for a screw.

Save the screw! You need it to reattach the expansion card to the case. You can toss out the slot cover.

REMEMBER

5. **If necessary, move cables out of the way or remove another expansion card or a mass storage device to allow ample room to install the expansion card.**

Some expansion cards can fit into only one slot, and some fit rather snugly.

6. **Ground yourself.**

Touch the metal part of the PC case.

7. **Swing the locking hook out of the way.**

The locking hook is found on one side of the expansion slot (the side away from the back of the case). The hook anchors the card, but move it out of the way first so that you don't break it when you insert the card.

8. **Insert the expansion card into the expansion slot.**

Gently press the card into the slot. Use the connector edge to guide you, but also the rear of the card, which slides into the same hole as the expansion card cover. The card must be fully seated; don't "fudge" it or force it.

9. **If the hook on the expansion slot doesn't automatically snap into place, reach down to swing the hook into the card, securing it to the slot.**

10. Connect any internal cables.

   If the card requires a power cable, attach it now. Attach other cables as well, which should be mentioned in the instructions you failed to read in Step 1.

11. Replace and reattach anything you removed or detached in Step 5.

12. Anchor the expansion card's slot cover to the case.

   Use the same screw you removed in Step 4.

13. Close the case, as described earlier in this chapter.

When you turn on the computer, the new hardware should be recognized instantly. Windows automatically installs necessary drivers and updates so that the PC can use the new gizmo.

If you experience any problems, you might have forgotten to connect a cable. The card may not be fully seated. It's rare, but the card might be defective. In this case, you must remove the card to ensure that the PC still starts (that the problem isn't elsewhere), and phone technical support or exchange the card for another.

>> Beyond display adapters, you might consider expansion cards that boost your PC's sound system, add USB ports, or provide other features. Honestly, the selection these days is rather thin.

>> Look on the back of your PC to examine the slot covers to determine whether a slot is empty. A blank slot cover, however, may not indicate that an expansion slot is available, because some expansion cards may not use the slot cover and some cards may use two.

TECHNICAL
STUFF

>> Before the PCIe expansion slot standard was PCI, which stands for Peripheral Component Interconnect (no "express"). Before then, the PC family featured a variety of expansion slot standards, including the original ISA slot type. ISA isn't a special acronym for anything; the slots needed a name, so the wizards came up with Industry Standard Architecture.

Adding or replacing an internal drive

Beyond giving your PC more memory, another way to be nice to Mr. Computer is to upgrade its storage capacity. You can replace or add internal mass storage devices just as you can replace or add many console components.

TIP

If your goal is merely to expand the PC's storage capacity, consider getting an external drive instead of adding more internal storage. For all-in-one, small-footprint PCs, and laptops, external storage is the only expansion option. See Chapter 2 in this minibook for details on adding external drives.

To add or replace an internal drive, you must access the console's drive bay, which is illustrated earlier, in Figure 4-1. This location is where internal storage roosts, and it places a limit on how much you can expand the storage system, for not only the number of drives but also their size or form factor.

Mass storage devices come in two popular sizes or form factors: 3.5-inch for most hard drives and SSDs and 2.5-inch for laptop hard drives. An obsolete, 5.25-inch form factor is used for optical drives and older hard drives. The PC console may sport 5.25-inch slots, though you can obtain an adapter to install a smaller, 3.5-inch drive in this slot.

Each drive requires two connections: data and power.

>> The data connection attaches the storage device to the motherboard. The current standard is SATA, which is a cascading acronym for Serial Advanced Technology Attachment. A SATA cable connects to the drive and the motherboard.

>> The power connection attaches the drive to the power supply. Unlike the SATA connectors, if the console lacks sufficient power connectors, you can use a splitter to provide power to multiple hard drives.

The types of drives you can add or replace are traditional spinning hard disk drives (HDD), solid-state drives (SDD), and optical drives (no fancy initialism).

To remove a drive, follow these steps:

1. **Open the PC case.**

   Follow the directions found elsewhere in this chapter.

2. **Disconnect the power and SATA cable from the drive.**

   Pinch the SATA cable connector to loosen its grip, and then pull out the cable. Remove the power cable.

3. **Remove the drive from the bay.**

   Some drives use screws to connect to the case. Up to three screws can be found on both sides of the drive. Some drive bays use rails or a caddy to insert the drive into the bay. Screws are the most common. Figure 4-6 identifies the screw hole locations, as well as other exciting items on a loose hard drive.

   If screws are attached to the drive's far side, you must remove the console's right-side panel to access the screws.

TIP

4. **If your task were only to remove a drive, close the PC case.**

   You can leave the cables hanging loose inside the case.

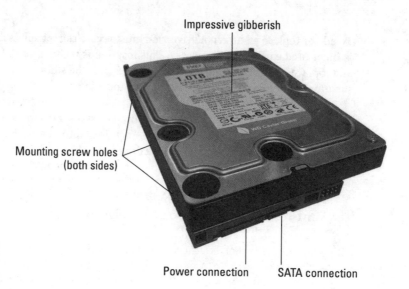

Impressive gibberish

Mounting screw holes
(both sides)

FIGURE 4-6:
A typical internal
hard drive.

Power connection   SATA connection

To add an internal drive, obey these directions:

1. **Open the PC case.**

2. **Locate the bay where you'll insert the drive.**

3. **If necessary, move items out of the way so that you can fully access the drive bay.**

   I've had to remove a display adapter to add a new drive to a PC. Just remember to reinstall and reconnect anything you move or remove in this step.

4. **Attach rails or a cage to the drive, if the drive bay uses that system.**

   The rails are, or the cage is, found in the drive already.

5. **Slide the drive into the bay.**

   If the drive uses screws to anchor itself to the drive bay, line up the holes on both the drive and the bay.

6. **Screw the drive into the bay.**

   It's best to use at least two screws to anchor the drive. The goal is to keep the drive from sliding around, and having two screws does the job.

7. **Attach the power and data cables to the drive.**

   The cables are different sizes and keyed, so you can't connect them incorrectly.

TIP

   If the drive is the PC's only drive or you want the drive to be the primary boot drive, attach it to the SATA 1 connector on the motherboard.

   Another tip: To help locate the SATA connections on the motherboard, follow a SATA cable from an existing drive.

8. **Replace and reattach any items you removed or disconnected in Step 3.**

9. **Close the case.**

Part of this step, covered in the earlier section "Closing the PC case," involves turning on the PC with the case open. It's best to determine that the hard drive starts with the case off and then close the case upon success. Otherwise, you can turn off the PC and quickly fix any problems.

Adding a new hard drive doesn't magically make it available to your PC. After the hardware installation, you must access the Disk Management console to partition the drive, assign a file system, and format the drive. Refer to Chapter 2 in this minibook.

TECHNICAL
STUFF

>> SATA is what I call a *cascading* acronym. It first translates as Serial ATA. ATA stands for AT Attachment. ATA was the standard developed for the IBM PC AT generation of computers, introduced back in the 1980s. AT stands for Advanced Technology. (Well, it was at the time.)

>> If the motherboard lacks sufficient SATA connectors, you can purchase a SATA expansion card to provide more. The expansion card might also offer *eSATA* connections, where the little *E* stands for *external*. Use the external connectors on the back of the expansion card to add external SATA drives.

>> Though you can use a splitter to provide power to several hard drives, you might consider instead upgrading the PC's power supply. Too many splitters imply that the power supply is reaching its output capacity. Refer to the earlier section "Upgrading the power supply."

>> Hard drives are cheaper and more plentiful, though SSDs are faster. Between the two is the hybrid drive, which is where solid-state storage augments spinning storage.

>> A worthy upgrade option for any PC is an NVMe drive. This drive uses the PCIe (expansion slot) interface and provides great speed at a reduced cost. NVMe stands for Non-Volatile Memory Express.

>> If your nostalgic desire is to add an optical drive, you must use a 5¼-inch bay. Before you add the drive, pop-out the drive bay cover on the front of the console; the optical drive sticks out the front of the PC so that you can access the discs. Optical drives are still necessary for compatibility with older software, to burn CDs, and to watch movies.

TIP

>> Better than adding an internal optical drive, consider getting an external, USB model. The external model can be connected to any PC or laptop that needs to read an optical disc.

DISK DRIVE SHOPPING

The number-one thing I look for in a new hard drive is capacity. You don't want to undercut storage, especially before you've stored anything on the drive.

For a second internal hard drive, I recommend a capacity at least that of the original hard drive. Otherwise, get as much storage as you can afford. Keep in mind that the true cost is measured by dollars-per-gigabyte. For example, a 5TB drive that costs $100 is a better value than a 3TB drive that cost $70. The first drive is 2 cents per GB; the second is 2.3 cents per GB.

Other technical details hover around a hard drive purchase like moons around Jupiter: drive speed, buffers and caches, and transfer times. And keep in mind that you want an *internal* drive, which might also be called a "loose" drive.

Finally, drives don't come with cables. If you're adding a new drive, ensure that it comes with a SATA cable. If not, buy one.

>> If you're replacing the PC's primary hard drive, the next step after installation and formatting is to recover Windows. See Book 3, Chapter 1. After that, you must reinstall any programs and personal files, which is covered in Book 4, Chapter 4.

>> It's possible to clone one hard drive to another, which is a complicated but elegant solution to increase hard drive capacity. See Book 5, Chapter 2 for details.

Power Management Issues

Power management hardware allows your PC to save energy. The hardware is part of the motherboard, so it's not a peripheral. Therefore, it's an inside-the-console item you may need to attend to for troubleshooting purposes. The good news is that resolving power management issues is done through software; a screwdriver is not required.

>> The power management system is responsible for the behavior of the PC's power button. This duty explains why the button isn't an on–off switch. It controls more than just the PC's power.

POWERFUL TERMS

Like most technology, PC power management is rife with specific terms and names for its modes of operation. Here's the short list:

hibernation: In this mode, the computer's current state is saved and the PC turns itself off. When you turn on the system again, the saved state is restored and you can continue working.

hybrid sleep: A cross between hibernation and sleep, this mode saves data for a fast recovery but doesn't quite turn off the computer. This mode is enabled by default in Windows 10.

Sleep mode: In Sleep mode, the computer slows down to save energy. Certain peripherals are disabled and the processor enters a low-power mode, but the entire system isn't shut down.

suspend: This is another name for *hibernate*.

>> Power management problems include issues with Sleep mode. Specifically, the PC is either unable to enter Sleep mode or unable to recover from it.

>> The power management standard is called the Advanced Configuration and Power Interface (ACPI). You'll find the ACPI items in the Device Manager window, listed in the System Devices category. See Book 3, Chapter 2 for details on the Device Manager.

Locating power management controls

Power management is enabled on all Windows 10 PCs. To check the settings, follow these steps:

1. **Press the Windows+I keyboard shortcut to summon the Settings app.**

2. **Choose System.**

3. **Choose Power & Sleep.**

   You see the basic Sleep mode commands, as illustrated in Figure 4-7. One section covers the screen; the other, the PC. The "plugged in" options appear only for battery-powered PCs, such as two-in-ones, laptops, and desktop PCs connected to a UPS (uninterruptible power supply).

The two main items for power management are the screen and then the computer itself (the stuff inside the console), labeled as *Sleep* in Figure 4-7.

For more detailed control over the PC's power management system, continue with these steps:

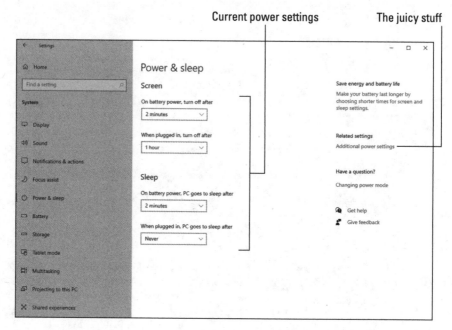

Current power settings   The juicy stuff

FIGURE 4-7:
Power
management
settings.

4. **Click the Additional Power Settings link.**

   The Control Panel's Power Options window appears.

5. **By the chosen power plan, click the Change Plan Settings link.**

   The Balanced plan is normally the one chosen, unless you've previously modified the plan to create your own. If so, click the link by that power plan.

   The Edit Plan Settings screen is similar to the Settings app's power management screen (refer to Figure 4-7), but it's not your final destination.

6. **Click the Change Advanced Power Settings link.**

   The Power Options dialog box appears, illustrated in Figure 4-8. This is the place where you can change individual power management settings.

Each item in the Power Options dialog box controls a specific aspect of power management or an individual piece of hardware. Choose an item in the tree to expand and view details. Click a link to set options. See the nearby sidebar, "Use the power button to turn off the computer," for an example.

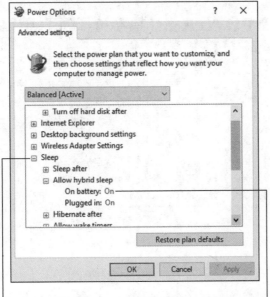

FIGURE 4-8:
The Power
Options
dialog box.

Click to expand an item   Click a link to display options

One item you may find in the Power Options dialog box is unique to laptops: Lid Close Action. You can choose what the laptop does — if anything — when you close the lid while the laptop is plugged in or on battery power. For example, if you prefer the laptop to hibernate when you shut the lid, in the Power Options dialog box choose Lid Close Action, and then select Hibernate from both the On Battery and Plugged In menus.

When you're done setting options in the Power Options dialog box, click the OK button. If the Save Changes button is enabled in the Edit Plan Settings window, click it to make your changes permanent.

>> After a given period of inactivity, or *timeout,* the power to the screen is disabled. Technically, the video signal is cut, which the monitor recognizes (or doesn't recognize), so the monitor sleeps or enters a low-power mode to save energy.

>> For the computer, Sleep mode powers down most of the electronics — primarily, spinning hard drives. The keyboard and mouse remain alert and potentially other hardware as well, such as the network adapter.

>> Upon a signal, such as a key tap or mouse wiggle, Sleep mode ends and the computer comes back to life. If not, or when Sleep mode fails, you have troubleshooting to do.

USE THE POWER BUTTON TO TURN OFF THE COMPUTER

One option you can configure in the Power Options dialog box is what happens when the computer is on and you punch the power button. Normally, you use the button to turn on the PC and then ignore the button thereafter. But the power button's function can be programmed.

In the Power Options dialog box, choose Power Buttons and Lid and then Power Button Action. Click the link to set what the power button does when you punch it. For example, to disable the power button, choose Do Nothing.

For a laptop or PC connected to a UPS, two options are available: Plugged In or On Battery. Set the power button's function for both conditions.

You can also set the function for the sleep button, though few computers these days have a sleep button.

TIP

>> You can't hurry Sleep mode, but you can lock Windows: Press the Win+L key combination. Windows displays the sign-on screen, and only those who have an account can access the system.

>> The screen saver isn't part of the PC's power-saving hardware. It's similar, in that the screen saver triggers from an inactivity timeout. Ensure that the screen saver timeout is less than the power management's screen timeout. Refer to Chapter 3 in this minibook for details on the screen saver.

Setting power management options for specific devices

Not only does the PC have power management software but specific devices do as well. The printer may fall to sleep after a period of inactivity, which saves power — especially when you leave the printer on all the time.

Another device that features its own power management is the network adapter. In fact, this power management setting caused a curious problem on my PC when the system would wake up from Sleep mode at odd times. It turns out that the network adapter was rousing the system. To fix the problem, I disabled that feature.

To check the status of an individual device's power management capabilities, such as the network adapter, use the Device Manager. Follow these steps:

1. **Press Win+X.**

2. **Choose Device Manager from the supersecret menu.**

The Device Manager window unfurls.

3. **Expand the Network Adapters item.**

You see an entry for each network adapter in the system. Also included are any Bluetooth adapters and IEEE port adapters. What you want is the Ethernet item.

4. **Double-click on the Ethernet item.**

You see the network adapter's Properties dialog box.

5. **Click the Power Management tab.**

If the tab isn't available, the adapter lacks power management smarts. Otherwise, you see two items, as illustrated in Figure 4-9.

Activate power management for this device

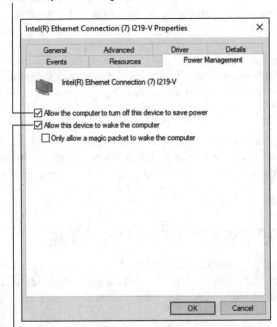

FIGURE 4-9: Power management for the network adapter.

On activity, the device can wake up the computer

Three settings are shown in Figure 4-9. The first lets the PC's main power-management software disable the device. The second lets the device itself wake up the computer. On my PC, I disable the second option for the network adapter because the computer is always receiving network traffic and it never goes into power-saving mode.

Other gizmos may also sport a Power Management tab in the Properties dialog box. Use this tab to control the device's energy saving settings. The only way to know for certain which gizmos have power management capabilities is to review items in the Device Manager window. For example, the UPS (uninterruptible power supply), keyboard, and mouse hardware all feature Power Management tabs in their Properties dialog boxes. In fact, you can configure the mouse or keyboard to *not* wake the computer from Sleep mode, by disabling their power management features.

See Book 3, Chapter 2 for more information on using the Device Manager.

Recovering from a PC coma

Occasionally, a PC may go to sleep and not wake up. It gets stuck. For a laptop, the battery level might be too low to start the system; otherwise, to turn off the computer, press and hold the power button until the system's power is off, and then release the button.

When you turn on the computer again, your next task is to update the PC's power management driver software. See the later section "Updating power drivers." Also, consider running Windows Update, in case the problem is related to the operating system. See Book 4, Chapter 2.

If the problem persists, don't use Sleep mode for your PC. For example, on one of my older, more stubborn computers, I don't use Sleep mode. Instead, I turn off the monitor when not using that computer and then turn off the computer at the end of the day.

Updating power drivers

To resolve most power management issues, ensure that your PC is using the latest ACPI power management software. The Windows Update service might install new drivers. For a more direct approach, follow these steps:

1. **Tap the Windows key.**

2. **Type** device manager **and choose the Device Manager from the list of items.**

   You don't need to type all of **device manager**; choose the matching program as it appears in the list.

3. **If prompted with a UAC warning, type the administrator's password to continue.**

4. **Click to open System Devices.**

5. **Right-click the item Microsoft ACPI-Compliant System.**

6. **Choose the shortcut menu item Update Driver Software.**

7. **Choose the selected item, Search Automatically for Updated Driver Software.**

   Windows looks online for any software updates.

8. **If the latest, bestest software is already installed, you see a notice; click the Close button. Otherwise, continue to follow the steps on the screen to update the computer's ACPI (power management) software.**

   You may be required to restart the PC to complete the installation process. If prompted, do so.

After updating the driver, try to repeat whatever action caused the PC's power management software to fail. For example, choose Sleep or Hibernate from the Start menu.

If the driver update didn't fix the problem, the power management hardware might be to blame. You can adjust the Sleep mode settings so that the PC never sleeps. Refer to the earlier section "Locating power management controls," and set the timeout values to Never. Disabling Sleep mode is a workaround, not a fix. If other problems occur in addition to power management failure, you may need to upgrade the motherboard or consider getting another computer.

Chapter **5**

Printer Problems

Printers are really their own computers, which means that they feature their own set of problems. Your computer is simply a visitor to the printer's realm, whether the printer is attached directly or available on a network. The computer passes off a document to print, and the printer prints the document. And along the way, various things can and do go wrong.

Between the Computer and Printer

Computers and printers may not hate each other, though it seems like they have a mutual distrust — like they were once married or shared a political debate program on a cable news channel. The evidence is clear: Try to print something and you'll experience the woe of the PC and printer being stubborn.

Configuring the printer in Windows

Like most computer peripherals, connecting a printer to a PC involves hardware and software steps.

For hardware, connect the printer to the computer. Attach a USB cable for a direct connection, or you can access any printer that's connected — wired or wirelessly — to the PC's local network.

The software steps to connect a printer to a Windows 10 PC are as follows:

1. **There are no steps.**

Unlike in the old days, the process for connecting a computer and printer just happens.

Years ago, you had to obtain (or write yourself) the software that forced the printer and PC to communicate. Yep: I've been around long enough that I not only had to hunt for a printer driver for each program, but I've also written printer drivers (software) using skills concealed in books.

Today, Windows instantly recognizes any printer directly connected to the PC, as well as any printer available on the network.

TECHNICAL STUFF

>> Printer software — the *driver* — is a part of Windows. If the driver required for a specific printer isn't available, Windows automatically fetches it over an Internet connection.

>> The introduction of Windows 95 marked a transition for PC users. Before then, all software came with its own printer driver. In Windows 95, the operating system took over printing duties. Even then, you had to manually install the printer. Staring with Windows Vista, printer software installation became automatic.

Connecting a printer

Printers share the love with a computer in two ways: directly or over the local network.

To directly attach a printer, use a USB cable. One end plugs into the printer, and the other into the PC. Easy as pie.

For network printers, the task is to connect the printer to the network. You can attach a network cable to the printer. In fact, if the printer is near the network gateway *(router)*, and the gateway has an available Ethernet port, you can plug it in using a standard networking cable.

Most commonly, printers access the local network wirelessly. Use the printer's control panel to connect to the local Wi-Fi network just as you set up your laptop or phone or another Wi-Fi gizmo.

Oh, and printers also plug into the wall for power.

To confirm that the printer is connected and available in Windows, follow these steps:

1. **Press Windows+I to conjure the Settings app.**

2. **Choose Devices.**

3. **Ensure that Printers & Scanners is chosen from the left side of the window.**

   You see a list of real and virtual printers displayed, as depicted in Figure 5-1.

Add a printer

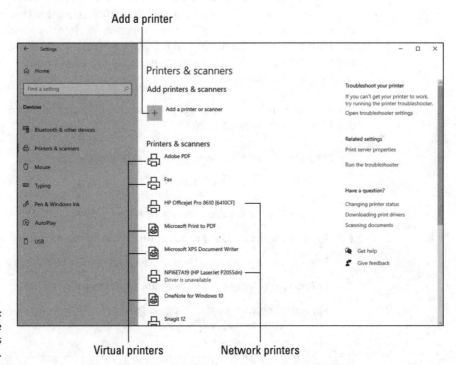

Virtual printers   Network printers

FIGURE 5-1:
Printers available
to a Windows
10 PC.

If the printer doesn't show up, you can add it directly: Click the Add a Printer or Scanner button and obey the onscreen directions. If this technique fails, ensure that the printer is on and connected to the PC. For a network printer, ensure that the network is operating properly and that the PC is using the same network. See Chapter 8 in this minibook for details on diagnosing network trouble.

REMEMBER

TECHNICAL STUFF

» You can't print when the printer is turned off. A printer can show up in the list of available printers, but when it's off, nothing prints.

» Printers don't come with USB cables.

» Back in the old days, printers used a unique printer cable, called a *parallel* cable. Those printers didn't come with cables, either.

» It's possible to share a printer connected to your computer with other computers on the network. The process is called *printer sharing.* It's better, however, to connect the printer to the network. Some gateways even come with USB ports specifically for a printer. Use this direct option to share a printer as opposed to sharing a printer directly connected to a specific PC.

Controlling the printer

All printers feature a control panel somewhere on the printer's case. The more advanced the printer, the more sophisticated its control panel. Low-end printers might have a couple of buttons and some lights. A printer that also serves as a scanner, copier, and fax might have a touchscreen interface with fancy graphics and online Help. Additionally, the printer's software in Windows may offer control over its features, such as scanning and faxing, or provide feedback for a paper jam or low ink levels.

If your printer has no control program or app, you can install one from the Windows Store. Obey these directions:

1. **From the Start menu, choose Microsoft Store.**

    You can type **Microsoft Store** and choose the matching item found in the results list, or you can scroll endlessly. If you haven't customized the taskbar, you can click the Windows Store button located on the taskbar.

2. **Type the name of your printer manufacturer into the Search text box.**

    For example, if you have a Hewlett-Packard printer, type **HP** into the box.

3. **Choose the printer control program from the list of results.**

    Many manufacturers use a single program to control all their printers. If not, in Step 2, search for your printer's name and not just the manufacturer.

When the app is installed, you can use it to control or gather information about the printer.

After the printer's app is installed, you can pluck it from the Start button's Programs menu, just as you start any program. In Figure 5-2, the HP Smart program is shown, which manages my office's HP OfficeJet Pro 8610.

>> Of all the printer features you can control, perhaps the most desperate one is to cancel a print job. See the later section "Canceling a print job."

TECHNICAL STUFF

>> Some older printers may feature an *On-line* or *select* button. It controls communications between the printer and the computer. When the button is on, the printer is ready to print. Taking the printer off-line or deselecting the button means that the printer is on and can be configured (or fixed) but nothing can be printed.

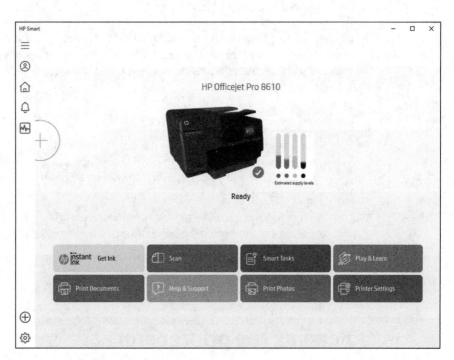

FIGURE 5-2:
A printer app.

Disconnecting a printer

You can unplug a USB printer from a computer at any time. Doing so doesn't uninstall the printer's software, but it does make the printer unavailable.

I can't think of any reason to disconnect a directly connected network printer or to configure a wireless network printer to forget its network.

On the software side, follow these steps to remove a printer from Windows control:

1. **Press the Windows+I keyboard shortcut.**

The Settings app appears.

2. **Choose the Devices tile.**

3. **From the left side of the window, choose Printers & Scanners.**

4. **Click to select the printer you want to remove from the list on the right side of the window.**

5. **Click the Remove Device button.**

6. **Click the Yes button to confirm.**

   The printer vanishes from the list.

Of course, the printer still physically exists. From this point on, however, Windows doesn't recognize it. The printer no longer shows up in any Print dialog boxes or on the Printers & Scanners screen (refer to Figure 5-1). Work through the steps to add the printer again.

>> To reconnect a printer physically, plug in the cable again.

>> For a printer you've removed (per the steps in this section), you must work through manual configuration to get it back — which may solve some printer issues. Click the Add (Plus) button in the Printers & Scanners portion of the Settings app.

>> Printers become disconnected when they're turned off or unplugged. This condition doesn't remove the printer from the list in the Settings app.

>> Like PCs, printers have Sleep mode. It's okay to leave a printer on all the time as it enters Sleep mode and consumes less power. If you're truly stingy about saving energy or you just don't print that often, turn off the printer.

Keeping the printer stocked

Printers require their own resources in order to operate successfully: ink and paper. You can't print without one or the other.

WARNING

>> Printers use standard, photocopier paper. You can buy fancy paper for color printing, photo paper, or even paper for iron-on transfers to T-shirts.

>> Avoid using erasable bond or fancy "dusted" papers, because they can gum up the printing mechanism. Overly thick paper stock is also prone to jam a printer.

>> The printer may not function — or you can damage the printer — if you attempt to print with an empty ink cartridge.

- The ink colors used for a color printer are cyan, magenta, yellow, and black. These are the *subtractive* colors (as opposed to the more familiar additive colors, which are red, blue, and green). Some photo printers may add second yellow and magenta inks.

- Yes, printer ink is expensive.

TIP

- One trick you can try to extend the life of laser printer toner is to rock the cartridge at the first low toner warning. Remove the toner from the printer, and then, using both hands, shift the cartridge gently back and forth. You can get a few extra pages from the toner, but you must replace it at the next warning.

Feeding envelopes

Most printers have an envelope slot, feeder, or tray. The better printers even let you stack up envelopes for mass mailings. Finding the tray is the first step in printing an envelope. The second step is to ensure that the envelope is properly oriented.

Somewhere on the manual feed tray you'll find icons for envelope orientation. Heed them.

When the printer lacks icons, print a sample envelope and see where the address shows up. This trick helps you determine how to orient the envelope, though you may have to complete one or two more sample runs before you get the orientation just right.

After working through envelope orientation, your next task is getting your software to print an envelope. It's not as difficult as it sounds: An envelope is merely a sheet of paper; one of a specific size. Use the Page Setup dialog box to choose the envelope size from the list of paper sizes. *Ta-da!* Just format the envelope "document" accordingly and then print.

- High-end printers often feature an envelope feeder option, which allows a massive number of envelopes to be shot through the printer at a time.

- Some applications, such as Microsoft Word, feature the Envelope command, which can be used to print a single envelope or more.

TIP

- Those peel-and-close envelopes work best in a laser printer. Because a laser printer uses heat to fuse the toner to the paper, the heat can also seal an empty envelope.

- See the later section "Using the Page Setup dialog box" for more information on selecting a paper size.

The Windows Side of Printing

You may access the printer in various programs, but it's Windows that does the work. The goal is consistency: Printing in every program is like saving and opening files. You don't need to learn new tricks, but you may not know all the tricks.

Printing in Windows

Because Windows handles all printing duties for you, the printing procedure works basically the same way in every program: Press Ctrl+P to summon the traditional Print dialog box or newer Print screen. Both items are illustrated in Figure 5-3.

Traditional Print dialog box   Print screen

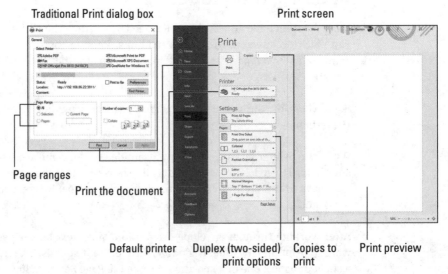

FIGURE 5-3:
Windows printer control.

Page ranges

Print the document

Default printer   Duplex (two-sided)   Copies to   Print preview
                   print options   print

Both locations offer the same control and details. The Print screen has the bonus of a print preview window, which is otherwise a separate command for programs that feature the Print dialog box. (Usually, it's the File ➪ Print Preview command.)

The printing process works like this:

1. **Save your document.**

Always save.

2. **Press Ctrl+P to summon the Print dialog box or Print screen.**

The Print command is found on the File menu. In the Microsoft Office suite, click the File tab and choose Print.

3. **Select a printer.**

   When you don't choose a specific printer, the default printer is used. It's flagged with a green check mark icon, illustrated in Figure 5-3. See the later section "Setting the default printer."

4. **Choose the number of copies.**

   This setting is preset to print one copy.

5. **Select the page range.**

   Use the text box if you need to print only a single page, a range of pages, or specific pages.

6. **Set other options.**

   Collating is a common option to set, determining whether multiple documents are printed a page at a time or one after the other. You might also see options for setting the paper size and orientation, though these options are typically set in the Page Setup dialog box. See the following section.

7. **Click the Print button to print.**

The document spews forth from the printer. Or, if something else happens, see the later section "Printer Problems and Solutions."

REMEMBER

>> The printer must be on, ready to print, and stocked with plenty of paper and ink for the printing process to be successful.

>> Print jobs flow from the PC to the printer at a quick pace. The process is called *spooling*. For low-end printers, spooling takes place on the PC; high-end printers feature their own memory, so spooling takes place on the device.

>> Save paper! Use the Print Preview command before printing. Proof your document. Print only when everything is ready to print.

>> The Print toolbar button either opens the Print dialog box or instantly prints the document. When a document instantly prints, default settings are used.

>> The Range option allows you to set the starting and ending pages, selected text, or specific pages or a range of pages. Separate individual pages with commas; a range of pages, with a hyphen. For example:

```
2,4,9–16
```

This range prints pages 2 and 4 and pages 9 through 16.

>> When a Selection option is available, only the text or items selected in the document are printed.

PRINTING WINDOWS

The Print Screen (or PrtSc) key on the PC's keyboard once actually printed the text on the screen. Called a *screen dump*, after you pressed that Print Screen key, every character on the screen spewed out of the printer, like a snapshot. This feature has been lost since the PC went graphical in the early 1990s.

Today, the Print Screen key still functions, though it doesn't deal directly with a printer. When you press the key, a snapshot of the desktop is taken. The graphical image is stored in the Windows clipboard, and you can paste it into any document that accepts graphics. The Alt+Print Screen keyboard shortcut works similarly, but takes a snapshot of only the current window.

If you really want to print the screen, you can press the Print Screen key, paste the image into a graphics program, such as Paint, and then print the image from that program.

TIP

TECHNICAL STUFF

» *Duplex* printers print on both sides of a sheet of paper. When this feature isn't available, print all odd pages first. Reinsert the pages in the printer face down, and then print all even pages.

» The Collate option prints multiple documents one after another. When documents aren't collated, all the first pages print, and then all the second pages, and so on.

» The infamous printer error message "PC Load Letter" means that the printer is out of paper. PC stands for Paper Cartridge, and Load Letter means to load letter-size paper.

Using the Page Setup dialog box

A companion to the Print dialog box is the Page Setup dialog box. Its purpose is to set the page margins, paper size, orientation, and other page-level formatting items. These options are part of the printing process — specifically, dealing with the paper. A typical Page Setup dialog box is shown in Figure 5-4.

To access the Page Setup dialog box, choose File➪Page Setup. In some programs, look for the Page Setup command on the File tab. In Microsoft Office applications, page setup options are found on the Layout tab.

Paper source

Paper size   Margins

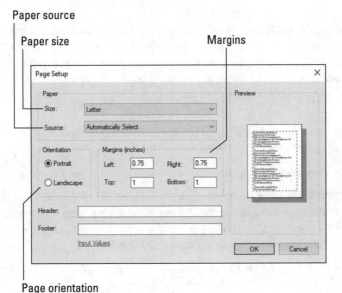

FIGURE 5-4:
A typical Page
Setup dialog box.

Page orientation

Here are the items you can set in the Page Setup dialog box, each of which relates to some aspect of printing:

Margins: This option sets the print area, leaving space near the edge of the paper. Some printers cannot print to the full edge of the page, so set the margins in a bit, not only to make the printed page look good but also to prevent printing errors.

Paper size: This is more of a page-size option because, in a program, the "paper size" is virtual. Only when you print does the paper size become important. And the printer dutifully looks for the right paper size and may refuse to print on another paper size — unless you use a "shrink to fit" option, if available in the Print dialog box.

Paper orientation: As with paper size, the orientation setting is more virtual than anything. The printer automatically prints in portrait or landscape orientation; you don't need to change the paper tray.

Paper source: When the printer has more than one paper tray, the source is chosen in the Page Setup dialog box, not in the Print dialog box. An example of using this feature is a printer stocked with plain paper in Tray 1 and company letterhead in Tray 2.

Printer Problems

TIP

Settings and options present in the Page Setup dialog box relate directly to whichever printer you've selected as the default. To use another printer's features, such as a specific paper tray, choose that printer in the Print dialog box, but do not print! Then use the Page Setup dialog box to set options specific for that printer, such as paper size and paper trays.

>> The Print dialog box might share some of the same settings as the Page Setup dialog box.

>> Some Print dialog boxes have a button or link to the Page Setup dialog box.

>> A few printers can print on an entire sheet of paper, in which case you can set the page margins to zero all around. Otherwise, the printer requires a half-inch of space on one end of the paper for the feeding mechanism. Information cannot be printed on that half-inch.

>> The standard printer paper tray accommodates American Letter size (8½-by-11 inches) as well as European A4 size paper. Use adjustments on the paper tray to change the size.

TIP

>> A paper tray can often accommodate smaller paper sizes as well, such as 6-by-4-inch photo paper. You must adjust the paper tray to snugly fit that paper size. Further, you must set the paper size in the Page Setup dialog box. After you complete both steps, the printer generates the output you desire.

>> The manual paper tray is the manual feed slot on most printers. This slot is used frequently for loading special paper, such as envelopes. All printers use the slot automatically when paper is present, though the Paper Source setting in the Print Setup dialog box can override this feature.

REMEMBER

>> When you choose another paper size in the Page Setup dialog box, don't forget to stock your printer with the new paper size. The printer's display may remind you of the paper swap, or it may not.

Setting the default printer

The default printer is the one that Windows uses automatically. It's preset in the Print dialog box and assumed as the printing output device for all programs. For any quick-print commands, such as the Print button in Microsoft Office, the default printer is the one selected automatically.

In earlier versions of Windows, the default printer was either the first printer installed or chosen specifically. In Windows 10, you can direct Windows to choose a default printer, which is the last printer used. To control this setting, follow these steps:

1. **Press the Windows+I keyboard shortcut.**

2. **In the Settings app, choose Devices.**

3. **Choose Printers & Scanners on the left side of the window.**

4. **Scroll down the right side of the window to locate the check box labeled Let Windows Manage My Default Printer.**

5. **Place a check mark in the box.**

   This action directs Windows to set the default printer as the last printer used.

If you'd rather set a default printer yourself, ensure that the check box is empty in Step 5, and then continue with these steps:

6. **Click to select the printer you want to use as the default.**

   A series of buttons appears below the printer: Open Queue, Manage, and Remove Device.

7. **Click the printer's Manage button.**

   A screen dedicated to the specific printer appears. It lists options for trouble-shooting, printing a test page, and so on.

8. **Click the Set As Default button.**

   This printer is now the computer's default printer.

The default printer features a green check mark on its icon (refer to Figure 5-3). This icon appears on at least one of the printers listed in various locations in Windows — unless you chose to let Windows set the default printer, as shown in this section's steps. When Windows sets the default printer, it uses the last printer you chose in the Print dialog box or on the Print screen.

REMEMBER

You can always choose any printer when you print. The default is preset; otherwise, you choose whichever printer you desire in the Print dialog box. You must remember to do so before you click the Print button.

Working with print jobs

When you print something in Windows, you create a *print job*. The program hands off information to the Windows print spooler service, which sends the document to the printer. Once there, the job prints as fast as the printer can go.

A typical print job might print quickly, depending on how much printer memory is available. Multiple jobs stack in a printer queue, with each job printing one after the other. To view the queue, open the printer's window. Heed these directions:

1. **Press the Windows+I keyboard shortcut to bring up the Settings app.**

2. **Choose the Devices tile.**

3. **From the left side of the window, select Printers & Scanners.**

4. **Choose a printer on the right side of the window.**

5. **Click the Open Queue button.**

    The queue window appears. Any print jobs waiting are shown in a list.

Most of the time, the queue window is empty; modern printers are fast. When jobs do appear in the queue, you can control them: Click to select a job, and then use the Document menu to pause or cancel. You can also resume or restart a paused or canceled print job.

For example, if the printer is off-line or malfunctioning, select a print job and from the menu choose Document, Pause. Fix the printer, and then back in the printer's queue window, from the menu choose Document, Resume to continue printing.

>> You can change the order of items waiting in the queue: Drag a print job up or down in the list.

>> You can get to the printer queue window quickly if you see — and double-click on — the wee printer icon that appears in the notification area on the taskbar. This icon, shown in the margin, vanishes when the printer queue is empty.

>> In addition to the print queue window, you may see the printer's app appear while printing. Depending on the app, it can also be used to control print jobs in the queue.

Canceling a print job

The best way to cancel a print job is to go to the printer itself. Yes, stand up, leave your chair, and walk over to the printer. Press (or tap) the Cancel button on the printer's control panel. Printing stops almost immediately. If not, one or two pages may continue to print, but then printing stops.

The only time printing continues is if more print jobs are in the queue. Refer to the preceding section for information on viewing the queue and killing off print jobs.

TIP

>> For a printer without a Cancel button, take the printer off-line: Press the On-line or Select button. A few lines or pages may continue to print, but eventually the printer stops. Remove the last sheet of paper, if necessary. Then reset the printer or, if the printer lacks a Reset button, turn it off.

>> Look at your printer now to locate the Cancel button. It should be obvious, not on a menu or hidden on a secret panel. The button features a red X icon.

Printer Problems and Solutions

The first step in diagnosing printer problems is to determine where the problem lies: with the printer itself, with Windows, or with the application you're using. The Print Preview command helps you determine whether your software is up to snuff or that the printer has gone hinkey.

"It printed on the wrong side of the page!"

Printers eat paper and ink. Know where the paper is inserted and how it's oriented. For blank sheets, the orientation doesn't matter. But when printing on letterhead or printing a check, ensure that the paper is set in the tray the correct way.

To assist you with the paper orientation, an icon near the paper tray shows the proper orientation, as illustrated in Figure 5-5. If the icon isn't found or obvious, consider marking the printer's paper tray with a Sharpie so that you know which way the paper goes. Use Figure 5-5 as your guide.

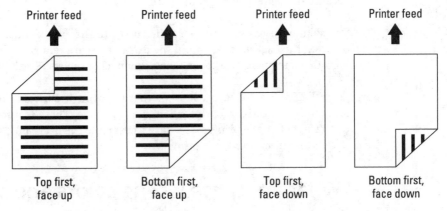

FIGURE 5-5:
Paper orientation for a printer.

"Print preview lied!"

A program's print preview feature can help determine whether a problem is with the printer or specific to your software. Even so, sometimes the print preview image *lies*.

First, remember that some printers cannot print on one edge of the paper. For the other three edges, the margin may be all the way to the edge of the page, or it might be a half-inch or so away from the edge. The fourth edge, however, is required by the printer to feed the paper. Regardless of what the print preview says, you can't print on that edge of the page. The solution: Decrease the document's margins.

Second, some features aren't implemented properly. I'm thinking specifically of Microsoft Word's annoying page border feature. The problem is with Word, not with the printer, but it's difficult to determine because the print preview window shows the border present. (To fix the page border on a page in Word, set the border from the *text*, not from the edge of the paper.)

Finally, ensure that you haven't set your application or the printer itself to print in *Draft mode*. This mode is used for quickly printing a document without fancy text formatting or graphics. If you need these types of features, disable Draft mode in your application or in the printer's Properties dialog box.

"What's this extra page?"

You may not be able to see it on the screen, but extra cells in a spreadsheet or blank lines in a document are printed just like other items. The page is blank because the items you're printing are invisible.

The solution in Word is to move the cursor to the end of a document and keep pressing the Backspace key until the extra pages are removed. In Excel, click the View tab, and in the Workbook Views group, choose Page Break Preview.

Cover pages and document info sheets may print if such an option is set. The program may prefix the print job with a title page. These features are set in the program, not by the printer. You have to examine the program's printing options to see why the extra page is printed.

"What are these wrong colors and streaks?"

Weird or faded colors indicate that a color ink cartridge is low. Some printers inform you of this situation, but many don't. The solution is to replace the low ink cartridge.

Dark streaks down the page might indicate that ink or another gunky substance has infiltrated the printer's paper feeding mechanism. But for a laser printer, the streaks often mean that the toner is old. Replace the toner cartridge.

If the printer features a head cleaning utility, run it to see whether it resolves the streaking color issue.

"I just loaded paper, but the printer says the tray is empty!"

This situation happens to me all the time: Remove the tray and slide it in again. Often the tray isn't fully inserted, and printer trays are an in-all-the-way-or-not-at-all type of device.

Also be aware that some printers insist upon loading specific paper stock when the document formatting requires it. Return to the application and confirm the paper type and page options. Ensure that the printer's paper tray is configured for any specific paper stock and that such paper is loaded.

"The paper keeps jamming!"

The number-one cause of printer jams is, of course, paper. Paperless printers seldom jam. You probably have a printer that uses real paper, so it will jam someday.

The first solution to a printer jam is to find the jam and remove the paper. If the printer is smart enough to tell you where the jam occurred, heed its advice. Otherwise, follow the paper's path from tray to output: Open various printer hatches and covers to remove the errant sheet. Resume printing.

» If the page that jammed needs to be printed again, use the Print dialog box to print only the single sheet that jammed.

» Some printers may not recover from a paper jam until you open and close the cover.

» Some printers are smart and recover well from a jam, reprinting the page that was jammed.

» Don't confuse a paper jam with a misfeed. Remove the paper tray and pull out the paper. Fan it out, to puff some air between the pages. Ensure that the paper tray is fully inserted. Try printing again.

Using the Printing Troubleshooter

Of the many troubleshooters offered in Windows, one is specific to the installed printer. Heed these steps to summon that troubleshooter:

1. **Press the Windows+I keyboard shortcut to bring forth the Settings app.**

2. **Choose Devices.**

3. **Ensure that Printers & Scanners is chosen from the left side of the window.**

4. **Click to select the printer.**

5. **Click the Manage button.**

   The printer's management screen appears.

6. **Click the Run the Troubleshooter link.**

   The troubleshooter attempts to find problems.

Keep in mind that the printer troubleshooter looks only on the PC for any issues. It doesn't check the printer itself.

TIP

» Some printers may have a self-diagnostic mode or troubleshooting utility on the Control Panel. For example, an inkjet printer might have a head cleaning utility you can run, which resolves streaking issues.

» The printer's control program may also offer troubleshooting information and help. Refer to the section "Controlling the printer."

Chapter **6**

Peripheral Perils

Traditionally, a *peripheral* is any hardware attached to the PC. The device is *peripheral* to the heart of the system. This location doesn't imply that the device is optional; a keyboard is a peripheral, but its presence is necessary to operate the computer. Likewise, a monitor is technically a peripheral, but on an all-in-one PC, it's integrated into the console.

For this chapter, the term *peripheral* applies to gizmos not covered anywhere else, which includes items both inside and outside the console.

» Refer to Chapter 3 in this minibook for information on PC monitors and graphics.

» Chapter 5 in this minibook covers the printer.

Hardware Troubleshooting

Keep in mind that change causes most PC issues. If you have a hardware problem, ponder what's changed: Have you added new hardware? Updated software? What else is new or different? Understanding change doesn't fix the problem, but it leads you in the right direction.

Checking the Device Manager

The best way to instantly check whether a peripheral is malfunctioning is to check the Device Manager. Obey these directions:

1. **Press the Windows+X keyboard shortcut.**

Appears the supersecret menu.

2. **Choose Device Manager or tap the M key.**

The Device Manager program starts, showing an inventory of the computer's hardware by category.

Figure 6-1 illustrates a typical Device Manager window. What you're looking for are items flagged with a yellow Warning icon. These are hardware devices that Windows has recognized as operating improperly. (No such items are flagged in the figure.)

When you find a flagged item, open it. The item's category is expanded, and the problematic item is visible. Double-click on the flagged item. Follow the directions in the dialog box that appears, to resolve the issue.

>> The Device Manager window may confirm your suspicions about a failing peripheral, or it might surprise you. I've discovered several issues flagged in the Device Manager window that I was unaware of. Most of them were hardware conflicts, which Windows helped resolve.

>> See Book 3, Chapter 2 for more details on the Device Manager, including how to resolve problems and errors flagged in the window.

REMEMBER

>> Just because hardware isn't flagged as malfunctioning in the Device Manager window doesn't mean it's working properly. Windows is hardware tolerant. A gizmo could be dying or failed completely, and it won't show up in the Device Manager window. If so, you have more troubleshooting to do.

Hardware list

Computer name

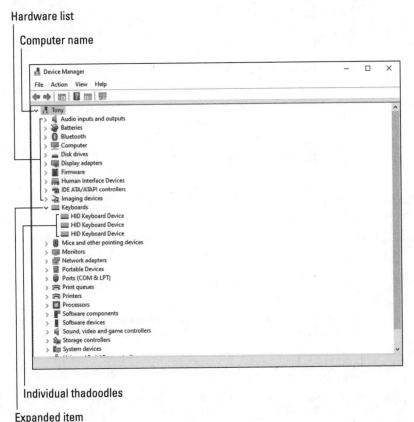

FIGURE 6-1:
The Device
Manager.

Individual thadoodles

Expanded item

Diagnosing USB issues

Pretty much any peripheral uses a USB cable to attach to your PC. The cable attaches directly to the console, or it attaches to a USB hub, which then attaches to the console. In fact, you can have quite an array of hubs and wires to make available dozens of dinguses for your PC peripheral passions.

The gamut of USB connections available to the PC are visible in the Device Manager window. Follow the steps in the preceding section to summon the window. Open the Universal Serial Bus item to view the lot, as illustrated in Figure 6-2. Note that both ports (where you plug in the USB cable) and devices (peripherals) are shown in the list.

As with other items in the Device Manager window, unruly USB items are flagged with a yellow circle if something is awry.

So, what can you do?

Peripheral Perils

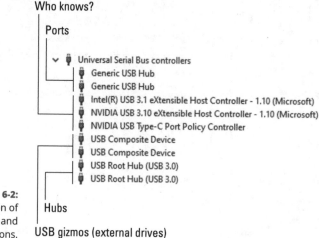

Who knows?

Ports

∨ 🔌 Universal Serial Bus controllers
  🔌 Generic USB Hub
  🔌 Generic USB Hub
  🔌 Intel(R) USB 3.1 eXtensible Host Controller - 1.10 (Microsoft)
  🔌 NVIDIA USB 3.10 eXtensible Host Controller - 1.10 (Microsoft)
  🔌 NVIDIA USB Type-C Port Policy Controller
  🔌 USB Composite Device
  🔌 USB Composite Device
  🔌 USB Root Hub (USB 3.0)
  🔌 USB Root Hub (USB 3.0)

FIGURE 6-2:
The pantheon of
USB ports and
connections.

Hubs

USB gizmos (external drives)

Unplug the device and reconnect it. This process wakes up the gizmo and solves most connection issues — unless the device has a separate power cord. In this case, keep the USB cable connected and cycle the device's power: Turn it off, wait, and then turn it on again. If the device lacks an on–off switch, unplug it instead.

TIP

>> USB stands for Universal Serial Bus. Say "you S bee," not "usub."

>> Some powered USB devices, such as hard drives and scanners, must be plugged directly into the console. Even when they're plugged into a powered USB hub, they may still have problems. To resolve the issues, ensure that devices such as hard drives and scanners are connected directly to the console.

>> Some keyboards, particularly the ones with fancy lights, require *two* USB connections. Check them both.

>> Touchscreen monitors require a USB connection. If touchscreen input isn't working, check the USB cable.

>> A PC can sport as many as 128 unique USB gizmos attached at once. That's the limit on the USB standard.

>> To add more USB ports, attach a USB hub to the PC.

>> Hubs come in two flavors: powered and unpowered. A powered USB hub also plugs into the wall.

>> Version 3.0 is the current, fastest implementation of the USB standard. Version 2.0 is still around, and USB gizmos can connect to either device, though USB 3.0 devices are best used on USB 3.0 ports.

>> USB 3.0 ports and connectors are color-coded blue.

TIP

>> USB ports colored red or yellow indicate a power-on port. These ports can be used to charge cell phones and other electronics when the computer is turned off. Providing the computer remains connected to wall power, use the yellow or red USB ports to charge a mobile device.

>> If your PC lacks USB 3.0 ports, you can add them by installing a USB 3.0 expansion card. The expansion card also increases the number of USB ports available on the console.

Doing the hardware swap

A surefire way to detect peripheral problems — and fix them — is to swap out questionable hardware with something that works. This technique applies to not only peripherals but also any PC component. It's just that peripherals are easier to swap.

The process works like this:

1. Disconnect the questionable device, such as a keyboard or mouse.

For powered devices, disconnect the power before you disconnect. For storage devices, attempt to properly dismount or eject the device. Specific directions are found in Chapter 2 in this minibook.

2. Attach a replacement, something you know that works.

For example, attach another mouse or keyboard.

3. Test the replacement.

If the replacement works, you know that the problem lies with the specific piece of hardware.

When you're done swapping, you can swap back the defective item, but eventually you'll need a replacement. You can use the spare as a replacement — if it's a spare. Often, I swap hardware, such as a monitor, between computers I'm actively using. For that situation, using the replacement is impractical.

>> Most components you swap can't be fixed, either by using software or by wielding a screwdriver. That's why it's best to replace the part.

>> The drawback to this troubleshooting technique is that not everyone has a spare keyboard, mouse, or monitor lying about.

>> This method can work for internal items as well, though it's much more arduous to swap out an internal drive, memory, or an expansion card. In that case, you can buy a replacement straight out.

Peripheral Perils

Running a hardware troubleshooter

Windows 7 introduced hardware troubleshooting and diagnostic tools, all carefully hidden in the Control Panel. Windows 10 inherited these troubleshooting tools, but spread them all over town. The key location to look for hardware troubleshooters is in the Settings app.

If any hardware or other issues arise in Windows, notices appear atop the Settings app window. Follow these steps to proceed with hardware troubleshooting:

1. **Press the Windows+I keyboard shortcut to call forth the Settings app.**

2. **Check for hardware issues flagged at the top of the Settings app window.**

   If you don't see any special icons or notices at the top of the window, pending issues aren't present. But you should still confirm that these notices can appear:

3. **Choose the Privacy tile.**

4. **On the left side of the window, choose Diagnostics & Feedback.**

5. **On the right side of the window, locate the item Recommended Troubleshooting.**

   You may need to scroll down the window a few lines to find this item.

6. **From the menu, choose the option Ask Me Before Fixing Problems.**

   This choice ensures that troubleshooting notifications appear atop the Settings app window.

The individual hardware troubleshooters are still available, but you must venture to the specific hardware item's area in the Settings app to find this service. These troubleshooters are located by clicking the Device tile and choosing a hardware item on the left side of the screen. For example, when you choose the Mouse item, an option appears on the screen titled Troubleshooting My Mouse.

REMEMBER

To use Windows to assist with hardware troubleshooting, visit the Settings app. If the issue isn't flagged immediately, venture to the Device tile and choose a specific hardware item. A troubleshooting link appears somewhere on the item's control screen.

Audio Anxieties

You can blame two things for relating noise to computers. The first is Hollywood, where for some reason they believe that text displayed on a computer screen makes noise. Trust me: No one would use a computer if the display were noisy.

The second noise-related thing to blame is the early teletype machines. These beasts were used as the first computer terminals. (And hence the term *TTY* to describe a terminal.) A teletype used a bell to alert the operator. Early computer terminals came equipped with a single tiny speaker for the same reason.

Fast-forward several dozen years and today's computers have not only internal speakers but also an extensive set of external, state-of-the-art, surround sound speakers and a digital sound system to match. With all that hardware, something is bound to go wrong.

Testing the speakers

The PC console has one, internal speaker. It's okay for beeps and boops, but to make sound that frightens the neighbors, you want a little more oomph. That means external speakers. Or, if you don't want to scare the neighbors, you can use headphones and just scare yourself.

The easiest way to ensure that noise is coming from the speakers is to use the volume control in the notification area on the taskbar: Click the Volume Control icon, illustrated in Figure 6-3. You hear an audible "beep" (or another amusing tone) when you click the control as shown in the figure.

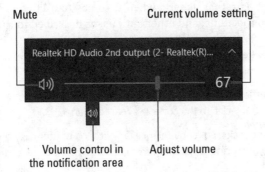

Mute   Current volume setting

Realtek HD Audio 2nd output (2- Realtek(R)...

67

FIGURE 6-3:
Testing the PC's volume.

Volume control in the notification area   Adjust volume

For more speaker testing, bring up the Sound dialog box. Follow these steps:

1. **Right-click the Volume icon in the notification area.**

   The icon is shown in the margin.

2. **From the pop-up menu, choose Open Sound Settings.**

   The Sound part of the Settings app appears.

3. **Choose the output device.**

From the menu, select which hardware you want the computer to use for generating sound. If the current device doesn't work, select another item from the menu.

4. **Adjust the Master Volume control to test audio output.**

Slide the controller and then release the mouse button to hear sound (or not).

If changing the output device doesn't work, click the Troubleshoot button located below the Master Volume control.

>> To mute the speakers in Windows, click the Mute button in the volume control's pop-up window, as shown in Figure 6-3.

>> Your PC's sound hardware may have its own program, which you can use to test the speakers. Look for such a program on the Start button.

>> See the later section "Fixing silence" for information on determining whether the speakers are broken.

Connecting speakers

The term *speakers* is rather generic when it comes to a PC. You'll find quite the variety, terms, connections, and other options, as described in this list:

Internal speaker: Most PCs have a speaker inside the console. It's a cheap, tiny speaker, and you don't want to use it.

Rear speaker jacks: The standard PC setup is to plug a set of stereo speakers into the audio output jacks on the console's rear I/O panel.

Front speaker jacks: For convenience, a typical computer case provides duplicate speaker (and microphone) jacks up front, where you'd connect a headphone.

S/PDIF: High-end audio systems might employ the Sony/Phillips Digital Interconnect Format. It requires special optical cables and equipment used only by serious audiophiles and has separate S/PDIF connectors: one for input (S/PDIF in) and another for output (S/PDIF out).

USB speakers: You can plug USB speakers or headphones into any USB port on the computer.

Monitor speakers: Some monitors, specifically those that also double as HDTVs, feature built-in speakers. These may connect into either the rear speaker jacks or the USB port, though some monitors may accept audio input over the HDMI or DisplayPort connection.

Traditional audio connectors are color-coded on your PC, as shown in Table 6-1. The pink and green jacks are the most common, used for audio input (a microphone) and speakers or headphones, respectively. Other colors are nonstandard, though the table lists popular colors.

TABLE 6-1

PC Sound Jack Color Codes

Audio Connector Color	Connection
Black	S/PDIF output
Black	Surround sound left or right
Brown	Surround sound center or subwoofer
Gray	Line-in jack (for audio equipment)
Lime green	Speakers or headphone
Pink	S/PDIF input
Red (or pink)	Microphone
White	S/PDIF input

>> Small footprint PCs and laptops have only one set of speaker jacks.

>> Headphones can also be connected to a speaker jack. When you do so, a prompt appears, asking which type of audio device was connected. Ensure that you choose headphones so that the sound output doesn't damage your hearing.

>> You cannot hear sound from the speakers when you plug them into the microphone jack. Likewise, the microphone may seem undermodulated when it's plugged into the line-in jack.

>> External speakers require power! Avoid using speakers that need batteries. Instead, use speakers with a power adapter. Speakers can also draw power from a subwoofer, or from the PC's USB port.

>> A bit beyond the standard stereo speakers are speakers that come with a subwoofer. In this configuration, it's usually the subwoofer that connects directly to the console. The stereo speakers then connect to the subwoofer.

>> Some gaming keyboards feature audio connectors. These are for convenience, either as a pass-through for standard audio connection or as a bonus set of audio connectors.

>> At the pinnacle of computer speaker technology is *surround sound*. It involves multiple speakers situated around the computer to create realistic, 3D sound. Setting up such a thing requires a degree in audio engineering, though enthusiastic and motivated computer users can often handle the task.

Peripheral Perils

Fixing silence

The biggest issue with computer sound is not hearing anything. This situation happens often. To fix the problem, follow a step-by-step process to find and eliminate the cause. Here's how I do it:

1. **Test the speakers as described in the earlier section "Testing the speakers."**

   The computer merely sends out a signal. It's up to the speakers to generate the sound.

2. **Ensure that the speakers are connected to the computer.**

   Are the speakers plugged in? Are they plugged into the right jacks? If a subwoofer is connected, is it plugged in? Is it getting power? Is it even working?

   Speakers need power to make noise.

REMEMBER

3. **Check to see whether the speaker's volume control is turned up enough or that a hardware switch doesn't mute the speakers.**

   The volume control and switch are often found on the headphone's cable or on the headphone ear can.

4. **If you have another set of speakers, swap them out with the current set to see whether the speakers themselves have died and left behind a silent shell.**

5. **Check the Windows volume control. (Refer to Figure 6-3.)**

   Is the volume high enough? Is the volume control muted?

6. **Check the volume mixer or volume control to ensure that individual audio devices haven't been muted.**

   The volume mixer or volume control allows you to set levels for various sound-generating items in the computer. To display the volume mixer, right-click the volume control on the taskbar (shown in the margin) and choose the Open Volume Mixer command from the pop-up menu. Such a mixer is shown in Figure 6-4.

   Ensure that devices or applications listed in the Volume Mixer window haven't been muted.

7. **Check the sound hardware configuration.**

   Some PCs with speaker jacks on the front and back must be configured to allow audio input from either place. For example, your PC may allow speakers to be plugged in the rear jacks but not in the front jacks at the same time. When your PC offers this type of configuration, use the special sound software that came with the computer to confirm that all the sound jacks are working as you expect. (It's not a Windows-specific solution.)

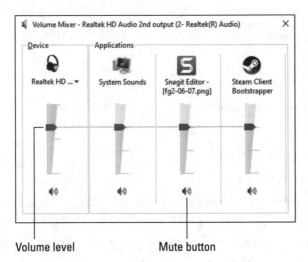

FIGURE 6-4:
The Volume
Mixer.

Volume level   Mute button

8. **Confirm that the sound device is working properly.**

Open the Device Manager to confirm whether the sound hardware is hinkey.
The Device Manager is covered earlier in this chapter.

If all else fails, check your ears. Are other things making noise in the room? If so,
the problem is probably the computer.

REMEMBER

Things go wrong in a computer when something changes. If the sound just went
out, try to recall what you just changed. It may help lead you to the solution.

» Some speakers use both the green audio jack and the USB connector. The
USB connection is used for power with the audio signal coming from the
audio jack. This type of speaker is mute when either the audio or USB
connection isn't made.

» If the computer has never made sound, contact the manufacturer or dealer.

Testing the microphone

For a microphone to work on your computer, it must be plugged into the proper
audio jack. Table 6-1 says it's the red or pink jack. Plugging a microphone into any
other audio jack results in less-than-satisfactory results. Well, unless it's a USB
microphone, which simply plugs into the USB port. In fact:

TIP

The best way to troubleshoot microphone issues is to use a USB microphone. I find
them far more reliable than the standard audio jack microphones.

Even if you have a USB microphone, heed these steps to perform some cursory troubleshooting:

1. **Ensure that the microphone is properly connected and stuff.**

2. **Right-click the Volume icon on the taskbar.**

   The icon is shown in the margin.

3. **Choose Open Sound Settings.**

   The Settings app opens, with the Sound options visible.

4. **Below the Input heading on the right side of the window, ensure that the proper audio input device is chosen from the menu.**

   If your microphone doesn't appear on the list, the problem lies with the device or its connection.

5. **Observe the meter below the heading Test Your Microphone.**

   The meter activates on sound input. If it doesn't move, the problem is with the microphone or its connection.

If all else fails, click the Troubleshoot button in the Input category to test the microphone. Work through the steps to see if Windows can help resolve the issue.

REMEMBER

Your computer may not be configured to use the specific microphone jack that your microphone is plugged into. If your PC came with specific audio software, use it to configure the audio jacks to accept microphone input.

» You don't want to spend too much or too little on a PC microphone. Cheap microphones don't work well, record poorly, and sound annoying with audio chat and online communications. Professional microphones require a mixer or pre-amp to connect with a computer.

TIP

» I use a microphone headset, which provides both headphones and a microphone. It's perfect for online communications and gaming. And I'm not implying that I've been playing computer games when I should have been writing this book. No way!

Running the audio troubleshooter

In addition to the Troubleshoot buttons on the Sound screen in the Settings app, Windows features an audio troubleshooter, which is easily accessed from the Volume Control icon on the taskbar: Right-click the icon (shown in the margin) and choose the Troubleshoot Sound Problems command. Continue following the interactive directions on the screen.

Updating audio device drivers

The software side of your PC's audio system requires a device driver to control the sound hardware. To confirm that your PC is using the latest version of that software, follow these steps:

1. **Press the Windows+X keyboard shortcut.**

The supersecret menu appears.

2. **Choose Device Manager.**

3. **Expand the item Audio Inputs and Outputs.**

4. **Right-click on the item that's causing issues.**

If an item is flagged with a yellow Warning icon, well, there's the trouble! Otherwise, locate the input, output, or other specific hardware gizmo that's generating the issue.

5. **From the shortcut menu, choose the Update Driver Software command.**

6. **Choose the option Search Automatically for Updated Driver Software.**

Windows probes the Internet, looking for better software to drive your PC's audio hardware.

If a better or more up-to-date driver is found, install it. If not, the problem must lie elsewhere.

As a solution, you can opt to install a sound expansion card. This card is more sophisticated than the simple audio included on the PC's motherboard. Refer to Chapter 4 in this minibook for details on installing an expansion card.

Another option is to go USB: Get USB speakers and a USB microphone, or a single USB headset. As I write elsewhere in this chapter, I find USB microphones far more reliable than the models that connect to the PC's audio port.

Keyboard and Mouse Woes

Two important peripherals provide vital input for the computer: the keyboard and the mouse. The keyboard is the traditional input gizmo, often dubbed the standard input device. The mouse came along when computers went graphical, because it's easier to move a mouse pointer across the screen than to whack the right-arrow key 2,000 times.

TECHNICAL STUFF

>> Despite its necessity, the keyboard is still considered a peripheral. Even on a laptop, where the keyboard is integrated into the device, the keyboard is a peripheral.

>> The monitor is considered the computer's standard output device. Refer to Chapter 3 in this minibook for details on that peripheral.

>> The keyboard is so essential to the PC's operation that when it's not detected, the startup sequence stops. The BIOS error message "Keyboard not found; press any key to continue" is considered a classic Catch-22 of computer industry logic.

Troubleshooting basic input dilemmas

Before slamming the mouse into your computer desk or slapping your palms wildly on the keyboard, try some basic troubleshooting:

1. Ensure that the computer is on.

If the computer case's tiny power lamp is illuminated, the computer is on. When the computer's power supply fan is whirring, it's on. If the computer isn't on, refer to Chapter 1 in this minibook for help.

2. Check the connections.

Is the USB cable plugged in? If so, disconnect it and reconnect it, and that magic may fix the problem.

3. Test the keyboard or mouse for signs of life.

For the keyboard, press and release the Caps Lock key. The Caps Lock lamp on the keyboard illuminates when the keyboard has power. If so, the problem lies elsewhere.

Optical mice use a lamp to detect movement. Flip the mouse over and look at the lamp; if it's on, the mouse should function. This trick doesn't work, however, for infrared mice, where humans can't see the lamp.

If it appears that the keyboard and mouse are receiving power and functioning, the problem lies with the PC itself. Restart the system to see whether this step fixes the problem.

REMEMBER

>> Wireless keyboards and mice don't work when the battery is low. Some wireless input devices direct Windows to display a low battery notification. Heed it. Otherwise, replace the batteries or recharge the device.

>> You can't fix a dead keyboard or mouse; just buy a replacement.

Taming a wild mouse

When the mouse jumps around too much, you may have activated the snap-to feature. To undo this option, follow these steps:

1. **Press the Windows+I keyboard shortcut.**

The Settings app appears.

2. **Choose Devices.**

3. **On the left side of the window, choose Mouse.**

4. **Click the Additional Mouse Options link.**

The Mouse Properties dialog box appears.

5. **Click the Pointer Options tab.**

The Pointer Options tab, illustrated in Figure 6-5, contains a slew of useful tools for dealing with the mouse pointer in Windows.

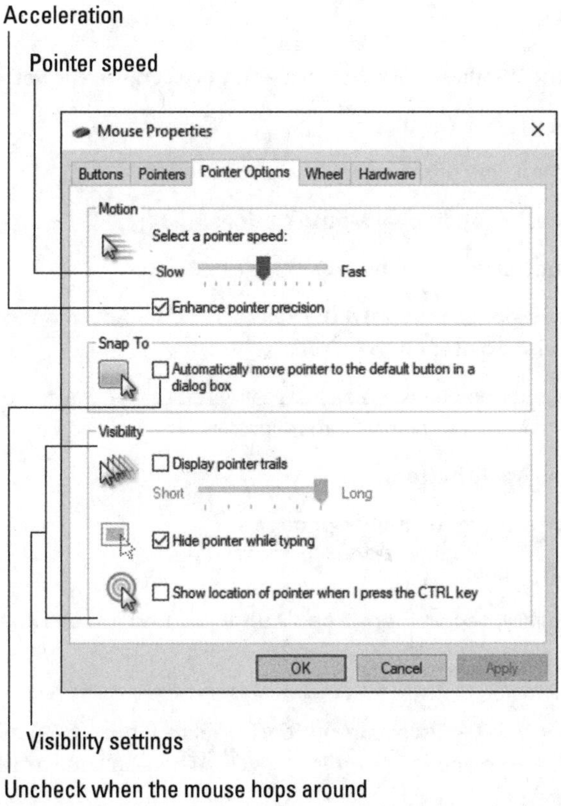

Acceleration

Pointer speed

FIGURE 6-5: Mouse pointer options.

Visibility settings

Uncheck when the mouse hops around

6. **Remove the check mark by the option Automatically Move Pointer to the Default Button in a Dialog Box.**

7. **Click OK.**

If these steps don't fix the problem, consider cleaning the mouse. See the later section "Cleaning the mouse."

Making the mouse pointer move faster or slower

The mouse pointer's movement on the screen mimics the mouse's movement on the desktop. The relationship between the two is the mouse pointer's speed, which you may find too fast or too slow. For example, if you find yourself lifting the mouse several times to "swipe" the pointer across the screen, the pointer is moving too slowly.

To adjust the mouse pointer's speed, access the Mouse Properties dialog box. Heed these directions:

1. **Press the Windows+I keyboard shortcut to conjure the Settings app.**

2. **Choose the Devices tile.**

3. **On the left side of the window, choose Mouse.**

4. **Click the link Additional Mouse Options.**

5. **Click the Pointer Options tab.**

6. **Use the slider gizmo below the Select a Pointer Speed option to throttle the mouse pointer on the screen.**

   A fast mouse pointer can zip across a large screen — or two monitors — with ease. A slow mouse pointer is more precise.

7. **Click the Apply button.**

8. **Practice moving the mouse pointer.**

   Gauge the speed.

9. **If necessary, repeat Steps 6 and 7 until you find a speed you like.**

10. **Click OK to confirm the settings.**

The Enhance Pointer Precision option (refer to Figure 6-5) adds a modicum of intelligence to the mouse pointer's speed. When you move the mouse quickly,

Windows accelerates the mouse pointer. When you move the mouse slightly, Windows slows down the pointer speed. It's a good feature to have active.

TECHNICAL STUFF

Some computer mice use a custom Mouse Properties dialog box, different from the one shown in Figure 6-5, or a special tab is added. Either way, adjusting the mouse speed may take place differently for some mice.

Improving mouse pointer visibility

The Pointer Options tab in the Mouse Properties dialog box contains a host of options to help you make the mouse pointer more visible. The options are clustered in the aptly named Visibility area. (Refer to Figure 6-5.) Here are the settings you can consider:

Pointer trails: The Display Pointer Trails option "ghosts" the mouse pointer to form a cometlike tail wherever the mouse wanders. Activate this feature to make it easy to follow the mouse pointer on the screen. Pointer Trails doesn't necessarily make it easier to *find* the mouse pointer.

Hiding the mouse (or not) while typing: The Hide Pointer While Typing option is normally selected. That way, the mouse pointer (or cursor) vanishes while you compose text. Just wiggle the mouse to locate the pointer, though uncheck this item to keep the pointer visible always.

Mouse ping: I call the Show Location feature *mouse ping*. When it's active, you use this feature to quickly locate the mouse pointer. Just tap either Ctrl (Control) key on the keyboard and you see a series of concentric circles hone in on the mouse pointer's position. The effect is similar to a sonar display.

If you still have difficulty locating the mouse pointer, choose a different look for the pointer. In the Mouse Properties dialog box, click the Pointers tab. Choose a larger version of the standard mouse cursor or something else unique, as illustrated in Figure 6-6.

To visit the Pointers tab, follow Steps 1 through 4 in the preceding section and then click on the Pointers tab in Step 5. Choose a new pointer scheme from the Scheme menu, or you can double-click a specific pointer type and choose a new pointer image file from the Browse dialog box.

TIP

Click the Apply button in the Mouse Properties dialog box to preview the new pointers. Click OK to lock in your choices.

Peripheral Perils

Select a pointer scheme   Selected pointer preview

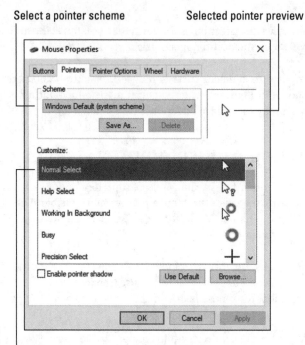

Double-click to choose a different pointer

FIGURE 6-6:
Mouse pointer choices.

Using a left-handed mouse

Up to 10 percent of the population are southpaws, naturally choosing to use their left hand instead of their right. Manufacturers make left-handed computer mice, but more importantly, you can switch the primary mouse button from left to right — so that this button is under the index finger on your left hand. To do so, follow these steps:

1. **Press the Windows+I keyboard shortcut.**

The Settings app appears.

2. **Choose Devices.**

3. **Choose Mouse on the left side of the window,.**

4. **Click the link Additional Mouse Options.**

The Mouse Properties dialog box appears, Button tab forward. If not, click the Buttons tab.

5. **Set a check mark by the option Switch Primary and Secondary Buttons.**

6. **Click OK.**

You can now use your left index finger to click the mouse's right button and get all that good left-click action.

REMEMBER

All the manuals, web pages, computer books, and other documentation on Planet Earth assume that the main mouse button is the *left* button. When you switch buttons as described in this section, the main mouse button is the *right* one. Also, when the directions say to right-click, you do a *left-click*. Remember that!

Honing the keyboard

The computer keyboard presents an impressive slab of buttons, all innocent little momentary on–off switches. The only two hardware items you can control from Windows are the keyboard's repeat delay and repeat rate:

Repeat delay: This interval sets the time between when you press and hold a key and the key repeats itself.

Repeat rate: This rate determines how fast a key repeats after the repeat delay time passes.

The best way to understand these two settings is to mess with them. Obey these steps:

1. Tap the Windows key.

2. Type keyboard

3. From the search results list, choose Keyboard Control Panel.

The Keyboard Properties dialog box appears. If the Speed tab isn't forward, click it. This tab, shown in Figure 6-7, is where the repeat delay and repeat rate values are set.

4. Adjust the sliders beneath Repeat Delay and Repeat Rate to speed things up or down.

Nothing is affected until you click the OK button, so experiment with each item. I recommend changing the settings individually as opposed to both at once.

5. Click the Apply button.

6. Click the Test text box.

7. Press and hold a key on the keyboard to check the rates.

The repeat delay is the pause before a key repeats; the repeat rate is how rapidly characters appear after the delay.

8. Repeat Steps 5 through 8 to hone the settings.

9. Click OK when things are set up just so.

Peripheral Perils

Repeat speed

Pause before repeat action

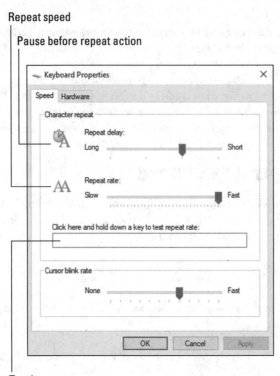

FIGURE 6-7:
Keyboard repeat
and delay
settings.

Test here

When a key gets physically stuck, it repeats like crazy, no matter what. A stuck key indicates a mechanical problem with the keyboard, not anything that software can fix. You can try cleaning the keyboard as described in the next section. If cleaning doesn't work, however, consider buying a new keyboard as the best solution.

TECHNICAL STUFF

Low-end computer keyboards use a magnetic membrane to detect key presses. When this membrane breaks, such as when a key gets stuck, it cannot be fixed. Only more-expensive mechanical keyboards can be fixed: Pop off the bad key cap and remove whatever gunk is jamming the mechanism. Replace the key cap.

Vacuuming a keyboard

I know some people who are meticulous when it comes to cleaning a keyboard. For them, the best solution is to obtain a keyboard cover, which, just like the plastic sofa covers at Grandma's house, keeps the keyboard clean. Never mind how tacky a plastic keyboard cover looks.

For my own keyboard, I use a handheld vacuum cleaner to suck the crud from between the keys. You can also use a can of air, but I fear that the air blast just moves the crud farther from where I can reach.

Using a bent paperclip also helps to pull the crud from the keyboard. Tweezers help, but only before the crud sneaks down below the keycaps.

Sometimes, it helps to turn over the keyboard and give it a good shake. Be prepared for gross stuff to come out.

TIP

>> The best way to avoid a dirty keyboard is to not eat while you use the computer.

>> You can use a pencil eraser to clean the keycaps. Keep in mind that the more you use a computer keyboard, the more likely it is that certain key cap labels wear off. On my keyboards, it's always the A key's label that goes first.

>> If you use a pencil eraser to clean key caps, take a vacuum to the keyboard immediately afterward to rid the keyboard's guts of eraser stubble.

WARNING

>> I know some obsessive people who pop off the key caps before vacuuming the keyboard. This trick works, but on some keyboards you risk permanently damaging the key by removing the cap. Be careful.

Cleaning the mouse

The mouse needs cleaning more than any other part of the computer. Today's mice are optical, which means that any small bit of junk or hair that obscures the optical sensor causes the mouse pointer to behave erratically on the screen. A good cleaning fixes the problem.

To quickly clean the mouse, follow these directions:

1. **Ensure that the mouse pointer is positioned on the screen in a way that, if you accidentally click the mouse, nothing "bad" happens.**

    For example, you don't want the mouse pointer hovering over the OK button for the Completely Erase Hard Drive command.

2. **Turn the mouse upside down in one hand and use a pair of tweezers in the other hand to remove gunk from the mouse's optical "eye."**

    You might also use a blast of air to finish the job.

This technique works the same for nontraditional mice, such as trackball mice. For this specific model, remove the trackball and then clean the optical sensor. Also clean any hair that has accumulated around the ball supports inside the mouse.

» Removing hair and gunk from a mouse's optical sensor is a regular part of computer maintenance. You don't need to schedule the procedure; just wait until the mouse becomes erratic, and then check and clean the sensor.

» It's not necessary to clean the trackpad for a laptop, though you might give it a wipe with a cloth, if you like. Dirt on a trackpad doesn't affect mouse performance as much as hair and gunk block the optical sensor on a handheld pointing device.

Chapter **7**

Software Situations

The good news about software problems is that they're consistent. The bad news is that the operating system is software and it's in charge of everything. So, when you experience a software problem, hope that it's an issue with a program and not with Windows directly. Yes, even Windows can be fixed, but fixing other software — the programs you run on the PC — is far less painful.

Installation Issues

Most computers are dedicated systems, running only one program. They do it consistently and well. Your PC is not one of these computers, which is a good thing. Flexibility and an abundance of software is the key to the PC's success.

Adding software

To build the computer's software inventory, you install a new program. The primary source for the software is the Internet.

If you stridently obey Microsoft, new software is obtained from the Microsoft Store. Open the Store icon on the taskbar (if you haven't yet removed it) or find the Store app on the Start menu. Use the Microsoft Store to browse for, optionally purchase, and obtain new programs and apps for the computer.

Also common is to obtain software from the developer's website. After all, not every program inhabits the virtual shelves of the Microsoft Store. The process works like this:

1. **You visit the developer's website.**

2. **Venture to a specific download page.**

3. **Choose the software to install.**

    To assist with this step, you might have an installation key or other directions that explain what specifically you're looking for.

4. **Watch as the software is downloaded from the developer's website into your computer.**

5. **Run the installation program.**

    This step may involve registering the software, entering a special key, and completing other tasks. Mostly, the process is automatic.

6. **Use the program.**

    The program runs at once, or, as with all software on your PC, you can summon it from the Start menu.

Regardless of its Internet source, after the program is installed, you're done: Use the software.

Updates to the program might be available in the future. It's popular for a program to feature an updater or refresher utility. You're notified when a new version is available and given the opportunity to install the update, often free of charge.

>> Some software comes on installation media, such as a thumb drive or an optical disc. This practice is getting rare. Still, if the Internet is slow or unavailable in your location, you can obtain installation media rather than install over the Internet.

>> Software you buy at the store is mostly an empty box. Inside you find instructions for obtaining the software over the Internet, often with an installation key code used to unlock the program.

>> See the nearby sidebar "Which Windows version?" to answer the question of whether your PC has the 32-bit or 64-bit version of Windows installed. This question is often posted at software download sites.

WHICH WINDOWS VERSION?

Windows may seem like one operating system, but it has several layers. Beyond the various versions (Home, Pro, and so on), Windows comes in two flavors: 32-bit and 64-bit. The installed version depends on the PC's hardware as well as on your own preferences during installation. This detail is important to know when obtaining new software, because some programs are written specifically as 32-bit or 64-bit flavors.

For the most part, Windows installs in the 64-bit flavor. To confirm, press the Win+Break keyboard combination.

The System window details information about Windows, including the version and whether it's 32-bit or 64-bit. The version number is found below the Windows Edition heading in the System window. The flavor is found under the System heading, labeled System Type.

TIP

>> New software installed in Windows 10 is highlighted on the Start menu: Tap the Windows key and look for the highlighted entries. They represent new programs.

WARNING

>> Review Book 1, Chapter 2 for helpful information about locating a software developer's website. You want to ensure that you use their own website to obtain the software and not another, phony website. If you're careless, you might install malware on your PC.

Downloading software

No matter which web browser you use, after you download software, you see some questions displayed. The most important one is whether to run or save (open) the program. My advice is to save. This way, should something happen, you can still run the saved download without having to repeat the process of visiting the website and choosing the file all over again.

Downloads are saved in the Downloads folder, which is found in your personal file area in Windows. To open that folder and view its contents, obey these steps:

1. **Press The Windows+E keyboard shortcut to bring up the File Explorer window.**

2. **Choose Downloads from the navigation pane on the left side of the window.**

   If you don't see the navigation pane, choose View, Navigation Pane, Navigation Pane from the menu.

3. **Look for the file you downloaded.**

   By default, the Downloads folder displays the most recent files at the top of the list. The file you downloaded is most likely the top entry in the list.

4. **Open the file.**

   It may be called Install or Setup, or it may have a nice, long complex name with numbers and dots and dashes. These details help you keep various installation and update programs separate from each other.

5. **If you see a warning about the file coming from the Internet, click the Yes or Allow button to proceed.**

   The warning ensures that you don't accidentally run a file you didn't download. Because you deliberately downloaded the installation program, it's okay to run.

6. **Continue obeying the installation directions on the screen.**

The nifty thing about having the program saved in the Downloads folder is that you can rerun the program again if anything rotten happens during installation. See the next section.

>> Sometimes, the program you download is an installer, not the full program. The installer proceeds to access the Internet to obtain and install the full version of the program.

>> If you download a Zip file archive, you must open the archive to extract the files. Look for a Setup or Install program in the extracted files. Run this program to complete installation.

>> After installation is complete, I move the Install or Setup program to a subfolder named Programs. That way, I can keep the Downloads folder organized and relatively empty.

>> If you desire to be a nerd, you can visit the Downloads folder by typing the following text in a File Explorer window's address box:

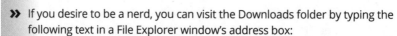

```
%USERPROFILE%\Downloads
```

TECHNICAL
STUFF

Type that text exactly and press the Enter key. Ta-da.

Dealing with installation issues

When a program doesn't install properly, the first thing you need to know is this: *It's not your fault.*

When the error is a missing file, it's not your fault. When the download or media cannot be read, it's not your fault. Keep in mind that you're not a software developer. It's not your job to track down missing files or repair defective discs.

What do you do?

After getting frustrated, repeat the installation process. Just start over. Reread the directions. Confirm that you have everything you need and that any required steps are taken in the proper order. You can try restarting Windows and proceed as before, but perhaps this time pay real attention to the messages during installation.

TIP

Sometimes, you must uninstall the program before you reinstall it. This trick works even if the program didn't fully install the first time. Refer to the section "Uninstalling software," later in this chapter.

REMEMBER

Be sure to check the website or software box for updates and notices. I missed one of the notices when I tried to install a program, and got frustrated. When I phoned the developer, the message I heard on hold reminded me to read the information on the website, which contained the solution I was looking for.

Banish the Unwanted

Perhaps the primary reason most people remove software from their computers is to make more room on the mass storage system. Some programs occupy a lot of space and, if you no longer use them, uninstall them. Still, even when storage space isn't a concern, you should feel free to evict any unwanted or seldom-used software on your computer.

Uninstalling software

You don't just yank a program from mass storage. This desire may be satisfying, but it's bad practice. Further, software is installed *all over* the storage system. To best remove software, you must follow specific directions:

1. **Open the Settings app.**

   Press the Windows+I keyboard shortcut.

2. **Choose the Apps tile.**

   A long list of installed programs appears.

3. **Select the program you want to remove.**

   Use the Search text box menu to help you locate a specific program, or just scroll through the list.

TIP

If your goal is to free storage space, choose Size from the Sort By menu. Then look for the largest programs in the list. Choose one you no longer or seldom use.

4. **Click the Uninstall button.**

5. **Heed the onscreen directions.**

The uninstall operation is performed by the software itself, not by Windows. The program removes its various elements and references. It does not remove any files you created, though it may disassociate itself from those files. (See the later section "Changing the file association.") Some uninstall programs may retain program settings, which is helpful if you reinstall the program.

WARNING

>> Do not delete or remove installed applications manually.

>> Malware doesn't appear in the list. To remove malware, you must use a special utility, such as Windows Defender. See Book 4, Chapter 3.

REMEMBER

>> Deleting a program's shortcut icon doesn't delete the program. Shortcut icons are found on the desktop, on the Start menu, and elsewhere in Windows. Some uninstall procedures remove these shortcuts; some don't.

TECHNICAL STUFF

>> Microsoft makes it very difficult to remove its own programs, those that piggyback on Windows such as Edge, Paint, and others. Under normal situations, it's not necessary to remove these programs and apps. If you desire to do so, you must run the PowerShell command-line tool as system administrator and use the Remove-AppxPackage command followed by specific details to purge the programs and utilities. This process is quite advanced and beyond the scope of this book.

>> See Book 5, Chapter 2 for more information on freeing disk storage.

SYSTEM RESTORE AND UNEXPECTED UNINSTALLATION

Sometimes, a System Restore operation has the unintended consequence of messing up a program you recently installed. The effect is that a program may appear to be installed but is missing vital files that were "unhooked" by the System Restore operation.

Because you probably ran System Restore to recover from a disaster, I don't recommend undoing the System Restore. Instead, reinstall the program that's screwing up. Doing so reconnects the items that System Restore disconnected.

Removing bloatware

In the early days of the PC, the computer came with its operating system preinstalled, but nothing else. Well, the BASIC programming language was available. It was provided so that you could write your own software. I'm glad those days are over.

Replacing the notion that you can write your own software is the desire of computer manufacturers to include "bonus" programs preinstalled on the computer. The abundance of this software, dubbed *bloatware*, isn't as obnoxious as it once was, but still you may find unwanted and unused software on your computer. The solution: Remove the software.

Uninstalling bloatware is done just like uninstalling any PC software: Refer to the earlier section "Uninstalling software."

>> Some bloatware arrives uninstalled. For example, you may see a "sign up" or "preview" icon on the desktop, which visits an online site to download special software. Just delete those icons if you don't plan to use any of the services or programs.

WARNING

>> Be careful! Some of the bonus software on your PC might seem to be bloatware but isn't. Software such as custom utilities or firmware upgrade tools are required.

TIP

>> No, you don't have to live with the antivirus software preinstalled on your PC. You can remove it, but I recommend doing so only after any "free" or prepaid term has been completed.

Cleaning up the uninstall leftovers

It's most disappointing after removing software to see a message along the lines of "Some elements of the program were not removed." Ugh. Thanks for the letdown, Mr. Computer. Imagine trying to pull something like that on your mom when you were a kid: "Mom, I finished cleaning my room, but some parts of the floor remain unvacuumed."

Some programs don't uninstall all their pieces because other programs might use them. This consideration is only polite. After all, when you're done eating, you don't remove the salt, pepper, butter, ketchup, and other items from the table when others might still be using them.

My advice: Don't sweat it. The program is gone, which is what you wanted.

The Good and Evil of File Association

File association is the operating system magic that makes a file's icon look the way it does. Its appearance relates to the program that created it or that can open the file. This effect is controlled by the operating system, which associates files with programs. This system works great! When it doesn't, you must fix the file association faux pas.

Understanding file association

Every icon on the desktop and in a File Explorer window represents a file. A *file* is merely a chunk of information on the PC's mass storage system. It's a dull topic, but relevant because the last part of the file's name, the *filename extension*, is how Windows identifies the file's type.

A file *type* is a category, like graphics files or Excel worksheets. Windows uses the file type information (the filename's extension) to determine which program opens a file, which programs to list on the file's shortcut menu, and which icon to slap on the file. The official term for all this nonsense is *file association*.

For example, the file named Kayak_adventure.docx has the filename extension docx. Normally, that extension is hidden in a File Explorer window, but the extension is still part of the name. The docx extension is associated with Microsoft Word. Therefore, the file appears with a Word document icon. When you double-click the icon, Microsoft Word opens and loads the file for editing. This is how file association works.

>> Windows keeps track of dozens of filename extensions, noting which programs open which files.

>> The filename extension is the final part of a filename. It begins with a period and is followed by one or more characters. Most extensions are three or four characters long.

>> The File Explorer program normally hides filename extensions. This concealment doesn't mean that a file lacks an extension, merely that Windows is trying to be sneaky. See the next section.

>> Some files lack extensions, in which case they're not associated with any program. Likewise, not every extension is known to Windows. See the later section "Dealing with unknown file types."

>> One major problem with filename association is that installing a new program can reassociate existing files on your computer. For example, programs opened by Paint may suddenly be opened by Photoshop. To prevent this

situation, most programs ask before they make the reassociation. If not, you can reassign file associations; see the section "Changing the file association," later in this chapter.

TECHNICAL STUFF

» File association based on the filename extensions is a terrible system. It's relatively easy to change a filename's extension, which modifies the association without altering the file's contents. This change can cause trouble, which is why you're warned whenever you attempt to rename a file's extension.

Hiding or showing file extensions

Windows is afraid that you'll discover the secret to file association and you may offend the gods by changing a file's extension. I'm certain that, somewhere on the Microsoft campus, a flock of programmers sit and cower in terror at the thought. Still, it's *your* computer, and if you want to see the silly extensions — change them, even — you can do so.

As the Lord Commander of my PC, I prefer to see the extensions, not only in a File Explorer window but also when I use the Save As or Open dialog box. One command changes whether you see the extensions. To hunt it down, obey these steps:

1. **Tap the Windows key.**

2. **Type** file explorer options

3. **When you see the File Explorer Options Control Panel item in the search results, choose it.**

   The File Explorer Options dialog box appears. It's part of the Control Panel, but also accessible from within any File Explorer window.

4. **Click the View tab.**

5. **Uncheck the item Hide Extensions for Known File Types.**

6. **Click OK.**

Filename extensions are now displayed in every folder window, as well as in the Open and Save As dialog boxes.

Having the filename extensions visible lets you see a full filename, but it also adds a caveat:

WARNING

Don't change a file extension unless you know what you're doing! Just leave it alone.

Why show the filename extensions? First, it's honest. You're seeing the real file-name and not an abbreviation. Second, and most importantly, you can more easily diagnose file association problems with the extensions visible.

Changing the file association

Windows harbors a secret location where you can view all filename extensions currently associated with programs and change these programs. Please don't tell anyone else about this location; make them purchase this book. But for you, follow these steps to access the Set Associations window:

1. **Press the Windows+I keyboard shortcut.**

   The Settings app appears.

2. **Choose the Apps tile.**

3. **On the left side of the window, choose Default Apps.**

4. **Click the link Choose Default Apps By File Type.**

   A long list of file extensions appears. Next to each one is a tile representing the program designed to open the type of file.

As an example, scroll to the txt filename extension, which commonly identifies plain-text files. You see that the txt extension identifies a text document and is associated with the Notepad program, as illustrated in Figure 7-1. If it's not associated with Notepad, the program listed is the one that opens when you double-click a plain-text file (or a file with the txt filename extension).

To change a file association, click the associated program's tile. Any installed program capable of opening the given file type appears in the list (refer to Figure 7-1). Choose a new program from the pop-up list, or use the Microsoft Store link to browse for a program to use.

>> To reassociate the file with its original program, repeat these steps and choose that program in Step 6.

>> The file association can also be altered in the Open With window: Right-click on a given file type and choose Open With. Select a new program from the list and check the box Always Use This App to Open *xxx* Files. Click OK.

REMEMBER

>> Newly installed software can change file associations! You may be asked about associations during the installation process. Pay attention to that message, but understand that you can always reset the association as covered in this section.

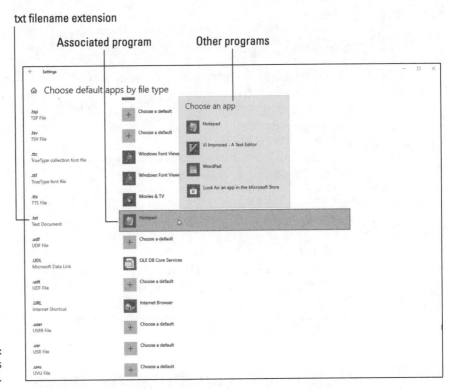

txt filename extension

Associated program   Other programs

FIGURE 7-1:
File associations
in Windows.

TECHNICAL STUFF

ASSOCIATIONS AT THE COMMAND PROMPT

Windows maintains two lists to do the file association tango. The first list, the file association list, contains filename extensions and their related file types. The second list links the file types with programs designed to open the specific file type. This system may seem like a lot of work, but it's not.

For example, consider that htm and html are both filename extensions for web page documents. The file type is `html file`. So, in the first list maintained by Windows, the following entries exist:

```
.htm=htmlfile
.html=htmlfile
```

The filename extensions htm and html are determined to be of the htmlfile type. This file type is further associated with a specific program, in this manner:

```
htmlfile="C:\Program Files (x86)\Google\Chrome\Application\
    chrome.exe"
```

(continued)

(continued)

By associating both filename extensions with the `htmlfile` file type, you make it easy for the computer to reassign the file type to another web browser; only the `htmlfile` entry needs to be changed. Otherwise, Windows would have to pluck out every file extension that might be opened by a web browser. The dual lists save time.

To review file associations at the command prompt, the `assoc` command is used. Type **assoc** by itself at the command prompt to list all file associations — the filename extension followed by the type. To see the type for a specific extension, type **assoc** followed by a file extension, such as **assoc .txt**. (The extension must start with a period.)

To see which programs are associated with a file type, use the `ftype` command. Type **ftype** alone to display all file types and their programs. Follow **ftype** with a file type to show which program opens that type, such as **ftype txtfile** or **ftype htmlfile**.

You can also use `assoc` and `ftype` to create or reassign file types and associations, though it's a technical booger way beyond the scope of this book; you need to know about pathnames and the exact locations of programs, which is a bother. Instead, use the methods for file association that are described in the main text.

Dealing with unknown file types

Attempting to open an unassociated file causes Windows to become all flustered and anxious. Rather than show actual embarrassment, however, Windows displays a dialog box, shown in Figure 7-2.

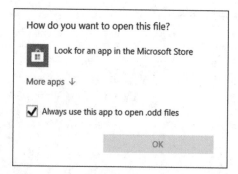

FIGURE 7-2:
An unknown
file type is
encountered.

Here's what you do:

1. **Don't click OK.**

2. **Close the dialog box.**

I'm serious. If the file isn't associated with anything, your computer cannot open it. You can try looking in the Windows Store, as the dialog box suggests (refer to Figure 7-2), but a better approach is to ask the source what to do with the file.

For example, when you receive a file with an unknown type as an email attachment, reply to the message and request that the sender resend the attachment in a common file format. This is the best thing you can do.

>> If the file was found on your PC's hard drive, leave it be. It may serve an important function for another program, in which case you have no business opening the unknown file.

>> You can try to search the web for the file type, just to see what's up. Even then, the file type may match some program you don't have and probably don't want.

Common Software Problems and Solutions

After all my years in troubleshooting, I know that people have a clutch of common questions regarding applications. Without getting overly specific and prattling on for far too many pages, in this section I give you some solutions for common software problems that I've experienced over the years.

"How can I stop this program from starting automatically?"

Some programs start right after you sign in to Windows. You can set some programs yourself, or Windows may automatically run programs or processes on its own. Therefore, you have a few locations to scour to find a startup program you want to kill:

>> The hidden Startup menu retained from older versions of Windows

>> The Startup tab in the Task Manager

>> The Run Once keys in the Registry

None of these places is easy to get to, but each is worthy of a check, just to see whether the pesky program is lurking in that location.

The old Startup menu

Years ago, the Windows Start menu featured submenus, one of which was titled Startup. The items (program shortcuts) placed on the Startup submenu ran automatically after you signed in to Windows. This location still exists, but is hidden. To get there, follow these steps:

1. **Press the Windows+R keyboard shortcut.**

   The Run dialog box appears.

2. **Type** shell:startup **into the box.**

   Type the text just as written here — no spaces.

3. **Press the Enter key.**

   The old Startup menu appears in the File Explorer window.

4. **Delete a program shortcut icon to prevent it from automatically starting.**

   Deleting the shortcut does not uninstall the program.

Be aware that some programs must start when you sign in so that their features are available to you. These programs include keyboard shortcut programs, antivirus software, and other programs you might want to keep active.

TIP

A second location to look for automatic startup programs is in the "all users" version of the Startup folder. Type the following command in the Run dialog box (Step 2 in the preceding list):

```
Shell:Common Startup
```

You may find further shortcuts in this folder. If you don't want the programs running, remove their shortcuts.

The Task Manager's Startup tab

A full list of all programs and processes that start when you sign in to Windows can be found in the Task Manager's window. Heed these steps:

1. **Press Ctrl+Shift+Esc to pop up the Task Manager.**

2. **If necessary, click the More Details chevron.**

   You need access to the full Task Manager window.

3. **Click the Startup tab.**

   A list appears, showing all startup programs.

Your goal on the Startup tab isn't to delete the program, but rather to disable it from automatically starting.

For example, if you don't want an updater program to run, select it in the list on the Startup tab. Click the Disable button to prevent the program from automatically starting.

Restart the computer to test the effect of disabling a startup program. Many of those listed in the Task Manager's window are support programs that make things such as malware checking, cloud computing, and automatic updates possible.

WARNING

Don't disable anything at random! Placing these startup programs in a non-obvious location was done for a reason. Disabling even one can alter your computer's behavior, performance, or security.

To reenable a disabled program, repeat the steps in this section, but click the Enable button after selecting a program.

The Run Once keys in the Registry

Programs that want to be sneaky place their startup commands in the Registry. To access this secret location, follow these steps:

1. **Press the Windows+R keyboard shortcut to summon the Run dialog box.**

2. **Type** regedit **and click the OK button.**

3. **If prompted with a UAC warning, click the Yes button to continue.**

    The Registry Editor starts. It contains Windows settings and other information, most of which can be reset by using other features in Windows. Still, people think it's cool to edit the Registry.

4. **Open the following Registry key:**

    ```
    HKEY_LOCAL_MACHINE
    \SOFTWARE
    \Microsoft
    \Windows
    \CurrentVersion
    \Run
    ```

    Choose each folder in succession: Start with the HKEY entry, and then open SOFTWARE and then Microsoft, and so on.

    The Run folder lists keys that represent programs that start automatically in Windows. Many of these programs are services, which are background utilities that support things like cloud storage and software update utilities. Still, some developers may sneak in a program.

5. **To remove an item from the Run folder, right-click it and choose the Delete command. Click the Yes button to confirm.**

6. **Check the RunOnce entry.**

   It's the next key in the Registry.

7. **Check the current user key as well:**

```
HKEY_CURRENT_USER
\SOFTWARE
\Microsoft
\Windows
\CurrentVersion
\Run
```

   and

```
HKEY_LOCAL_MACHINE
\SOFTWARE
\Microsoft
\Windows
\CurrentVersion
\RunOnce
```

WARNING

Be careful about messing with the Registry! If you accidentally delete or alter something important, the computer won't run properly. The solution is to run System Restore, which recovers the old Registry settings. See Book 3, Chapter 5 for details on System Restore.

"I need to run this older program"

One of the many troubleshooters available in Windows is designed to look for issues with older programs: the Program Compatibility troubleshooter. As with any software troubleshooter, sometimes it's brilliant and sometimes it's silly. Here's how to try it out:

1. **Tap the Windows key to pop up the Start menu.**

2. **Type** run programs

3. **Choose the matching result, Run Programs Made for Previous Versions of Windows.**

   The Program Compatibility troubleshooter appears.

4. **Click the Next button.**

   A list of installed programs (eventually) appears. Your job is to pluck from the list the program with which you're having issues.

RUNNING OLDER SOFTWARE

Windows 10 crossed the threshold of compatibility for ancient DOS programs and early Windows software. Whereas you could finagle Windows to run older software in previous versions, Windows 10 puts its foot down.

The best way to run older software is to emulate DOS or Windows on your PC. I recommend a program called DOSBox, which is available free at www.dosbox.com.

You can install and use the DOSBox emulator to attempt to run older software, but it's not the easiest solution. In fact, my best advice is to obtain an updated version of whatever program you want to run.

5. **Choose a bothersome program from the list.**

TECHNICAL STUFF

If the program isn't listed, choose the top item in the list: Not Listed. Use the Browse button on the next page to locate the program. The Browse dialog box isn't forgiving; to proceed, you must know the filename and exactly where it's located.

6. **Click the Next button.**

Proceed to work through the troubleshooter.

I recommend that you use the option Try Recommended Setting. Further, test-run the program to see if the magic works. For some programs, it works! For others, if the troubleshooter can't get the program to work, it probably won't work. Refer to the nearby sidebar, "Running older software."

"This program is broken!"

Some programs have built-in repair features. To check whether this feature is available on a given program, you must first attempt to uninstall the program. Yeah, this step sounds scary, but it's how the process works. Obey these directions:

1. **Press the Windows+I keyboard shortcut to summon the Settings app.**

2. **Choose the Apps tile.**

3. **Select the program you want to fix.**

For example, Microsoft Office.

4. **Click the Change button.**

   If the Change button doesn't appear, look for an Advanced Options link. If either is missing, click Uninstall. Remember that you're looking for a Repair option. Do not proceed with removing the program when the Repair option doesn't present itself. In this instance, choose Cancel; repair isn't available.

5. **Proceed with repairing the program.**

   The steps after this point vary.

As an example, when you click the Advanced Options link for Microsoft Office, you see a summary screen for Office. The Repair option appears on this screen.

When repairing a program doesn't work, your last resort is to reinstall it. The installation program may recognize that you're reinstalling and attempt a fix. It may even ask you to uninstall the program before it's reinstalled. That's okay: Reinstalling a program doesn't erase your files. It may just fix the problem.

"How can I purge the recently opened file list?"

The file may be gone, deleted, and dead with no possibility of recovery, yet its name still stubbornly appears in one of those Recently Opened Files menus. For some reason, this problem annoys folks more than anything else!

The official name for the list of recent files is the *MRU list*. MRU stands for *most recently used*, and Windows features a host of MRU lists.

TIP

In many nice programs, you can remove an item from an MRU list by right-clicking its entry: Choose the Remove from List command.

In those few naughty programs, you need to edit the MRU list directly. You use the Registry Editor to purge the lists. Obey these steps:

1. **Make a note of the filename you want to purge from an MRU.**

2. **Press Win+R to summon the Run dialog box.**

3. **Type regedit and press Enter.**

4. **If prompted with a security warning, click the Yes button, type the administrator's password, or click the Continue button.**

   The Registry Editor opens.

5. **Press Ctrl+F to summon the Find dialog box.**

6. In the Find box, type the filename you want to purge, and press Enter.

The Registry is searched for that filename.

You want to ensure that the filename that's located dwells in an MRU list. In Figure 7-3, you see the MRU list for the Paint program. Its key is titled Recent File List, which is a major clue that you're looking at the list of recently opened files in the Paint program.

7. When the filename is found, delete the entry from the Registry.

Right-click the key, as shown in Figure 7-3. Choose Delete and click the Yes button to confirm.

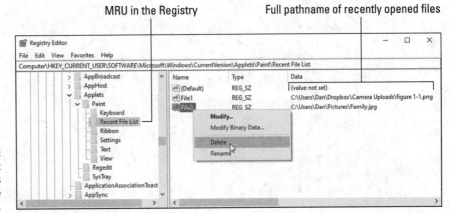

MRU in the Registry   Full pathname of recently opened files

FIGURE 7-3:
The Paint program's MRU list in the Registry.

The change doesn't appear until you close the Registry Editor window and reopen the application that listed the missing file.

The Registry Editor is covered in Book 3, Chapter 7.

Chapter **8**

Network Nonsense

Thanks to the Internet, every home and small business office features a network. Even a lonely, single computer connected to the Internet is on a network. This revelation means you have networking duties to perform, which includes resolving network nonsense.

» Another part of network troubleshooting involves security. See Book 4 for details on PC security.

» The Windows Firewall is yet another networking software tool. See Book 4, Chapter 3 for details on the firewall.

The Network Big Picture

Computer networking involves its own set of jargon, gizmos, and procedures. You mustn't shy away from the terms and technology! This book, your Internet service provider (ISP), and even the tech support person in Wamboolistan use the same lingo and make various assumptions about what you know. If you're not yet up to speed with computer networking, it's time to immerse yourself.

Understanding networking

Networking is about communications and the sharing of resources. The goal is to move information from one resource to another without having to walk or at least lean over so far in your chair that you spill onto the floor.

The shared resources include

Storage: This resource is like any computer storage, though it's available to all computers on the network. Included are computers connected to the network that share folders, but also network storage.

Printers: Printers are more commonly connected to a network today than they are directly connected to a computer. By doing so, everyone on the network can share the printer without each computer requiring its own printer peripheral.

Modems: Broadband modems are built for networking. They connect and interface with the Internet — the Big Network — and the modem is available to all computers on the local network for shared Internet access.

To share these resources, you use a wired or wireless network, or a combination of both. But at its core, networking is about sharing.

>> Computer networking became standard in the early 1990s. So, no matter what type of computers or software you use, the same networking standard is employed. That standard is referred to as *Ethernet*.

>> Another term for your small office or home network is *LAN*. This acronym stands for *local area network*.

>> The Internet is often called a WAN, for *wide area network*. Many modems and gateways feature a WAN port, which is where you connect the Internet.

>> *Network storage* refers to a mass storage device that doesn't necessarily belong to a specific computer. Also called a *file server,* this device offers high-capacity storage to all computers on the network.

>> Network storage can be broadened to include cloud storage as well. Traditionally only "local" storage, connected directly to the network, is considered.

Reviewing network hardware

Creating and configuring your own home- or small-office network isn't difficult, especially because it's a one-time operation. Even easier is adding devices to a wireless network. This simplicity doesn't underscore the need to know basic network hardware and the terms to describe the various boxy-things.

The network hardware consists of these items:

NIC: This part of the network dwells inside your computer. NIC stands for *network interface card*, though I've also seen it defined as network *information* card. Regardless, just say "nick" and you'll be fine.

Gateway: The gateway manages traffic on the network and coordinates incoming and outgoing network traffic with the Internet. This hardware might also be called a router, though for small-office and home networks, it's technically a gateway.

Broadband modem: The modem provides communications between your local network and the Internet. This hardware is also considered a network resource because its services are shared (thanks to the gateway) with various gizmos on the network.

Ethernet cable: For a wired network, the cable connecting network hardware is known as an Ethernet cable. One end connects to the gateway. The other end connects to each individual computer or printer or other gizmo on the network. The cable is also known as a CAT 5 or CAT 6 cable, where CAT is short for *Cat*egory 5, not kitty cat.

Switches, or hubs: These optional items allow a network to accommodate more wired devices. For example, you can connect a switch to the gateway or connect switches with each other. The goal is to expand the network.

Figure 8-1 illustrates a typical network, one that uses both wired and wireless connections. All the network devices (PCs, printers, laptops, tablets) shown in the figure have a NIC, though it's not illustrated directly.

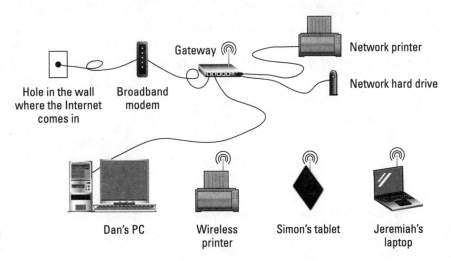

FIGURE 8-1:
A typical network.

Hole in the wall where the Internet comes in — Broadband modem — Gateway — Network printer — Network hard drive — Dan's PC — Wireless printer — Simon's tablet — Jeremiah's laptop

Perhaps the most basic network configuration is a single PC connected to a broadband modem. This setup might not be the most secure; I recommend using a gateway (router), to provide more security. Therefore, the best and simplest network is a PC connected to a gateway connected to a broadband modem.

REMEMBER

>> What you call "the router" is really a gateway. This term is used often in networking.

>> A wired NIC's presence is evident by the networking cable jack. This location is where the network cable connects. The jack is often called an *RJ-45,* though that's not its official designation.

>> Broadband modems come in various types, depending on how the network is accessed. They can be cable modems, satellite modems, cellular modems, and so on.

>> The old telephone modem is referred to as a *dialup* modem. It's used to access another computer or the Internet over standard phone lines. A dialup modem isn't a network resource.

>> The Ethernet cable features the same connections on either end. You can't plug in the cable backward.

>> Even on a wireless network, an Ethernet cable is required to connect the gateway to the broadband modem.

>> A wireless gateway is also known as a *hub* or *base station.* It also features at least two Ethernet ports: one for the broadband modem and another to add a wired device — or a switch, which provides for more ports and additional wired connections.

>> A *mesh* network is a wireless network that uses wireless hubs or base stations. One hub is the primary one, but the others help extend the wireless signal over a wide area. The primary hub acts as the gateway, connecting to the broadband modem.

>> Some gateways feature one or more USB ports. These can be used to connect a hard drive or printer to the network, which is illustrated earlier, in Figure 8-1.

>> Locations where a network cable connects (the NIC, the gateway, for example), feature status lights that blink when data is transmitted. These flickering lights are normal and, in fact, provide diagnostics that the network connection is active.

TIP

>> If you plan to run network cable through the ceiling or air ducts, get *planar* cable, which is designed for such purposes.

>> This is the last bullet point.

TECHNICAL
STUFF

NETWORK SPEED TRIVIA

The speed at which information flies over the local network is measured in Mbps and Gbps, which stand for *megabits per second* and *gigabits per second*, respectively. A typical local network might run at 100 Mbps. A Gigabit Ethernet network runs at ten times that speed, or 1 Gbps.

The speed limitation for a network is all hardware based. If all the gizmos — NICs, switches, gateway, and modem — can support Gigabit Ethernet, the network zooms along at that speed. Otherwise, the speed is throttled by the slowest hardware.

Gigabit Ethernet gizmos are often labeled *GbE,* or sometimes *1 GigE.*

Network Hardware Connection and Configuration

It's my best wish that the computer network is already set up and configured. Once this task is complete, you need only wait until it stops working and then fix it. Otherwise, you must first set up the network. Knowing about this process is useful because many troubleshooting procedures involve repeating these steps to ensure that the network hardware is working.

Plugging in the network

Ethernet cables plug into Ethernet ports on a PC or laptop. The cable goes in only one way, and you can use either end of the cable.

The other end of the cable connects to the gateway (router).

When the gateway runs out of ports, you can connect a switch to the gateway. The switch is a collection of Ethernet ports, one of which is an uplink. The uplink port connects to the gateway. Some switches lack a specific uplink port, in which case any port is used for the connection with the gateway.

The gateway itself connects to the broadband modem, which is covered in the next section.

>> See the later section "Connecting to a wireless network" for details on connecting to a network wirelessly.

>> Wired networking can be an art form, but one that's best appreciated when the art is invisible. The goal of a wired network is not to have the wires draped around the room like popcorn strings on a Christmas tree.

>> You have no reason to ever disconnect a network cable. Once plugged in, it pretty much stays plugged in unless you're troubleshooting network hardware or replacing the computer.

>> Many items on the network also require a power source: The gateway, broadband modem, and any switches all must be powered.

Connecting the gateway and modem

Though it be a technical beast, a gateway isn't difficult to set up. In fact, after it's set up, you rarely, if ever, need to reconfigure or mess with the gateway. It's a solid little gizmo.

The most important item to configure on the gateway is its administrator password. Follow the directions provided with the gateway to access its administrator account. Immediately change the password. Write down the password on a slip of paper and keep the paper with the gateway. You don't want to lose the password.

On the hardware side, the gateway features connections on its rump, as illustrated in Figure 8-2. The connections may be labeled as they are in the figure, though some gateways use icons instead of text. A Wi-Fi base station may not sport as many wired ports or other options shown in the figure.

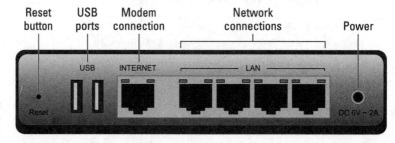

FIGURE 8-2:
Connectors on a typical gateway.

The modem has a few connections as well. The two you want to find are the Internet connection and the Ethernet port used to connect to the gateway. Some modems may have additional Ethernet ports, but the Internet and gateway connections are vital.

As with the gateway, broadband modems lack a power button. That's because they're on all the time. The modem has a power cord, and the way you reset the modem is to unplug it, wait, and then plug it back in.

TIP

» Gateways and broadband modems are meant to be on all the time. I've never seen one with a power switch.

» Label the power brick/plug for the modem and gateway. Using a Sharpie, write on a piece of paper and tape it to the plug, or use a label making machine. It helps to know which plug goes to which device, should you need to restart the network.

» The USB ports are used to connect external storage or a printer to the network. Once connected, these resources can be accessed by all network computers.

» The gateway's password is different from a Wi-Fi network's password. For a Wi-Fi router, you must set both the administrator's password to access the gateway *and* the Wi-Fi network's password or other method of authentication. Use different passwords for each.

» One important item to find on the gateway is its reset switch. It might be a tiny button or a hole into which you stick a bent paperclip. (Refer to Figure 8-2.) The only time you need to use the switch is when you forget the gateway's administrator password. Otherwise, you can ignore it.

» Flickering lights on a gateway or broadband modem are normal. The lights signal activity, which is important when diagnosing problems. The absence of lights or flickering indicates a down network or some other problem.

» Not all gateways feature the connections shown in Figure 8-2. Some lack USB connectors. That's okay: If the gateway doesn't have USB ports, use an Ethernet cable to connect a printer or hard drive to the network.

Configuring a gateway

The gateway requires two steps for its setup. First comes the hardware connection: It must be attached to the modem as well as to the local network. Further, it needs power, so you must plug in the gateway.

The software side of gateway configuration is vital, especially for a wireless network. That's because the gateway provides first-line defense for network security. The Bad Guys adore an unsecured gateway.

The specifics for setting up a gateway vary from device to device. The general process works like this:

1. **Connect the gateway to the local network, but not to the broadband modem.**

   The local network might simply be one PC that connects to the gateway. For a wireless gateway, the connection is made wirelessly, often by using a specific app on a mobile device. Specific directions come with the wireless gateway.

   Often, the gateway lists setup directions and default passwords on a sticker. Look on the bottom of the gateway for such information.

   TIP

2. **Plug in the gateway to the power outlet.**

3. **On the connected computer (or any computer on the connected network), open a web browser.**

   Most gateways feature their own web server. You access the gateway's web page to configure the thing. Some gateways might use their own configuration program instead of a web browser.

4. **Type the gateway's IP address into the web browser's address bar.**

   The IP address looks something like http://192.168.0.1 or possibly http://10.0.0.1. The quick-start guide for the gateway (or the details printed on the gateway itself) gives you the proper address.

   When you're successful, you see the gateway's login screen.

5. **Use the default administrator name and password to log in to the gateway.**

   After signing in, you see the gateway's configuration program. The most important thing to do next is to reset the administrator's password.

6. **Change the gateway's administrator password.**

   Write down the password on a sheet of paper. Do this before you type in the password. I suggest writing

   ```
   Gateway Admin name:
   Gateway Admin password:
   ```

   The Admin name can be *admin*, which is the default for most gateways. The password should be nice and strong, not easy to guess. You'll rarely type it in again and you're writing it down, so it need not be memorable. But you must write it down and specify that it's the gateway's administrator password. Doing this step now saves you headaches in the future.

7. After you change the password, sign out of the gateway and sign back in again using the new password.

TIP

It's okay to have the web browser software memorize the gateway's password; save the password, if prompted.

8. Ensure that the gateway's firewall is active.

The firewall most likely is active, but check to confirm. Use the gateway's web-based interface in your PC's web browser to navigate to the firewall's options screen.

9. For a wireless network, name the network.

Locate the option that lets you assign a network name or SSID. You can hide the name for more security, but set the name now.

10. For a wireless network, think of a network access password.

This password is different from the gateway's administrator password. So, on the same sheet of paper you used in Step 6, write down the password — for example:

```
Wi-Fi network name:
Wi-Fi network access password:
```

Write down the password before you use the gateway's software to set the password, and then set the password.

11. If prompted, restart the gateway.

At this point, the gateway is up and running.

12. Close the web browser window.

13. Connect the gateway to the broadband modem.

Because you've secured the gateway, it's safe to open 'er up to the full onslaught of the Internet.

14. Take the piece of paper with the gateway's password(s), and stick it underneath the gateway.

That way, you'll never lose the vital information.

The gateway retains all settings and changes you've made, providing you've used the program to set and save those changes. You don't need to reconfigure the gateway after a power outage.

TECHNICAL STUFF

>> SSID is the *service set identifier,* a fancy term for a Wi-Fi network's broadcasted name.

CHECK YOUR PC'S IP ADDRESS

One of the gateway's jobs is to manage computers and devices on the local area network (LAN). To keep the gizmos in line, each is assigned or designated a specific Internet Protocol (IP) address. It's like a street number, but far more cryptic.

The easiest way to assign IP addresses to network devices is to use the DHCP. The Dynamic Host Configuration Protocol assigns a unique IP address to each device the network finds. It manages the IP addresses and ensures that no two devices use the same address.

To check your PC's IP address, you need to do some digging. The information is found in the Settings app: Choose the Network & Internet tile and then choose Status from the left side of the window. On the right, click the Properties button. The IP address information is listed on the next screen.

Two sets of IP addresses appear: IPv4 and IPv6. IPv4 is the older, more familiar version, which consists of four numbers separated by dots. IPv6 is newer, longer, and more confusing. Both values are assigned to the PC by the gateway.

If your PC features two network connections, each one has its own IP address. So, a laptop with both wireless and wired NICs features two sets of IP addresses when both adapters are connected to a network.

>> If you forget the gateway's administrator password, you can reset the gateway: Look for the reset button and follow the directions on the gateway for a reset. Typically, you press and hold the button for about 5 seconds. After you reset, you must configure the gateway all over again, as described in this section.

>> Though you may never touch the gateway again, one thing you might do in the future is update the gateway's software. As with any software update, the new version may offer improved security and fix problems. The message alerting you to the upgrade's availability provides directions for performing the upgrade.

Connecting to a wireless network

A wired network is cinchy to connect to: Plug in an Ethernet cable. *Boom!* You're done.

Well, you won't hear a *boom* sound. If you do, proceed to the "Network Trouble-shooting" section, later in this chapter.

To connect to a wireless network, you might not have to do a thing: Windows remembers previously connected wireless networks and, as long as the password hasn't changed, the network is reconnected instantly.

To connect to a new wireless network, follow these steps:

1. **Click the Internet icon on the taskbar.**

The icon is shown in the margin, which indicates that no network connection is available.

2. **Choose a network from the list.**

Figure 8-3 illustrates how Wi-Fi networks may look in the Settings app.

3. **Click the Connect button.**

4. **If prompted, type the network password or security key.**

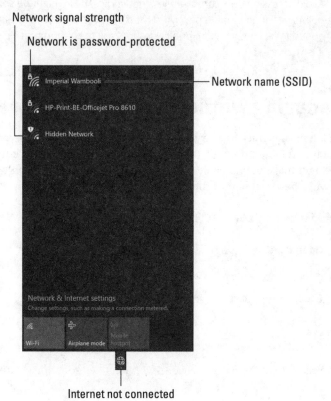

FIGURE 8-3:
Available Wi-Fi networks.

Upon success, the "not connected" icon on the taskbar changes to the Wi-Fi Connected icon, as shown in the margin.

>> If you plan to frequent the network — such as at home, the office, or your favorite coffee shop — place a check mark by the item Connect Automatically, which appears after Step 2. With this setting active, you need only type a wireless network password once. After that, the computer automatically reconnects to the network any time it's in range.

>> If the wireless network password has changed, you must direct Windows to forget the network and then reconnect. See the later section "The Wi-Fi password has changed!"

>> If the gateway features WPS (Wireless Protected Setup) access, you can connect by typing a PIN or pressing a button on the gateway itself.

>> Some wireless networks have no passwords. For most public locations, such as airports or libraries, you must access a web page to sign in to the network or agree to terms. Although you're connected, full Internet access isn't granted until you visit a web page.

WARNING

>> Avoid accessing unsecured wireless networks. These might be spoofed access points designed to mine passwords and sensitive data. If you're in doubt about a Wi-Fi network at a public location, ask to confirm that it's legitimate. If it isn't, don't access it.

Managing wireless connections

Windows keeps track of every Wi-Fi network your PC has connected to. The information is retained to make it easier to reconnect to a network in the future. So, when you make your weekly visit to Café Pretentious, you don't need to ask the girl with the green hair at the counter for the Wi-Fi password.

To review memorized Wi-Fi connections, heed these steps:

1. **Open the Settings app.**

   Press the Windows+I keyboard shortcut.

2. **Choose the Network & Internet tile.**

3. **Choose Wi-Fi from the items on the left side of the screen.**

4. **Click the Manage Known Networks link.**

   You find a list of all Wi-Fi networks you've connected to and entered a password.

The list of Wi-Fi networks is probably quite long. Don't let the length puzzle you; if you use a Microsoft account to sign in to Windows 10, the list includes networks accessed from each of your Windows devices, including laptops and mobile gizmos.

The only thing you can do with a known network — the only "management" — is to delete a network's entry: Select the network name and click the Forget button. *Thwoop!* The network is gone, though you may not hear the "thwoop" sound.

Checking network privacy

When you first connect to a network, you may be asked whether it's a private network or a public network. The question is vital to network security.

Private: A private network is less restrictive. You set this network for your home or office, where you're assured of which devices and computers are connected to the network.

Public: The public network option is used for locations where you're unsure of who is on the network — for example, when accessing a wireless network in a café or at the airport.

The private/public network setting is determined when you first access a network. If it isn't, you can check on the connection status and change the setting later.

To confirm the current network's privacy setting, follow these steps:

1. Press the Windows+I keyboard shortcut.

The Settings app opens.

2. Choose the Network & Internet tile.

3. With Status chosen from the left side of the window, click the Properties button.

The Network Profile heading shows the current network status, Public or Private, as illustrated in Figure 8-4.

To switch between public and private network settings, choose a new setting from the window, as shown in Figure 8-4.

The changes you make don't affect the entire network. After all, if you just joined a wireless network in a cybercafé, why would your computer be allowed to lord it over all other computers on the network? No, the public/private thing merely tells Windows how to treat the network.

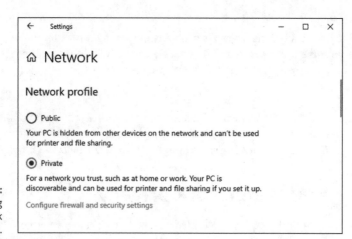

FIGURE 8-4:
Checking
the network
security level.

The Software Side of Networking

One of Windows many duties is to oversee network communications and sharing. As with network setup, the good news is that network configuration is done once and forgotten — unless you have trouble.

Looking at the network

The Network window has nothing to do with managing the network, though it gives you an overview of available network resources. It also shows you that the network — the local part, at least — is up and running.

Figure 8-5 illustrates what a Network window may look like.

To summon such a window, heed these brief steps:

1. **Press the Windows+E keyboard shortcut to conjure a File Explorer window.**

2. **Choose Network from the address bar.**

   Or, you can click on the Network item in the navigation pane on the left side of the window, as illustrated in Figure 8-5.

I visit the Network window frequently to confirm that the local network is up and running. Even when the Internet is down, the local network lets you share resources, access files on other PCs, and print.

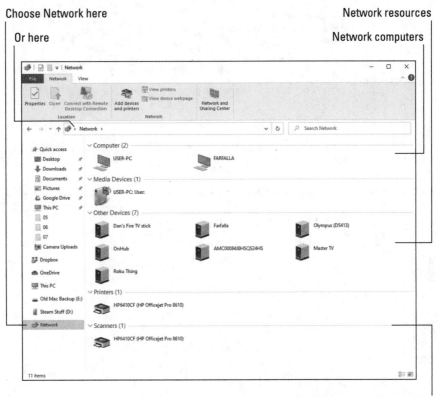

Choose Network here

Or here

Network resources

Network computers

Network printers and scanners

FIGURE 8-5:
The Network
window.

WARNING

A public network may still show computers in the Network window. *Be careful!* Those computers are sharing their resources on a network with low security. Accessing the computers is risky.

Checking the Internet connection

The hardware way to check on an active Internet connection is to look at the broadband modem. Are all its lights on and blinking? If so, the Internet might be okay; a signal is present, though the Internet itself may be offline.

The simple software way to check the Internet connection is to point the mouse at the Networking icon on the taskbar. The two icons are shown in Figure 8-6 — one for a wired connection and another for wireless. Hover the mouse over the taskbar icon to see the pop-up window. If it says *Internet Access*, the Internet is online and available.

FIGURE 8-6:
An Internet
connection's
taskbar
notifications.

 Wired access

 Wireless access

 No access/local
access only

You can confirm the Internet connection status in the Settings app. Heed these directions:

1. **Press the Windows+I keyboard shortcut to call forth the Settings app.**

2. **Choose Network & Internet.**

At the top of the Status screen, you see a graphical and simplistic representation of the PC's current network connection, similar to the one that appears in Figure 8-7.

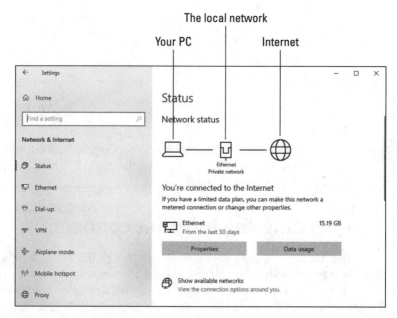

FIGURE 8-7:
The current
network status.

If any part of the network is down or malfunctioning, the Network status graphic shows where the problem is: your PC, the local area connection (the LAN), or the Internet.

>> When the Internet is down, you can phone your ISP to see whether it's a technical issue on their end. If so, you must wait for the service to become available again.

>> Also see the later section "Resetting the broadband modem." This is the solution to try when the ISP claims that nothing is wrong with the Internet.

>> It's possible that the Internet is available, but not the website you're trying to access. If so, try another site. Websites go offline from time to time, though it's usually only for a short while.

Enabling sharing options

The local network performs its task of sharing files, devices, and resources — if you've enabled that feature. The settings can be simple or complex, but for basic, local network sharing, you need to check only one spot. Obey these directions:

1. **Press the Windows+I keyboard shortcut.**

The Settings app appears.

2. **Choose the Network & Internet tile.**

3. **From the left side of the window, choose Wi-Fi or Ethernet.**

4. **Click the Change Advanced Sharing Options link.**

The Advanced Sharing Settings window lists three collapsible areas, illustrated in Figure 8-8. Each area controls sharing options for a specific type of network. In the figure, the Private network's settings are shown.

5. **Ensure that network discovery is active.**

Network discovery controls what you see in the Network window (refer to Figure 8-5). This option is what lets you access other computers and resources on a private network.

6. **Ensure that file and printer sharing is active: Choose the option Turn On File and Printer Sharing.**

This option lets you share folders on your PC's storage system and any printers attached directly to your computer.

7. **Expand the Guest or Public part of the window: Click the chevron.**

Only one area in the Advanced Sharing Settings window is open at a time. In the Guest or Public profile area, you can set options for guest network access.

8. **Turn off both items in the Guest or Public category.**

I don't recommend guest access on the network.

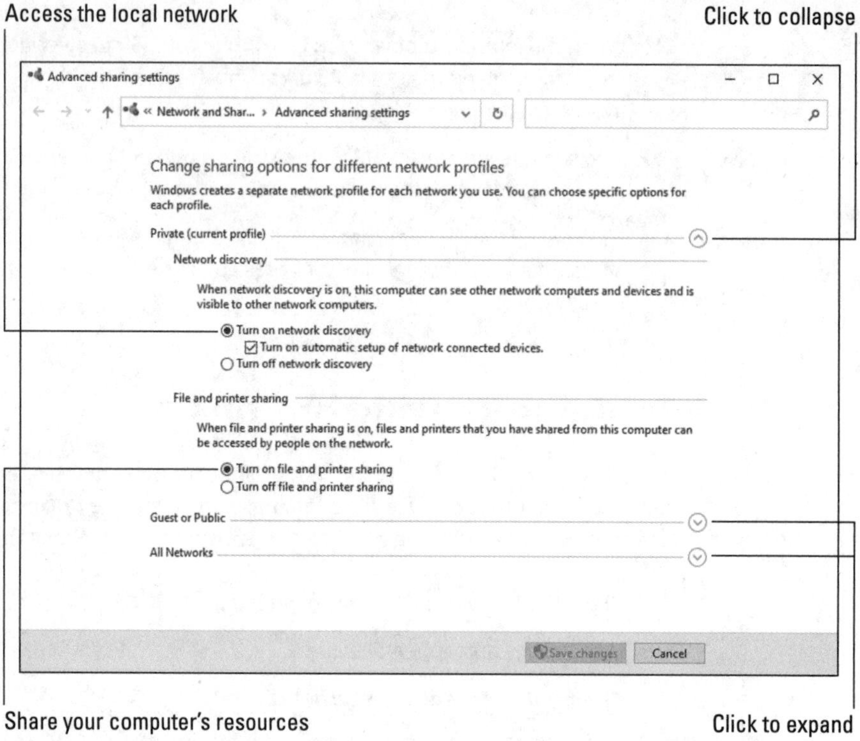

Access the local network   Click to collapse

Change sharing options for different network profiles

Windows creates a separate network profile for each network you use. You can choose specific options for each profile.

Private (current profile)

Network discovery

When network discovery is on, this computer can see other network computers and devices and is visible to other network computers.

◉ Turn on network discovery
  ☑ Turn on automatic setup of network connected devices.
○ Turn off network discovery

File and printer sharing

When file and printer sharing is on, files and printers that you have shared from this computer can be accessed by people on the network.

◉ Turn on file and printer sharing
○ Turn off file and printer sharing

Guest or Public

All Networks

Save changes   Cancel

FIGURE 8-8:
Confirming
network sharing
options.

Share your computer's resources   Click to expand

9. **Expand the All Networks part of the window: Click the chevron.**

10. **Ensure that two items are enabled: 128-bit Encryption and Password-Protected Sharing.**

11. **Click the Save Changes button to lock in any new settings.**

The button is available only when you've altered a setting; otherwise, you're good.

After you've confirmed the proper settings, you can access network resources, and other computers on the network can access your PC's resources — if you share them. Sharing folders is an example of a resource your PC can share. See the next section.

>> The sharing options apply to only the current network. An Internet computer can't bust into the local network to access your PC — unless you disable the firewall. See Book 4, Chapter 3 for information on the Windows firewall.

>> Sharing works both ways. If all PCs on the network have sharing enabled, you can access shared files and folders on those PCs as well. See the later section "Accessing shared folders on the network."

Sharing a folder

You don't have to share a folder on the network. No one thinks less of you for not doing so. If you want to share the contents of a folder with others on the network, follow these steps:

1. **Right-click the folder you want to share.**

You must see the folder to share it, not be "in" the folder. Use the File Explorer program to view the folder; the keyboard shortcut is Windows+E.

2. **Choose Properties from the shortcut menu.**

Ignore other "share" commands on the shortcut menu.

3. **Click the Sharing tab in the folder's Properties dialog box.**

4. **Click the Advanced Sharing button.**

The Advanced Sharing dialog box appears.

5. **Place a check mark by the option Share This Folder.**

6. **If you feel generous, type a more descriptive share name.**

The folder's name appears in the Shared Name box. This is the name that appears on the network as a shared folder.

7. **Click OK to close the Advanced Sharing dialog box.**

8. **Click the Close button to dismiss the folder's Properties dialog box.**

At this point, other computers on the network have read-only access to the folder, which means they can open files or copy them from your PC but cannot add files to the folder, delete files already in the folder, or modify the folder.

If you want to grant full access to the network folder, after Step 5, click the Permissions button. In the Permissions dialog box, look for the Permissions for Everyone table. Place a check mark by Full Control in the Allow column. Click OK.

WARNING

>> For security purposes, share only specific folders, not a folder tree. Do not share your entire user account folder or the root folder of a storage device.

>> To unshare a folder, repeat the steps in this section but remove the check mark in Step 5.

>> You can share only folders, not individual files.

TIP

>> A better way to share folders is to use cloud storage. A service such as Dropbox allows you to access shared files quickly over the Internet without having to mess with the peculiarities of Windows networking.

Accessing shared folders on the network

The Network window is your gateway to shared folders available on the local network. The process works like this:

1. **Choose Network from a File Explorer window, or from a Save As or Open dialog box.**

2. **Open the icon for the computer hosting the shared folder.**

   Or, you can open any computer icon to see which folders are shared.

3. **Open the shared folder.**

4. **If prompted, enter your name and password into the box.**

   The name and password represent an account on the network computer. If you don't have an account on that computer, you can't access the folder.

If you configured network sharing as I describe in the preceding section, permissions are granted for all users: "Everyone." Otherwise, you must have an account on the computer to access the shared folder.

Mapping a network folder to a drive letter

For network locations you frequent, consider mapping the shared folder to a drive letter on your computer. This shortcut lets you quickly access the folder — and keep it available whenever you use Windows.

To map a network folder to a drive letter, heed these steps:

1. **Browse the network for the folder you want to access.**

2. **Right-click the folder's icon.**

3. **Choose the Map Network Drive command.**

   The Map Network Drive Wizard appears.

4. **Choose a drive letter for the network folder.**

   For example, if the shared folder is titled Photos, you might choose drive letter P. Only available drive letters are chosen.

5. **Ensure that the item Reconnect At Sign-In is selected.**

   You want to have the network drive/shared folder available all the time.

6. **Click the Finish button.**

   The new "drive" appears in the This PC window in the Network Locations category.

You may be required to type your account name and password to access the network location. The good news is that this process needs to be done only once. After that, the shared folder/drive is automatically mounted when you sign in to Windows.

REMEMBER

>> I map shared folders to drive letters M and above. This choice means the letters won't conflict with any local media that I may attach to the PC in the future.

>> Refer to Chapter 2 in this minibook for additional details on drive letters and all that jazz.

>> The network location must be available for you to access the drive. If the resource (another PC or network hard drive) is offline, the drive letter appears dimmed in the File Explorer window. It becomes available after the network resource is again available.

Network Troubleshooting

No matter the network woe, I look at the hardware first. That's because it's easy: Cables must connect. Power must be on. Lights must blink. Getting those items out of the way first helps, but that type of hardware visual inspection is only the first step in a larger process that eventually involves software as well.

Checking the Device Manager

If the NIC is goofing off, the Device Manager window knows about it. Follow these steps:

1. **Press Win+X to bring up the supersecret menu.**

2. **Choose Device Manager.**

3. **Look in the Network Adapters category for issues.**

Malfunctioning hardware is flagged with a yellow warning icon.

If the Device Manager smells trouble, open the flagged item. The Properties dialog box may offer a suggestion for a fix. Usually, resetting the device is required. See the next section.

>> When the NIC is part of the PC's firmware (on the motherboard), it's impossible to replace. You don't want to buy a new motherboard just to fix a sour NIC. Instead, I recommend getting a USB Wi-Fi NIC and using it instead.

>> USB Wi-Fi NICs also work on laptops.

>> Yes, you can have multiple network adapters in a PC. You don't even need to disable the bad one; just choose the good one when prompted to make the initial network connection.

TECHNICAL STUFF

>> To disable a NIC, double-click its entry in Device Manager. In the NIC's Properties dialog box, click the Driver tab. Click the Disable Device button to direct Windows to ignore the hardware. Disabled devices are flagged in the Device Manager window. You can reenable them, but when the gizmo doesn't work, there's no point.

>> Also see Book 3, Chapter 2 for more information on the Device Manager.

Resetting the network software

The process of resetting the PC's network software is part of Windows own Network Troubleshooter. It's a general fix, and one that Windows tries first. Follow these steps to reset the network:

1. Press the Win+X key.

2. From the supersecret menu, choose Network Connections.

The Settings app opens and takes you right to the network status screen.

3. Click the Network Reset link.

4. Click the Reset No button.

Sit back and wait.

Resetting the network helps resolve issues such as conflicting IP addresses. This problem is the gateway's fault, so if you experience this problem, you might also look into either updating the gateway's software or getting another, newer gateway.

Upgrading the NIC's driver

The software that controls the NIC might get sour or need an upgrade. This new driver might be installed as part of the Windows Upgrade process, or it might be something you must check manually.

To manually update the NIC driver, obey these steps:

1. Set a system restore point.

See Book 3, Chapter 5 for more information.

2. **Press Win+X and choose Device Manager from the supersecret menu.**

3. **In the Device Manager window, open the Network Adapters item.**

   You may see more hardware listed than one simple network adapter. What you're looking for is the wireless or Ethernet adapter.

4. **Double-click to open the wireless or Ethernet adapter.**

5. **In the adapter's Properties dialog box, click the Driver tab.**

6. **Click the Update Driver button.**

7. **Choose the option to search automatically for a newer driver.**

8. **If Windows determines that a better driver is to be found, follow the directions to install that driver.**

   You may be prompted to restart your PC to complete the driver update. Do so.

See Book 4, Chapter 2 for information on Windows Update.

Resetting the broadband modem

Occasionally, you may lose your connection to the Internet. The local network is okay: You can still access network printers and storage just fine, but the Internet is unreachable.

The first things to check are the lights on the modem: Is the modem receiving a signal? If not, the problem is with your Internet service provider (ISP).

You can call your ISP and listen for a recorded message alerting you to any known outages. Before you venture through to a tech support person, reset the broadband modem: Turn the device off and then on again.

REMEMBER

Broadband modems lack a power switch. Unplug the modem. Wait 30 seconds. Plug it back in.

By *cycling* the modem's power, you can often wake it up and it reconnects to the Internet. If not, you can contact the ISP to alert them to the outage and see whether anyone can assist you.

TIP

>> When resetting the modem doesn't work, turn off the modem *and* the gateway. Wait a spell. Turn the modem back on. Wait. Turn on the gateway. At that point, the entire system should be up and running and your PCs can see each other and access the Internet.

>> A friend of mine who works for an ISP's tech support center says that resetting the broadband modem fixes about 90 percent of Internet connection problems.

Restarting the entire network's hardware

TIP

The ultimate network fix is to restart the entire network. It's a simple process to perform — not a regular activity or routine maintenance — but it takes time. Still, restarting the network is a good, general cure-all for many network ills. The procedure works like this:

1. **Turn everything off.**

   Computers. Printers. Hard drives. Switches. Gateway. Broadband modem. If it's connected to the network, you turn it off.

   You don't need to disconnect any Ethernet cables.

2. **Turn on the broadband modem and wait for it to start properly.**

   It takes a few moments for the modem to find a signal and chat it up with the Internet. When all the modem's status lights are on and the modem is happy, you can move on to the next step.

3. **Turn on the gateway.**

   Wait for the gateway to start up and get happy.

4. **If you have a switch connected to the gateway, turn it on.**

5. **Turn on a computer connected to the network.**

   Let the computer start up as normal. Observe network errors, if any.

6. **Log in to the computer and connect to the Internet.**

   When you can get on the Internet, the network is up and working properly. The network has been reset.

7. **Repeat Steps 5 and 6 for each computer on the network.**

8. **Start up any network printers and hard drives.**

Throughout these steps, observe any problems. When you find a problem, you find the problem hardware. Replace that hardware, or just don't connect it to the network. For example, I had a bum switch on my office network. Only by restarting the entire network did I locate the bad switch and replace it.

Working through these steps is necessary only when you're having trouble with the entire network. There's no need to restart your network every few months or so, yet some people do so anyway. Such toil is unnecessary.

Network Problems and Solutions

The network might be up and running fine, but you still are experiencing angst. Perhaps one of your questions is listed in this section, along with the appropriate, snappy, accurate answer.

"What's this firewall warning?"

The firewall works like a network traffic cop, not only with the Internet but with the local network as well. See Book 4, Chapter 3 for details.

"Where did that network PC go?"

Here are some things to check for finding wayward network PCs:

>> Ensure that the network PC is turned on. A computer that's turned off cannot be accessed — don't let that surprise you!

>> Computers that are hibernating or in Sleep mode cannot be accessed on the network.

>> Likewise, a shared printer that's turned off or connected to a PC that's unavailable cannot be accessed on the network.

>> Confirm that the computer's user hasn't discontinued sharing that folder.

If all these solutions fail, consider restarting your PC. And if *that* fails, restart the network. Refer to the earlier section "Restarting the entire network's hardware."

"I can't get a wireless connection!"

The biggest problem with connecting to a wireless network is that you don't have your computer's wireless NIC activated. There are two places to look.

First, check for an external switch or keyboard shortcut on a laptop computer that turns wireless networking on or off.

Second, confirm that the laptop isn't in Airplane mode: Press the Win+A keyboard shortcut to view the Action Center. Check the Airplane Mode tile to ensure that it's not active.

REMEMBER

Place your laptop into Airplane mode unless directed by flight personnel. Once it's aloft, you can activate Wi-Fi if you intend to use the in-flight Internet service: From the Action Center, choose the Network tile.

"The Wi-Fi password has changed!"

Some of your old haunts may change their Wi-Fi passwords from time to time. If so, inquire about the change and get a new password. In Windows, you must forget the network in order to reset the password. Refer to the earlier section "Managing wireless connections."

After you forget a network, reconnect. You'll be prompted for the new password, which you can enter at that time.

"What's a metered connection?"

Most wireless networks don't care how much data you use. Other networks may feature a data limit, or *cap*, like the mobile data limit applied to smartphones by cellular providers. This type of limited Wi-Fi network is known as a *metered* connection.

When you use a metered connection, you're either paying by the gigabyte or given a specific gigabyte allotment of data. With this limitation active, you must ensure that the laptop doesn't exceed the amount you've been granted. Specifically, you want to limit background activity that Windows would otherwise consider routine network access.

To apply metered network restrictions to your network connection, follow these steps:

1. **Press the Windows+I keyboard shortcut to bring up the Settings app.**

2. **Choose Network & Internet.**

3. **With Status chosen from the categories on the left side of the window, click the Properties button.**

4. **Below the Metered Connection heading, set the toggle switch to the On position.**

   This setting affects only the currently connected Wi-Fi network.

With the metered connection active, some programs self-limit their Internet activity. You may also see notifications about using certain programs or when accessing network services.

"The hotel network keeps forgetting my laptop!"

Whenever a network forgets your computer (for example, after a few hours of connection), it's most likely because the DHCP lease has expired. The quick solution is to reestablish the connection: Sign in to the location's website again.

DHCP is the Dynamic Host Configuration Protocol. It's the system that allocates IP addresses to network computers. For a Wi-Fi network, the gateway may limit the DHCP lease to a few hours. That means you must reestablish a connection to the gateway when the lease expires.

The business hotels I frequent generally set the lease time to 24 hours. Some coffee shops set the lease time to 2 hours.

TECHNICAL STUFF

You can use the Command Prompt window to force a DHCP lease renewal. Follow these steps:

1. **Tap the Windows key.**

2. **Type** command prompt

3. **Choose the Command Prompt desktop app from the search results list.**

   The Command Prompt window opens, reminding you how crummy it was to use a computer in the 1980s.

4. **Type** ipconfig /renew **and press the Enter key.**

5. **Close the Command Prompt window.**

The command `ipconfig /renew` forces all network adapters on your PC to immediately request a new DHCP list from the server (the gateway). If this command doesn't work, try this one instead:

```
ipconfig /renew6
```

The `/renew6` option might be required for gateways that use IPv6, which is a technical flapdoodle you don't need to worry about.

Network Nonsense

Chapter **9**

Shutdown Issues

t's been decades since the PC featured an actual on–off switch. It was big and red, like a paddle. You'd reach around the right side of the console and — *thwack* — the power went off, just like that. Those were good times.

The old on–off switch was so effective that many users mistakenly used it to quit a program. Today's users are smarter, but so is the on–off switch, which is now a power button. Further, the process of quitting Windows and turning off the PC is now accomplished as a software task. Theoretically, things run smoothly. When shutdown issues arise, you can crack your knuckles and get ready for some troubleshooting.

Such a Turn-Off

To best troubleshoot shutdown issues, it helps to understand the full PC shutdown process. As with starting a computer, certain things must happen in a specific order. Disaster looms at every corner!

> » Pressing the power button may initiate the Windows shutdown process. If not, you can reprogram the power button to do that. See Chapter 4 in this minibook.

WARNING

>> Yes, you can still flip a power switch to turn off a computer. If the power supply features a switch on the PC's rump, you can use it or you can unplug the computer. Don't ever do this randomly, however, because you can lose files and damage the hardware.

Walking through the Windows shutdown process

To shut down a PC, heed these familiar steps:

1. **Save your stuff!**

   I bet you didn't think this would be the first step. It's not only first — it's the most important.

2. **Close programs.**

   Again, this might be a surprise step. I always use the Alt+Tab keyboard shortcut to cycle through any open program windows, closing each one. This way, if an issue exists with the program, I can deal with it directly rather than wait for the shutdown process to find the problem.

3. **Tap the Windows key.**

   Up pops the Start menu.

4. **Choose Power and then choose Shutdown.**

   The Power item may appear as a single icon, as shown in the margin.

5. **Sit back and watch as the PC furls its sails and quietly turns itself off.**

   You may still need to turn off the monitor and any peripherals to fully complete the procedure.

Starting at Step 4, Windows takes over. It follows a to-do list that includes the following, general steps:

A user check takes place: On the unusual possibility that another user is also signed in to your PC, you're alerted. Do you really want to shut down? Those users may be running programs or have unsaved documents. This warning rarely appears, because maybe two people use the multiple-user feature and these people are gravely ill. If you do ever see this warning, click No to cancel shutdown. Also see the later section "Discovering that another user is signed in!"

Programs close: If you didn't close windows and exit programs, Windows does the job for you. It sifts through that list of running programs and sends each one the shutdown signal. If a program contains unsaved data, you're prompted to save the data to continue — or you can click the Cancel button, which stops the entire shutdown operation. When a program cannot be stopped, you're prompted to end it, which is discussed in the later section "Dealing with the Restart Anyway prompt."

Processes end: Beyond programs you start, other programs run in the background. These are called *processes,* and they include functions such as cloud storage synchronization utilities, antivirus, and other tools, many of which feature teensy icons in the notification area. These, too, are closed by Windows.

You're signed out: When programs and processes you started have been fully shut down, you're finally signed out. You can reach this stage if you merely sign out of Windows, which is one good way to fix stuck programs or other goofiness. It's faster to sign out than to restart Windows.

Windows kills itself: Okay, I'm being dramatic. After the programs and processes you started are killed off, Windows begins halting its own programs, processes, and services: It shuts down the network connection and turns off the print spooler and other, miscellaneous items that run all the time. During this phase, Windows ensures that everything quits nicely and no data is lost.

The power is cut: When Windows is done with itself, it sends a signal to the computer's power management hardware to turn off the power. The PC turns itself off.

The shutdown process may seem overly formal. After all, a program stops when it's told to stop or when the electricity stops. Yet this process is far better for the PC's hardware and software than just flipping a big red switch.

>> By properly shutting itself down, Windows deals with the issue of *digital detritus.* For example, an improper shutdown may cause a program to leave pieces of itself lying around like rubble after an explosion. This clutter builds. Or, perhaps the network connection is left open, so all network traffic slows. A procedural shutdown avoids these issues.

>> Another disadvantage to an improper shutdown is that errors aren't detected. When the computer is shut down properly, you may see a warning regarding defective software or bad hardware. Often, that's the only way to identify and troubleshoot an issue.

TECHNICAL STUFF

>> Back in the old days, not every PC had power management software. When Windows was done shutting down, it would display a message telling the user that it's "safe" to turn off the computer.

Reviewing shutdown options

You have several choices on the Power menu for quitting your computer duties. The menu is affixed to the Start menu and illustrated in Figure 9-1.

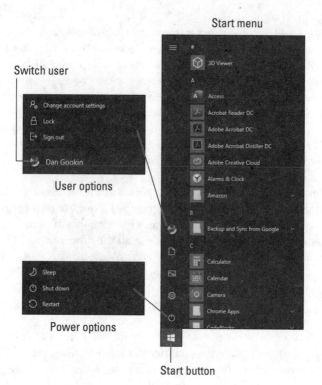

Start menu

Switch user

User options

Power options

FIGURE 9-1:
Power options.

Start button

Tap the Windows key to view the Start menu. The two icons worthy of note are illustrated in Figure 9-1.

 The power icon's menu shows power-related options. These include Sleep, Shut Down, and Restart. Some PCs may also show the Hibernate option.

 The user icon shows either a generic image (shown in the margin) or your account photo (refer to Figure 9-1). Its name is the same as your sign-in name. The options on the user icon's menu deal with your account: Change Account Settings, Lock, and Sign Out. If more than one user has an account on the computer, the Switch Users option appears. Choose this item to view a list of other user accounts on the system.

Here is what each of the shutdown and account options does:

Change Account Settings: Not really a shutdown command; choose this item to open the Settings app to view your account's options.

Lock: Choose this item to lock Windows, which is similar to signing out though your programs continue to run. The keyboard shortcut is Windows+L.

Sign Out: This item exits your Windows session, terminating all programs and processes and presenting the main sign-in screen. It does not quit Windows.

Switch User: This option appears only when other user accounts are available on a single PC. Choose an account from the user list to allow that user to sign in to Windows, or select the generic Other User item. Your account is suspended while the other user has access to the PC.

Sleep: Choose this option to place the PC into a low-power mode, saving energy. To *restore*, or wake up, the computer, wiggle the mouse or tap a key on the keyboard. You need to sign back in to Windows to continue.

Hibernate: This option takes Sleep mode one step further: The goal is to save time and energy. When the PC goes into hibernation, information in memory is saved and the computer is shut down. When the computer starts up again, information is loaded back into memory and the system starts quickly. After you sign in, Windows looks just as it did before hibernation.

Shut Down: Choose this option to sign out of Windows and shut down the computer.

Restart: When this option is chosen, the computer shuts down and then starts up again. Choose Restart to fix common computer ailments, though the command is also necessary when installing new hardware or software.

 Duplicates for these items are also found on the sign-in screen, shown when Windows first starts or when you sign out. Look for the power icon, shown in the margin. Click this icon to view the Power Options menu, similar to the menu shown earlier, in Figure 9-1.

>> The Lock option allows you to secure your computer when you need to step away for a minute.

>> For Windows 10 computers with other users, such as a shared workstation at a large organization, ensure that you always sign out when you're done working. These systems are different from home and small office systems; by

not signing out, you make it more difficult for others to use the same computer.

TIP

>> Choosing the Sign Out option is faster than restarting Windows. Especially for minor irritations, sign out and then sign back in again to resolve program issues and other weirdness.

>> You can use the Switch User option to switch back and forth between different users on the same PC. This sounds nifty in theory, but outside of a large organization, few individuals use this feature.

>> Windows automatically enters Sleep mode after an inactivity timeout.

>> The hibernation option may not be available to all Windows 10 computers.

TECHNICAL STUFF

>> The Restart command is also known as *reset* or *reboot*. Some nerds may also refer to "cycling the power," though that's more of a hardware operation. For example, to cycle the power on a printer, you turn it off, wait, and then turn it on again.

Problems with Restarting

Two ugly restart issues are common. The first is the random, unexpected restart. The second is the automatic restart, or re-restart, which happens when the PC decides on its own that one restart isn't good enough.

REMEMBER

>> Restarting Windows often cures many minor ills.

>> Sometimes, it's simpler to sign out of Windows than to restart the PC. Signing out may fix a software issue in less time than the full restart.

>> Restarting a computer is a common and often necessary task. Even if you're a fan of leaving a PC on all the time, you'll find yourself restarting it every so often for many reasons, from installing or updating software to fixing bugs.

Experiencing a random restart

An unexpected restart is a sign of trouble. I'm not talking about the computer requesting a restart, as when you see a "Restart now?" prompt. No, I'm referring to the computer just blinking out and starting over in a rude and discourteous manner.

The random restart can happen before your eyes. Or, if you leave a computer on all the time, you may return after a break and see the sign-in screen — or worse, a troubleshooting startup menu.

Most of the time, a random restart indicates a hardware error. It could be a sign of any of these issues:

>> **Motherboard problems:** These are the worst because they're difficult to detect. The restart could be due to bad firmware, corrupted memory, or a defective processor.

>> **Graphics processor overheating:** Today's GPUs and their banks of memory need lots of cooling power. When the hardware gets too hot, the system restarts.

>> **Power supply issues:** Underpowered power supplies can lead to random restarts.

Motherboard problems are the worst. You can check with the computer dealer or manufacturer for diagnostic tools. These can detect problems with the processor, firmware, and memory, though such software tools may not spot the problem. The good news is that this type of hardware may still be under warranty.

If the graphics processor is overheating, you need to check the fans. This process requires opening the PC case and observing that the fans work. You can also hear the fans when the display adapter kicks into high gear. Ensure that the adapter has the proper power connections. You might also look into additional cooling for the console, in the form of a cooling fan expansion card.

Power supplies must be beefy enough to handle the PC's wattage load. If the power supply can't handle the draw, it fails. This is good news because power supplies are easy to replace and rarely, if ever, does a dead power supply damage the rest of the system. See Chapter 4 in this minibook.

>> Random restarts generally don't show up in the Windows error logs. The reason is that the glitch is just too fast for anything to be recorded. Still, check out Book 3, Chapter 8 for details on the Event Viewer.

>> Don't rule out software glitches that can cause random restarts. Poorly installed and corrupt software can randomly crash a computer. These errors are consistent, so if you know that running a specific program crashes the system, you can check for an update to the program.

>> Software updates might also fix random crashes. Updating a video driver or the power management driver might be in order.

Restarting automatically

An automatic restart, or a re-restart, occurs when the computer restarts, appears to boot again, but then you see a second restart.

When the second restart happens before the Windows logo appears, the computer has a hardware issue. An exception to this conclusion occurs when installing certain updates, because the second restart is required for whatever reason.

If the second restart happens after the Windows logo appears, what you're seeing is a software update installation. For example, some software updates need two restarts to install completely. A message on the screen alerts you to the second reboot. The important point with this process is not to interrupt the installation.

Windows is configured to automatically restart on an error. You can change this option, which is located in the well-hidden Startup and Recovery dialog box, illustrated in Figure 9-2.

Option to restart on system failure

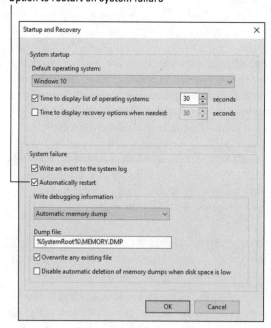

FIGURE 9-2:
The Startup
and Recovery
dialog box.

Follow these steps to visit that location:

1. **Press the Windows+Break key combination.**

   The System window appears.

   The Break key is also the Pause key on some keyboards. If the keyboard lacks either a Break or Pause key, tap the Windows key and type System. Choose the System Control Panel item.

2. **Choose the link Advanced System Settings on the left side of the window.**

   The System Properties dialog box appears.

3. **Ensure that the Advanced tab is chosen.**

4. **In the Startup and Recovery area, click the Settings button.**

   The Startup and Recovery dialog box is found!

The System Failure area of the System and Recovery dialog box gives Windows suggestions about what to do when things go kaput. The Automatic Restart option is activated by default; when the system crashes, Windows restarts. If this option is disabled, the PC turns itself off.

The only time I recommend disabling the Automatically Restart setting is when Windows gets stuck in a restart loop. When this happens, you must disable the option so that you can troubleshoot. Before you get to that point, however, you need to boot Windows in Recovery mode. See Book 3, Chapter 1 for details.

Shutdown Malaise

Shutdown problems don't carry the weighty burden of start-up issues or other typical PC problems. The reason being that shutting down is what you do at the *end* of the day. Also, shutdown issues don't often influence starting the computer. (Well, just hope that's the case.) Regardless, shutdown issues simply demonstrate that computer trouble has no trouble walking into or out of the door.

As a general suggestion for any shutdown issue, check the event log. Programs that refuse to quit or that improperly shut down are noted in the Windows system log. See Book 3, Chapter 8.

Upgrading software to fix shutdown issues

One key reason for shutdown issues is that the computer's software isn't up-to-date. The problem is significant for older PCs or any system that runs older software. Some stubborn programs just don't know when to quit. Keeping software current is the best fix.

>> Book 3, Chapter 2 covers the Device Manager, which may highlight malfunctioning hardware. If so, consider updating the hardware's device driver to resolve shutdown issues.

>> See Book 4, Chapter 2 about running Windows Update.

Turning off a stubborn PC

After you try the Shut Down command and it fails to respond, press and hold the power button. After about ten seconds, the computer turns itself off. This trick is especially useful for laptops, where you can't just pull the plug. And for desktop PCs, try this trick first *before* you pull the plug.

REMEMBER

Using the power button to forcibly turn off a computer is a desperate measure. Do not use the press-and-hold method as your normal way to turn off the computer. Try to *troubleshoot* shutdown issues, not ignore them.

Waiting for an update to install

The most common reason a PC takes a long time to shut down is that it's installing updates. This situation is confirmed when you read the screen; upgrade information appears, explaining the process and reminding you to be patient.

How long should you be patient? As long as it takes, but there is a limit. I've waited 20 minutes while my laptop said it was toiling with an upgrade at 20 percent. I figured it was stuck, so I pressed the power button until it turned off.

When the system restarts, it may attempt to recover the update or it may surrender and start again with the updates not applied. Refer to Book 4, Chapter 2 for information on fixing stalled updates.

WARNING

>> It's usually a bad idea to turn off a computer in the middle of an update. Doing so can render the system unable to start. Still, if you've waited and the update is stuck, the damage is done and you can power down the PC.

TIP

>> A good way to determine whether the computer is stuck or actually working is to examine the mass storage lamp on the console. When the light is flashing, the computer is busy. If the light isn't flashing, the computer is most likely stuck. In that case, force a shutdown as discussed in the earlier section "Turning off a stubborn PC."

>> The shutdown process may be slow simply because the PC is slow to begin with. Refer to Book 5, Chapter 3 for information on pepping up a slow computer.

Discovering that another user is signed in!

This situation happens rarely, but if someone else is using your computer and you try to shut down, Windows stops you. The other person can be logged in on the same console (by using the Switch Users command), or they might be using a shared folder over the network. Either way, Windows displays a warning.

First, don't freak out. No one is hacking your computer.

Second, unless it's an emergency, cancel the shutdown operation. That's the best choice because the other person may have open, unsaved files. Only when you *truly* need to shut down or restart should you proceed with shutdown.

Finally, figure out who the other person is and have them sign out of the console or disconnect from the network. This task is easy in a home or small office because you can just ask. After the user is signed out, continue with the shutdown.

If you must, you can shut down and ignore the warning. In that case, the other user is disconnected and any unsaved files are discarded.

Dealing with the Restart Anyway prompt

After you sign out, restart, or shut down Windows, the screen dims and you may see a prompt listing several programs. The prompt implies that these programs are having trouble quitting. Two choices are offered:

>> **Restart Anyway:** Choose this option to quit the programs that won't otherwise quit.

>> **Cancel:** Stop the sign-out, restart, or shutdown operation.

THE COMPUTER WAS IMPROPERLY SHUT DOWN!

In days gone by, when the computer was unplugged or otherwise unceremoniously shut down, you saw Windows waggle its finger at you when the PC restarted. The operating system didn't literally wag its finger. Instead, you saw a message along the lines of "Windows was improperly shut down." Then you witnessed a series of menu items.

This improper shutdown screen has vanished from Windows 10. I suppose that Microsoft reasoned it was unnecessary to alarm innocent users. If the PC was improperly shut down, it attempts to restart normally. If it can't, the Windows Recovery menu is displayed. Using this menu is covered in Book 3, Chapter 1.

This choice isn't easy, but the best thing to do is wait. Most of the time, the obstinate program terminates. If not, you must make a choice.

Whether I click Restart Anyway depends on which programs are stuck. If it's a background program or process, such as a cloud storage utility, I'm okay with terminating the program(s).

If the stubborn program is Word, or another application I've been using, it might be waiting for me to save a document. In that case, click Cancel. Return to the app and save your document. Then try to shut down again.

TECHNICAL STUFF

In some versions of Windows, the prompt is End Now instead of Restart Anyway.

3
Tools to Use

Contents at a Glance

Chapter **1**

Windows Recovery Environment

Windows comes packed with troubleshooting tools, but what happens when Windows itself is the problem? Or perhaps the PC has some issue that prevents Windows from loading? In those dire situations, you need a special utility, almost a second operating system, to help diagnose and repair the computer. That tool is called the Windows Recovery Environment.

Startup Keys and Recovery Options

Just as the PC first comes to life, you may see a splash screen displaying the man-ufacturer's logo. It's quick! On that screen, you may also see a series of keys and options. These are the *startup keys,* which you can use to troubleshoot your PC as well as perform other technical functions.

Reviewing the startup keys

Beyond the fancy logo, a PC's splash screen shows you options for starting the computer. These options appear quickly, shown as a list of one or more keys and their functions. Typical startup keys perform the following tasks:

Enter Setup (UEFI): Choose this option to run the PC's hardware setup program, called the UEFI. This option was once known as the BIOS Setup program.

Update the BIOS (firmware): This option applies an update to the PC's firmware, though I recommend performing this update using an update program in Windows as opposed to using the Update BIOS startup key.

Choose Boot Device: When this option is chosen, you see a list of devices that can start the computer, such as the primary mass storage device. This choice is a one-time option; otherwise, the default boot device (set in the UEFI) is chosen.

Each option is assigned a key, such as F2 to enter the setup program. The key assignments vary between different PC manufacturers, so don't expect any consistency. In fact, on some computers, the text listing the startup keys doesn't appear at all; to make it appear, you must set an option in the UEFI.

The point of the startup keys is to troubleshoot. Specifically, you can access the setup program (UEFI) to adjust the PC's hardware or choose a boot device to start the PC beyond the primary mass storage device and Windows. For example, you can troubleshoot by choosing the Recovery volume as the PC's boot device. That's one way to access the Windows Recovery Environment tools, such as when you can't get Windows to start normally.

TIP

>> See the nearby "What's a UEFI?" sidebar if the term puzzles you or you have difficulty pronouncing this acronym in your head.

>> Refer to Book 4, Chapter 2 for details on performing a firmware (BIOS) upgrade.

>> The startup keys may not appear if you've installed a boot loader on your PC. In this configuration, you see the bootloader, which generally has options for entering the UEFI as well as for choosing an operating system or a boot device.

>> You must be quick to choose a key when the computer starts! I've had to sit through several restarts to not only read all the text but also stab the proper key. When the Windows startup animation appears, you're too late.

>> The UEFI can set the boot order for storage devices attached to your PC. For example, you can direct the hardware to look for a bootable thumb drive. Normally, the primary storage device with a Windows boot partition is the main boot device.

WHAT'S A UEFI?

The UEFI is the Unified Extensible Firmware Interface, a program that configures the PC's firmware (the basic hardware), or what was once known as the BIOS. In today's PCs, however, a lot more goes on than in the early days. The BIOS is really only part of what the UEFI configures. Oh, and it's pronounced "you-fee."

Choose the UEFI option at boot-time to change PC hardware settings and other items specific to the system's hardware. For example, you can choose which boot device starts the PC, though it's best to choose Windows and not some random hardware.

Book 2, Chapter 1 offers more information about the UEFI.

>> The temporary boot device option may be titled Choose Boot Device or Select Startup Device or a similar title.

TECHNICAL STUFF

>> Years ago, the two common startup keys were F5 and F8. The F5 key summoned a boot manager, like today's Choose Boot Device option. The F8 key presented a startup menu, from which you could choose various PC repair and troubleshooting options. The F8 key's function has been replaced by the Windows Recovery Environment. Specifically, the Startup Settings item displays a menu similar to the old F8 key's menu. See the later section "Changing startup settings."

Locating recovery options in Windows

If you can start Windows, you may not have to worry about whacking the proper startup key, as described in the preceding section. That's because Windows presents various startup and recovery options within the Settings app.

To view the recovery options, follow these directions:

1. **Open the Settings app.**

   Press Win+I.

2. **Choose Update & Security.**

3. **On the left side of the window, choose Recovery.**

   The right side of the window lists options for Windows recovery and reset, as illustrated in Figure 1-1.

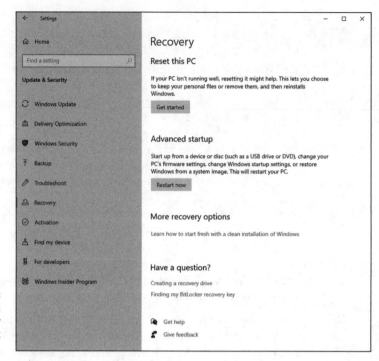

FIGURE 1-1:
Windows
Recovery
Environment
options.

These two options are presented:

> **Reset This PC:** This item is close to the reinstall-Windows-to-fix-anything philosophy that dominated tech support back in the 1990s and 2000s. See the next section.

> **Advanced Startup:** This item restarts the computer and runs the Windows Recovery Environment. The PC restarts immediately after you click the Restart Now button.

These items may not be echoed by the startup keys, but you can use Advanced Startup to access the UEFI or to review the list of startup devices. Accessing these features is covered in the later section "Windows Recovery Environment Duties."

Resetting Windows

The option to reset Windows 10 might help fix some problems by taking the drastic step of resetting Windows to the original version installed on the PC.

Before you complete these steps, I recommend that you first attempt to run the System File Checker program, covered in Chapter 4 of this minibook. This program selectively replaces corrupt files in Windows without the need to reinstall everything. That's a better first step.

The process of resetting the PC works like this:

1. **Press Win+I to bring up the Settings app.**

2. **Choose Update & Security.**

3. **Choose Recovery.**

4. **On the right side of the window, beneath the heading Reset This PC, click the Get Started button.**

   You're presented with two options.

   Keep My Files: This choice is best for fixing Windows issues you can't otherwise address. Windows is reinstalled, but your programs and personal files remain unchanged.

   Remove Everything: This choice resets the PC to a state similar to a new installation. All your data is removed; nothing is saved unless you've created a backup.

5. **Choose an option to reset Windows.**

WARNING

When you choose Remove Everything, all your files are erased.

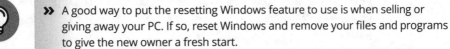

>> Resetting Windows is the same thing as reinstalling Windows, which was once a commonly accepted method to fix software problems. It's a bit of overkill for some issues. Yet Microsoft saw fit to add a Reset command for Windows 10, so perhaps there's some merit to the operation?

TIP

>> A good way to put the resetting Windows feature to use is when selling or giving away your PC. If so, reset Windows and remove your files and programs to give the new owner a fresh start.

>> The reset options are also available in the Windows Recovery Environment, described later in this chapter.

TECHNICAL STUFF

>> If you choose to reset the PC, you end up with the computer's original version of Windows 10. This version is instantly out-of-date. Subsequently, after resetting the PC, you need to run the Windows Update tool to get Windows current again. Windows Update is covered in Book 4, Chapter 2.

Using Advanced Startup

The Advanced Startup option in the Settings app allows you a quick short-cut to access the Windows Recovery Environment. When you click the Restart Now button, the PC immediately restarts and launches the Windows Recovery Environment.

>> Refer to the earlier section "Locating recovery options in Windows," for detailed steps on arriving at the Settings app's Recovery screen.

>> The Windows Recovery Environment is covered later in this chapter.

>> If you want access to all the Windows Recovery Environment tools, choose the option in the Settings app, as described in this section. If you use a separate system repair disk you've created, not all commands are available.

>> When you can't start Windows, you must use the startup keys to access the system recovery partition on the PC's primary storage device or use a system repair disk (thumb drive) to access the Windows Recovery Environment. Specific steps are covered elsewhere in this chapter.

The Sacred Recovery Volume

You can't rely upon Windows to fix your PC when your PC's primary storage device fails. In these circumstances, you need another storage device to start the computer. That tool is known as the Recovery volume.

The *Recovery volume* houses a host of tools you can use to diagnose and repair problems with the PC and Windows. You can use the Recovery volume to restore your system after a complete disaster, troubleshoot startup issues, or change the PC's configuration.

Checking to see whether the PC has a Recovery volume

You may be lucky and find that your PC dealer or manufacturer has already created a Recovery volume for you. It's found on a special partition on the PC's primary storage device. To confirm whether it's there, obey these directions:

1. **Press Win+X.**

2. **Choose Disk Management.**

   The Disk Management console appears. It lists all storage devices available to your PC, similar to those shown in Figure 1-2.

3. **Look for a recovery partition.**

   In Figure 1-2, the recovery partition is highlighted.

The *recovery partition* is a bootable storage device (part of the primary mass storage system) that contains the Windows Recovery Environment software. If you see this partition, you have access to the Recovery software when the PC first boots.

If you don't see the recovery partition, which is true for some low-end PCs and teensy laptops, don't despair! You can create a Recovery volume on a thumb drive, as covered in the next section.

TECHNICAL STUFF

>> Even if your computer already has a Recovery volume, I recommend that you create a second, thumb drive Recovery volume.

>> You don't see the recovery partition in File Explorer's This PC window. It's absence is explained because the volume isn't designed to be mounted into the PC's storage system.

>> Another unmounted partition is the UEFI, which is illustrated in Figure 1-2. The UEFI ("you-fee") program dwells on its own partition, which is mounted when you choose to run the UEFI as the computer first starts.

Creating a repair disk

Whether your computer lacks a Recovery volume partition or you just want to make a wise investment in a useful tool, create a repair disk thumb drive for your PC.

You can use any thumb drive or media card, but the capacity must be at least 8GB. This storage device is dedicated as a Recovery volume, so it can't have any data on it that you otherwise need.

To create the repair disk, obey these steps:

1. **Insert the thumb drive or other media into the appropriate slot on your PC.**

   You can use a thumb drive or media card, though I use *thumb drive* throughout this chapter.

Recovery partition (not mounted in Windows)

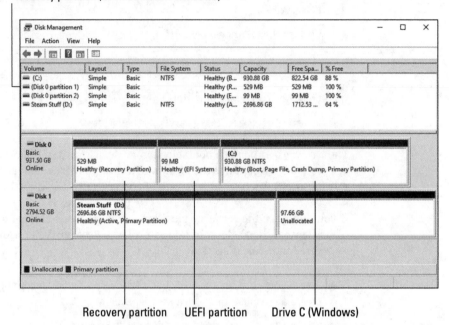

FIGURE 1-2:
The Disk
Management
console.

Recovery partition   UEFI partition   Drive C (Windows)

2. **Dismiss any AutoPlay notification or close any window that pops up when you insert the thumb drive.**

Oh, you can look at the media to ensure that it doesn't contain anything you would otherwise want to keep. If so, copy those files to the PC's primary storage device.

3. **Tap the Windows key to pop up the Start button menu.**

4. **Type the text** create recovery drive **and select this item when it appears in the search results list.**

5. **If prompted with a User Account Control (UAC), click the Yes button to start the Recovery Media Creator program.**

The Recovery Drive Wizard starts. The sole option in the window is preselected for you, so everything is ready to go.

6. **Click the Next button.**

The wizard calculates how much storage space is required for the drive. This process takes some time.

[Time passes. . . .]

Eventually, you see a list of available storage devices on which the repair disk can be created.

7. **Choose the thumb drive from Step 1 and click the Next button.**

   You see a final warning about deleting everything on the media.

8. **Click the Create button.**

   Windows builds the repair disk. This process also takes some time to complete.

   [Even more time passes. . . .]

9. **Click the Finish button.**

   The message in the wizard proclaims that the repair disk is ready.

10. **Properly unmount the drive and label it.**

    Refer to Book 2, Chapter 2 for information on unmounting media. Label the thumb drive in such a manner that you'll always know it's the repair drive for your specific PC.

TIP

If you have multiple PCs, create a repair disk for each one.

To use the repair disk, see the later section "Starting the Windows Recovery Environment from a repair disk or thumb drive." Its main purpose is to launch the Windows Recovery Environment, which is the next section's topic.

Windows Recovery Environment Duties

The Windows Recovery Environment is a special tool — actually, its own operating system — designed to help you resolve PC startup issues, fix Windows, and recover from various types of disaster. You may hear it referred to by other names, but the official term is the Windows Recovery Environment.

>> You have several options to access the Windows Recovery Environment, as covered in the following two sections.

>> In previous editions of Windows, the tools were called the Windows Recovery Environment Console. Recovery options also appeared on a special menu that showed up whenever you pressed the F8 key as the PC started.

TECHNICAL
STUFF

Starting the Windows Recovery Environment from Windows

If you can get the computer started and sign in to Windows, you can access the recovery tools from Windows itself. Obey these directions:

1. **Close your programs and save your data.**

That's because the computer will restart after you complete these steps.

2. **Press Win+I to start the Settings app.**

3. **Choose Update & Security.**

4. **Select the Recovery category on the left side of the window.**

5. **Click the Restart Now button.**

The computer immediately restarts.

The PC powers up and you see the main screen for the Windows Recovery Environment. This screen is described in the later section "Running the Windows Recovery Environment."

And now — the secret!

You can use the standard Restart command to enter the Windows Recovery Environment: Before you click the Restart command on the Start menu, press and hold the Shift key. When the PC restarts, the Windows Recovery Environment is loaded.

Starting the Windows Recovery Environment from a repair disk or thumb drive

Because you may not be able to start Windows, it's also possible to summon the Windows Recovery Environment tools from the Recovery volume on your PC or a repair disk thumb drive that you created. To access the tools, follow these steps:

1. **If you're using a repair disk, insert the media into the proper hole on the PC.**

Attach a thumb drive or insert a media card. You can perform this operation whether the computer is on or off.

2. **Start the PC if it's not already on; otherwise, restart.**

What you're looking for is the startup menu. Specifically, you want to jab at the key that presents various boot devices.

WARNING

Pay attention! That startup key prompt appears rather quickly. If you wait too long and the computer seizes or you see the Windows animation appear, you must try again.

3. **Press the startup key that allows you to select a boot device or startup volume.**

   On my PC, it's the F10 key, which is labeled Enter Boot Menu.

4. **Choose the recovery boot volume.**

   The PC displays a list of available storage devices, similar to those shown in Figure 1-3. This list is extremely unhelpful.

```
Boot Menu

LAN  : IBA GE Slot 00C8 v1403
SATA : PORT 6G 0 : WDC WD5000AAKX : Part 0 : Boot Drive
SATA : PORT 3 : HL-DT-ST DVDRAM
UEFI : SATA : PORT 6G 0 : Windows Boot Manager : PART 0 : OS
Bootloader
USB : SanDisk Ultra 1.26 : PART 0 : Boot Drive
UEFI : USB : SanDisk Ultra 1.26 : PART 0 : OS Bootloader

↑ and ↓ to move selection
```

FIGURE 1-3: A typical boot menu.

In Figure 1-3, you see the word *boot* a few times. These devices are used to start the PC. In fact, the *Windows boot manager* is most likely the partition with Windows itself. The thumb drive titled SanDisk Ultra is a repair disk, which is the one to select for booting into the Windows Recovery Environment should you be unable to start the computer.

If the list you see on your PC is as unhelpful as the one illustrated in Figure 1-3, just start choosing devices. You can skip the LAN device because it's the network adapter. The SATA devices are most likely internal storage. UEFI indicates startup programs, so you can avoid those entries. And in Figure 1-3, one item says DVDRAM, which is the PC's optical drive.

>> To confirm that you have a Recovery volume on your PC, refer to the earlier section "Checking to see whether the PC has a Recovery volume."

>> If you haven't yet created a repair disk, refer to the earlier section "Creating a repair disk." Do it now!

Windows Recovery Environment

Running the Windows Recovery Environment

The main screen for the Windows Recovery Environment is illustrated in Figure 1-4. This is how the screen appears when you use Windows to restart the PC (from the Settings app).

Choose an option

 Continue
Exit and continue to Windows 10

 Turn off your PC

 Use a device
Use a USB driver, network connection, or Windows recovery DVD

FIGURE 1-4: The Windows Recovery Environment.

 Troubleshoot
Reset your PC or see advanced options

Here is a quick summary of the top-level items:

Continue: Leave the Windows Recovery Environment and start Windows normally.

Turn Off Your PC: As it says.

Use a Device: Choose a startup device, like the boot menu shown in Figure 1-3 but prettier.

Troubleshoot: Display troubleshooting tools.

The only true option for troubleshooting is, well, Troubleshoot. Choose that item and you see two additional items:

Reset This PC: This choice displays the same items available in the Settings app. Refer to the earlier section "Resetting Windows."

Advanced Options: This choice displays additional options, illustrated in Figure 1-5.

The Advance Options item should be your first choice — unless you've already been there and nothing worked. In that case, you can choose Reset This PC and then choose whether to reinstall Windows and keep your files or wipe everything clean and reinstall Windows.

⊖ Advanced options

System Restore
Use a restore point recorded on your PC to restore Windows

Command Prompt
Use the Command Prompt for advanced troubleshooting

System Image Recovery
Recover Windows using a specific system image file

UEFI Firmware Settings
Change settings in your PC's UEFI firmware

Startup Repair
Fix problems that keep Windows from loading

Startup Settings
Change Windows startup behavior

See more recovery options

FIGURE 1-5:
Advanced options in the Windows Recovery Environment utility.

The seventh option is System Image Recovery, which is accessed by clicking the item at the bottom of the screen, See More Recovery Options.

If you use a Recovery volume or thumb drive to start the Windows Recovery Environment, you see fewer options than appear in Figures 1-4 and 1-5. After being asked to choose a keyboard, and selecting the Troubleshoot tile, you see options for System Restore, System Image Recovery, Startup Repair, Command Prompt, and Uninstall Updates.

The following sections review the options available.

Performing startup repair

When the primary storage device has trouble starting, you can run the Startup Repair option in the Windows Recovery Environment. This choice is the first step to fixing what might be a damaged hard drive or at least a screwed-up master boot record (MBR).

After you choose this item, the computer instantly restarts. You must sign in to Windows: Choose your username or the administrator account and type your password when prompted. At this point, a diagnostic program runs. When it's done, it may explain what's been fixed or not. You're given the opportunity to restart the PC or reenter the Windows Recovery Environment tool.

TIP

This item replaces a host of tools you'd otherwise use in a command prompt window. See the later section "Using the command prompt."

Windows Recovery Environment

Changing startup settings

The Startup Settings item in the Windows Recovery Environment tool is a throw-back to the old F8 key startup menu. When you choose this item, click the Restart button. You then see a menu full of basic, startup configuration choices, as illustrated in Figure 1-6.

Startup Settings

Press a number to choose from the options below:

Use number keys or functions keys F1-F9

1) Enable debugging
2) Enable boot logging
3) Enable low-resolution video
4) Enable Safe Mode
5) Enable Safe Mode with Networking
6) Enable Safe Mode with Command Prompt
7) Disable driver signature enforcement
8) Disable early launch anti-malware protection
9) Disable automatic restart after failure

Press F10 for more options
Press Enter to return to your operating system

FIGURE 1-6:
Startup settings.

You can use this menu to control how Windows starts. The most common items are 4 through 6, which cover Safe mode. See Chapter 4 of this minibook for specifics on each mode. A tenth item is available if you press the F10 key. This option allows you to enter the Windows Recovery Environment.

>> If none of the Startup Settings choices pleases you, press the Enter key to start Windows normally.

>> This item might not be available if you access the Windows Recovery Environment from a Recovery volume or thumb drive.

Using the command prompt

The Command Prompt option is available primarily for users who are familiar with the commands and know what to do when faced with ugly Text mode. If you can stomach the C: prompt, this choice is for you!

After selecting the Command Prompt item, you see a list of administrator accounts. Choose yours and type the password to continue. Next, a Text mode window appears. This window is the same cmd.exe program that you can run within Windows. Once it's started, you type commands to attempt to fix whatever problem exists with the PC.

Table 1-1 lists a smattering of the commands you can type at the prompt. This isn't a full list, but it gives you an idea of which issues the command prompt can address.

TABLE 1-1:

Command Prompt Commands

Command	What It Does
bcdboot	Runs the boot file creation and repair tool
bcdedit	Boots the Configuration Editor
bmrui	Runs the System Image restore utility
bootrec	Runs a disk repair utility
bootsect	Starts the boot sector restoration tool
chkdsk	Checks a volume for errors and then repairs them, if it can
exit	Closes the Recovery Console window in Windows Vista or restarts the PC for Windows XP
format	Formats a disk drive, preparing it for use
recover	Attempts to read an otherwise unreadable file
reg	Runs the Text mode Registry Editor
sfc	Runs the System File Checker

The commands shown in the table aren't complete; many have additional options and settings. And don't expect helpful documentation to pop up and greet you. Again, this tool is for experienced users.

In addition to the commands used for Windows repair, all standard Text mode commands and utilities are available at the command prompt. These include tools for file manipulation and commands for general system management.

Windows Recovery Environment

Perhaps the most valuable command is *bootrec*, which takes the place of several other commands that fix storage device issues. The *bootrec* command has several incarnations:

bootrec /FixMbr: Use this command to repair the primary storage device's master boot record. This solution addresses the "missing operating system" as well as "disk not found" errors.

bootrec /FixBoot: Use this command after the preceding command to ensure that the boot sector on the primary hard drive is working properly.

bootrec /ScanOs: This command displays a list of available Windows installations on attached media.

bootrec /RebuildBcd: Use this command to fix any reported problems with the Boot Configuration Data (BCD).

Many of these commands are run automatically when you choose the Startup Repair option found on the Windows Recovery Environment's Advanced Options screen. (Refer to Figure 1-5.)

REMEMBER

>> The command prompt accessed from the Windows Recovery Environment is more about fixing a hard drive that can't start than about addressing general Windows issues.

>> You can always start a command prompt window in Windows, or in Safe mode, to address other issues. See Chapter 4 in this minibook for information on Safe mode.

>> The command prompt program name is cmd.exe. To run it from Windows, press Win+R to bring up the Run dialog box. Type **cmd** and press the Enter key.

TECHNICAL STUFF

>> Future releases of Windows 10 may start the PowerShell instead of the old command prompt. Many of the commands are similar, though the PowerShell is more powerful — and more cryptic — than the command prompt.

Uninstalling updates

When a Windows update causes more woe than it's worth, you can choose the Uninstall Updates option from the Windows Recovery Environment's Advanced Options screen (refer to Figure 1-5). You're presented with two additional options: Uninstall Last Quality Update and Uninstall Last Feature Update. Because it's difficult to determine whether Windows has recently installed a quality or feature update, I recommend choosing one and then the other to help resolve the issue.

By uninstalling an update, you restore Windows to an earlier version. This process isn't the same as reinstalling the original version of Windows that came loaded on the computer. No, it merely rolls back all updates since the last official "build" of the operating system.

One good reason for using this tool would be to remove a bad update. Though you can try System Restore first, if that process fails you can restore the previous Windows build. This step may fix the problem.

>> My guess is that the Uninstall Updates tool came about because of bad Windows builds that would cause some computers to malfunction. In those instances, Microsoft is quick to release a patch, but until then you can try the option to restore a previous build and hope that it fixes the issue.

>> The restore-previous-build procedure isn't the same as choosing to reset the PC, which installs the *original* version of Windows that came with the computer.

Accessing the UEFI

Choose the UEFI Firmware Settings tile in the Windows Recovery Environment to restart your PC and launch the UEFI program. From there, you can edit hardware settings and change other basic aspects of the computer.

Yes, this item is a duplicate from the startup option to modify the firmware or, as an old-timer would say, "enter the BIOS Setup program."

Choosing System Restore

The System Restore utility is covered in Chapter 5 of this minibook. It's a vital tool for undoing misconfigurations. For example, if you install a new program and the computer no longer works, you can run System Restore to recover — to restore the system to an earlier point.

>> It's important that you activate System Restore and set restore points. Otherwise, this tool doesn't really work. More details are offered in Chapter 5.

>> System Restore is a first step. If it doesn't work, you can try the option Restoring a Previous Build. If this solution doesn't work, you can use the option Recovering a System Image, covered in the next section.

Recovering a system image

 The System Image Recovery item, shown in the margin, is found when you choose See More Recovery Options on the Advanced Options screen (refer to Figure 1-5). It's the only tile available. What this option does is use a system image to restore Windows.

A *system image* is like a backup copy of Windows — the system. If Windows can't start or you're otherwise informed that Windows is corrupt and you've tried other tools and they've failed, you can recover the system image.

>> For more details on restoring the system image, see Book 4, Chapter 4.

>> Before trying the option to recover a system image, run the System File Checker. See Chapter 4.

>> Recovering a system image is the first step in total hard drive recovery. After recovering the image, you restore your personal files and programs from a recent backup.

Chapter **2**

The Device Manager

Sometimes it's obvious when hardware fails: The gizmo doesn't work! You can reconnect a cord, swap out the hardware, or just look puzzled. The best way to confirm that you're not going crazy (if you can get the PC to start) is to use the Device Manager. Even when you don't suspect that a hardware problem exists, this handy tool can show you what's up — or down. It even assists in other troubleshooting tasks, such as disabling hardware and updating driver software.

Your Pal, the Device Manager

The Device Manager isn't a secret. In fact, it's not the only place in Windows where you can obtain or modify hardware details, but it's centralized. It gives you a quick overview of the PC's hardware, plus quick access to various device Properties dialog boxes.

Opening the Device Manager

The Device Manager is part of what was once called the Windows Administrator Tools. These tools were a collection of programs accessed from the Control Panel, though each could be run individually. In Windows 10, the Device Manager is accessed independently, without bothering with a tour of the old Control Panel.

To summon the Device Manager, heed these steps:

1. **Press the Windows+X keyboard shortcut.**

The supersecret menu appears.

2. **Press M to choose Device Manager.**

Or you can pluck Device Manager from the menu.

The Device Manager window is illustrated in Figure 2-1. It uses a *hierarchical,* or "tree," structure to list hardware categories on the PC.

Specific device

Hardware categories

PC   Specific device's Properties dialog box

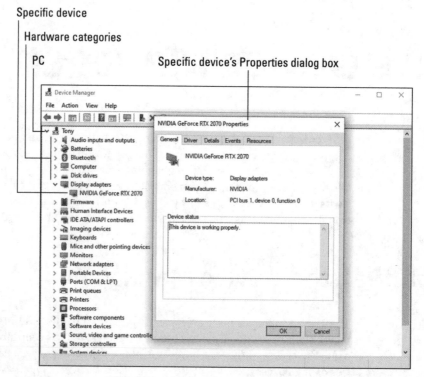

FIGURE 2-1: The Device Manager.

To view specific hardware, open a category. You see specific devices, such as the display adapter hardware shown in Figure 2-1. Each category has at least one piece of hardware. Several categories, such as Network Adapters, may have several items listed.

For additional details on hardware, double-click on a specific hardware item. You see the item's Properties dialog box, as shown in Figure 2-1. The Device Status area on the General tab in the Properties dialog box confirms that Windows believes the hardware to be running properly.

Any hardware errors detected are flagged in the Device Manager window: The hardware category is open, and a tiny yellow warning icon appears by the hardware entry. Further, the Device Status item in the device's Properties dialog box contains a description of the error. See the later section "Dealing with errant hardware."

TECHNICAL STUFF

» Windows is quite tolerant of misbehaving hardware. In fact, your PC's hardware probably fails more than Windows ever lets on. I'm not sure of the current data, but long ago a disk operation could fail ten consecutive times before an error message was displayed. The bottom line is that just because the Device Manager shows no problems doesn't mean that everything is working properly.

» Also see Chapter 3 for information on the System Information program.

Looking for hardware in the Settings app

The Device Manager is a holdover from Windows 7 and earlier. In Windows 10, Microsoft prefers that you use the Settings app for both PC configuration and certain troubleshooting duties, but it's just not yet enough to compare with your pal, the Device Manager.

To look for hardware in the Settings app, obey these steps:

1. **Press the Windows+I keyboard shortcut.**

The Settings app appears.

2. **Choose Devices.**

A list of devices appears on the right side of the screen, as illustrated in Figure 2-2.

Nothing in the device list (refer to Figure 2-2) tells you whether the hardware is malfunctioning. You can probably assume that it's all working, but the only option available is to remove the device. So this area, although it lists hardware, isn't as useful as the Device Manager.

Also accessible from the Control Panel, as well as from the Settings app, is the list of devices and printers. After Step 2 in this section, on the right side of the window, choose the Printers & Scanners link. You see the Control Panel's Devices and Printers screen, as shown in Figure 2-3.

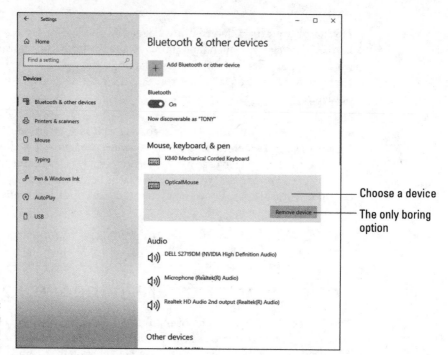

Choose a device

The only boring option

FIGURE 2-2:
Hardware gizmos listed in the Settings app.

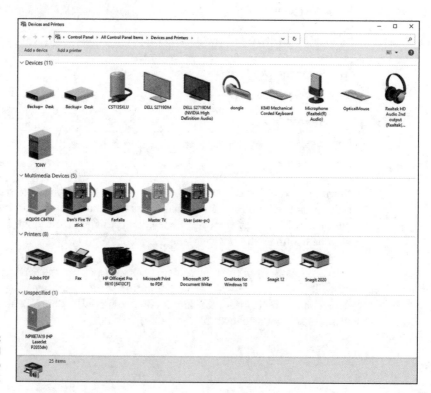

FIGURE 2-3:
Devices and Printers, but no troubleshooting.

As with the hardware gizmos listed in the Settings app, the Devices and Printers window merely lists hardware. Unlike the Device Manager, it doesn't show any hardware issues, nor does it list as many hardware devices.

TECHNICAL
STUFF

One curiosity between the Devices and Printers window and Device Manager is that double-clicking a hardware item in either window displays a hardware Properties dialog box. But — get this — it's not the same hardware dialog box, even for the same piece of hardware. So, for consistency's sake, I recommend that you use only the Device Manager for hardware troubleshooting.

Device Manager Duties

The Device Manager is useful when it flags malfunctioning hardware, but it also provides handy shortcuts to update drivers and to enable and disable various gizmos. The variety of activities contributes to this utility's usefulness.

Dealing with errant hardware

When Windows relents and finally admits that hardware is causing trouble, it flags the errant gizmo in the Device Manager window. The hardware category is expanded, allowing you to view the specific entry. A warning icon, shown in the margin, flags the hardware's icon.

To see what's up, double-click the entry in question. You see the device's Properties dialog box, with a description of the suspected trouble shown on the General tab. A solution might also be suggested. At this point, troubleshooting involves following the suggested solution.

If the solution that's presented doesn't fix the problem, you can try updating the software driver, disabling and enabling the device, or replacing the hardware.

Updating driver software

Hardware does nothing without software. For each hardware device in your computer — and listed in the Device Manager window — software is available to control the gizmo. That software is generically referred to as a *driver*. And, like other software in the PC, drivers need updating.

You can update a driver if you're experiencing hardware problems, when you receive a reminder from the manufacturer to update the driver, or you see a notification regarding a pending update. Security issues may also come into play, though for most hardware drivers it's not a major concern. Also, hardware manufacturers do recommend that you use the most current software.

To update driver software in the Device Manager window, follow these steps:

1. Set a restore point.

Refer to Chapter 5 in this minibook for details on System Restore.

2. In the Device Manager window, open the category containing the device.

For example, open Network Adapters for networking hardware.

To open the Device Manager, refer to the earlier section "Opening the Device Manager."

3. Double-click on the hardware you want to update.

A Properties dialog box appears.

4. Click the Driver tab.

The Driver tab in the device's Properties dialog box, which is beautifully depicted in Figure 2-4, contains several buttons dealing with updating the driver software.

5. To update the driver, or to confirm that the best driver is installed, click the Update Driver button.

You see a wizard appear, which guides you through the process.

6. Choose the option Search Automatically for Updated Driver Software.

Windows probes the Internet to see whether better driver software is available.

7. If the best driver is already installed, the wizard says so; click the Close button. If a better driver is found, heed the directions given to install the updated software.

Installation proceeds as the hardware driver is updated. You may be asked to restart the PC to complete the operation.

If the driver update doesn't work, nothing deleterious has happened. You still need to troubleshoot the issue, but you don't need to uninstall the driver.

If the driver update causes more problems, use the Roll Back Driver button in the Properties dialog box. (Refer to Figure 2-4.) If the issue is severe enough that you can't access the Device Manager, restart Windows in Safe mode or use the Windows Recovery Environment to remove the bad driver update.

» Refer to Chapter 1 for details on the Windows Recovery Environment. Safe mode is covered in Chapter 4 of this minibook.

» Drivers are routinely updated when the Windows Update utility runs. They may also be updated by the manufacturer. Refer to Book 4, Chapter 2 for details on Windows Update.

» Some hardware comes with its own updating programs. For example, the NVIDIA display adapter features a control panel program. That program alerts you to any pending driver updates. Check the notification area on the taskbar for such update reminders.

» You can also obtain driver software from the hardware manufacturer's website. In fact, that software may be better and more current than whatever Windows finds. Refer to Book 1, Chapter 2 for details on how to access the manufacturer's website to obtain software.

TIP

» If you don't know the manufacturer, use the device name at the top of the Properties dialog box (refer to Figure 2-4) as the search term in the Internet search engine of your choice. Peruse the results for a web page with *download, support,* or *driver* in its title.

Technical and official hardware name

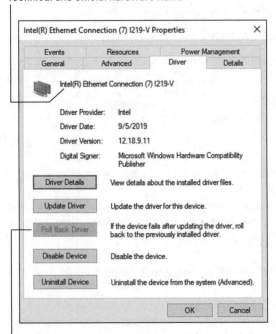

FIGURE 2-4:
Driver control for an Ethernet network adapter.

Uninstall the recent driver update

Disabling a device

Another nifty trick you can pull in the Device Manager window is to disable a piece of hardware. This technique is almost as good as uninstalling the hardware, but without disconnecting cables or using a screwdriver.

Once the device is disabled, Windows ignores it. This configuration may cause problems or, for troubleshooting, it may demonstrate that the disabled device was the source of the problems.

Disabling devices is also a good way to resolve conflict between two devices. For example, the PC's advanced audio system may conflict with the motherboard's audio, in which case disabling one might cause the other to work properly.

To disable a device, obey these steps:

1. **Open the hardware category in the Device Manager window.**

    Refer to the earlier section "Opening the Device Manager" for details on accessing the Device Manager window.

2. **Right-click the hardware you want to disable.**

3. **Choose Disable Device from the shortcut menu.**

    A warning appears. In some cases, disabling a device disables the computer. For example, if you disable the primary storage device, the system goes down. For peripherals, however, disabling a device is a handy troubleshooting tool.

4. **Click the Yes button to confirm.**

    The device doesn't pop out of the computer's case. No, it still appears in the Device Manager window, but with a disabled tag, as shown in the margin. Windows continues to run (as best it can) without the device.

At this point, you confirm that the problem or conflict you were having has been resolved. If so, you can keep the device disabled, though I would instead recommend that you uninstall it — if possible.

TIP

To reenable a device, right-click it and choose the Enable command. Immediately, the hardware is added back into the Windows inventory.

>> Another way to disable a device is to uninstall its driver. In the device's Properties dialog box, on the Driver tab, click the Uninstall button. (Refer to Figure 2-4.) Remove the driver and restart Windows, though at this point Windows may attempt to reinstall the driver. It won't do so, however, when a device is disabled.

>> Just like the warning icon that flags malfunctioning hardware, you see any disabled items when you first open the Device Manager window.

Chapter **3**

MSCONFIG and the Task Manager

For diagnosing and repairing Windows startup issues, nothing beats MSCONFIG. The utility is called System Configuration, but it's better known as MSCONFIG. Regardless, it's a handy tool for controlling how Windows starts and which services are started, as well as a central location for accessing other Windows tools and utilities.

The System Configuration Utility

I use the System Configuration utility so frequently that it's generally the default item that appears in the Run dialog box. To display this dialog box, press the Windows+R keyboard shortcut and type **msconfig**. Press Enter.

Figure 3-1 shows the General tab in the System Configuration window. The next section explores all the tabs and offers an overview of how to use the utility.

IT'S CALLED "SYSTEM CONFIGURATION," BUT EVERYONE SAYS "MSCONFIG"

I'm guilty. For years, I've called the program by its name, MSCONFIG. (Say "em-ess-config.") Then I noticed that the program window is titled System Configuration. Whatever. If you say "MSCONFIG," the nerds know what you're talking about.

Tabs

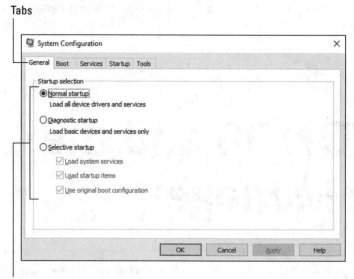

FIGURE 3-1:
The System
Configuration
utility.

Options and settings

The Run dialog box lets you type a command to run a program, which works well when you know a program's filename. (The program's filename is frequently not the same name as the program.)

**TECHNICAL
STUFF**

Exploring MSCONFIG

Each tab in the System Configuration window deals with a different part of the system. The first three tabs control startup options:

General: This tab contains basic startup options, including settings to go into Safe mode or to disable certain startup files.

Boot: This tab controls the operating system startup process, including the multiple operating system selection menu and other startup menus and options.

Services: This tab lists all services run in Windows.

The General tab and Boot tab seem quite similar, though the General tab relates to the current Windows installation. The Boot tab, shown in Figure 3-2, lets you switch between different versions of Windows (which is near-impossible to configure), but more importantly, it's the gateway to Safe mode, which is covered in Chapter 4 of this minibook.

The Services tab lists Windows startup and background programs, as well as processes related to your account's background programs. This tab is shown in Figure 3-3.

Safe mode option

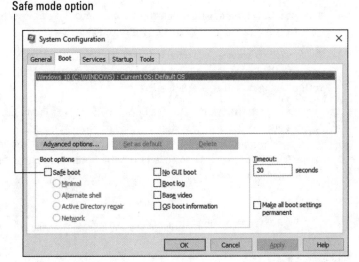

FIGURE 3-2: MSCONFIG's Boot tab.

You can use the Services tab to disable a part of Windows that might be causing trouble. See the later section "MSCONFIG Startup Options." Also see the nearby sidebar, "What's an application? A process? A service?"

The next two tabs in the System Configuration window perform tasks not directly related to startup issues. They are

> **Startup:** No, I didn't lie; this tab is empty. Its function has been moved to the Task Manager window.

> **Tools:** This tab lists shortcuts to handy troubleshooting tools in Windows.

The Startup tab is (well, was) similar to the Services tab in that it lists startup processes, or background programs. More detail is found in Chapter 6, which covers the Task Manager.

MSCONFIG and the Task Manager

CHAPTER 3 **MSCONFIG and the Task Manager** 267

The Tools tab lists other programs you can use for troubleshooting, information-gathering, diagnosing, and other gerunds I can't think of right now. See the next section.

The general procedure in MSCONFIG is to modify a setting and then click the OK button. You're prompted to restart the PC. The changes you made take effect when the system reboots.

>> It's common for the General tab to show Selective Startup as the PC's configuration. This setting is chosen automatically when you modify the Windows startup process; for example, when you turn off a startup program or disable a service. Only by enabling all startup services and programs is the General tab's Normal startup option chosen (refer to Figure 3-1).

>> To view which services are disabled, click the Services tab (refer to Figure 3-3) and click the Date Disabled column header. You see a list of disabled services sorted by the date they were deactivated.

>> Available operating systems on the Boot tab (if any) are limited to Windows. To start another operating system on the computer, you use a boot loader that appears when the PC first starts. This is how Linux can be run on the same PC as Windows; it's controlled from the boot loader, not from the System Configuration utility.

Sort the list to see any disabled services

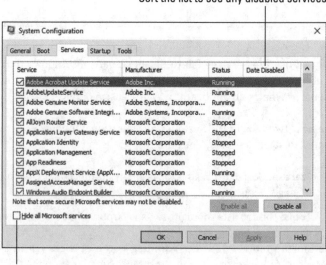

FIGURE 3-3:
The Services tab.

Check to see only your account's services

WHAT'S AN APPLICATION?
A PROCESS? A SERVICE?

TECHNICAL STUFF

When you get into software troubleshooting in Windows, you discover that the term *software* is too general. Sure, you can use the word *program* to describe files that contain code or computer instructions. But to troubleshoot, you must know some weird terms, how the weird terms are used, and where these weird things are controlled. Here's the lot of them:

app: Short for *app*lication, this term refers to programs designed for mobile devices. It's also trendy to refer to newer, Windows 10 programs as apps.

application: This term gets abused frequently, but traditionally it refers to productivity software, such as Microsoft Excel or Adobe Illustrator. Any program in Windows that appears as a button on the taskbar, however, is considered an application.

firmware: This is software encoded on a chip, which serves a specific purpose. The type of chip is known as ROM, for *read-only m*emory, though on today's PCs the chip can be rewritten. Also referred to as the BIOS.

process: A process is a program that Windows runs. Unlike applications, which show up on the taskbar and appear as windows on the screen, a process may not have a window. It runs invisibly. Some processes, however, appear as tiny icons in the notification area.

program: Software written for a specific purpose contained in a file is called a program. This term is rather broad, as programs that serve specific purposes go by different names.

service: A service is a task carried out by either an application or a process. A single process can sponsor multiple services. For example, an antivirus program may run as a process, and it may sport several services that monitor your computer for signs of malware.

software: These are the instructions that tell the computer hardware what to do.

thread: A thread is a program within a program. The processor can run many threads at the same time, and any individual program can use this feature to accomplish several things at a time.

Reviewing the troubleshooting tools

The richest feature in the MSCONFIG utility is found on the Tools tab. It's a treasure trove of various utilities in Windows that help you to diagnose, report, and troubleshoot various issues.

To start a tool, follow these steps:

1. **Select a tool in the list.**

2. **Click the Launch button.**

   This step is important! Don't click OK or you close the System Configuration window. Click Launch instead.

Commands available on the Tools tab are listed in the sections that follow. These sections are presented in the default order that they appear in the System Configuration window.

About Windows

Choose this item, also known as the WinVer utility, to see the About Windows dialog box, shown in Figure 3-4.

Windows name

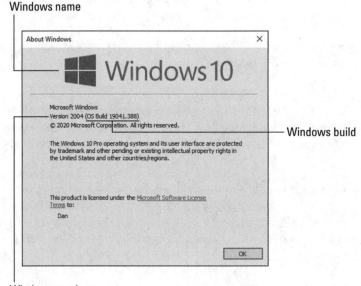

FIGURE 3-4:
Details about the current Windows version.

Windows version

Alas, the About Windows dialog box doesn't offer as much useful information as I'd like to see. It proclaims Windows name, version, and build number, as illustrated in the figure. It doesn't tell you whether you have the 32-bit or 64-bit version of Windows. To get this information, you need to bring up the System dialog box. See the later section "System Properties."

Change UAC Settings

User Account Controls (UAC) alert you when you're about to change a setting that affects all of Windows. For an administrator-level account, which is just about everyone, these warnings aren't obtrusive. For a standard-user account, which is just about no one, they pop up all the time.

To set the annoyance level of the UAC warnings, use the User Account Control Settings window. Adjust the slider up or down to set the degree to which you are annoyed or warned.

>> UAC warnings show up when you click on a button flagged with the UAC shield, shown in the margin.

>> If you see a UAC warning when you didn't click on a shield-flagged item, click the No button or Cancel button. Do an antivirus scan. See Book 4, Chapter 3.

>> Standard-user accounts must type an administrator password to proceed with changing items that affect system-wide settings. Because few users have standard accounts, this situation rarely occurs.

Security and Maintenance

Part IV of this book covers PC security. The Security and Maintenance tool, once known as the Action Center under Windows 7, is now its own app, Windows Security. It displays the status of various security options, including virus and threat detection, firewall, and other useful tools.

From the MSCONFIG utility, choosing the Security and Maintenance item opens the Security and Maintenance window from the Control Panel. Any current security issues are flagged; click the appropriate button or heed the warning to proceed.

Windows Troubleshooting

This item takes you to the Update & Security screen in the Settings app, where you can view the various troubleshooting tools. Refer to Book 1, Chapter 2 for more details on running a troubleshooter.

Computer Management

The Computer Management console is another location in Windows where several important tools are clustered. These tools include the Task Scheduler, Event Viewer, Performance Monitor, Device Manager, and Disk Management console.

Figure 3-5 shows the Computer Management console window. Each of the other items acts like a plug-in for the window. In fact, you can run them all individually, which is how I describe them in this book.

>> Click a chevron to expand or collapse a plug-in in the Computer Management console window.

>> The Shared Folders item in the Computer Management console can be useful when diagnosing network issues. Choose Shared Folders and then Shares to view folders available on your PC and the network. This item also lists open files that might prevent a system shutdown. Refer to Book 2, Chapter 9 for more details on shutdown issues.

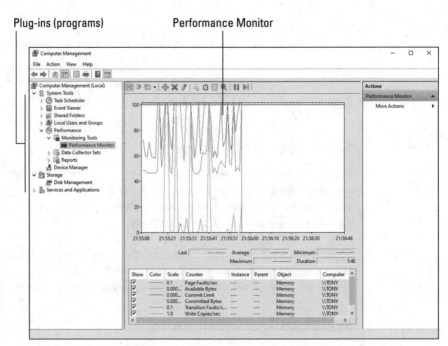

Plug-ins (programs)   Performance Monitor

FIGURE 3-5:
The Computer Management console.

System Information

The System Information window lists details about your PC's hardware and software environment. It's an excellent diagnostic tool.

See Chapter 8 in this minibook for more details on using the System Information window.

Event Viewer

The Event Viewer provides a good way to review your PC's activities — and a lot of activity is going on in the computer, even when it looks like it's just sitting still.

See Chapter 8 in this minibook for details on using the Event Viewer.

Programs

The Programs and Features window in the Control Panel lists all software installed on your computer. You use the window to uninstall or change programs, which is far more involved and offers more control than the Apps portion of the Settings app.

System Properties

The System Properties tool in the MSCONFIG utility launches the System window, which shows a summary of the computer's operating system, basic features, and network information, as shown in Figure 3-6.

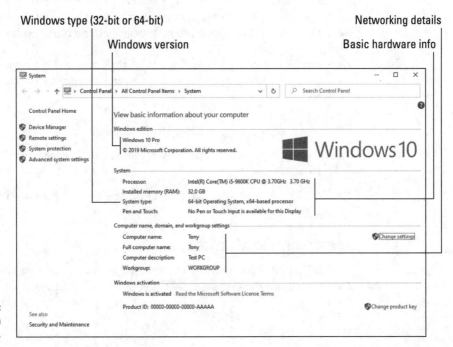

FIGURE 3-6: The System window.

The System window provides a gateway to other popular locations in Windows, such as the Device Manager.

>> The About Windows tool shows additional version information for Windows. Refer to the earlier section "About Windows."

>> The keyboard shortcut to summon the System window is Win+Break.

Internet Options

The Internet Options tool summons the Internet Properties dialog box. This dialog box controls options for Microsoft's own web browser, Edge. It doesn't change settings for third-party web browsers, such as Google Chrome.

This tool comes from an earlier time, when Microsoft made it difficult to install a non-Microsoft web browser in Windows. At the time, the Internet Properties dialog box controlled basic Internet settings. Today, it's simply an extension of the Microsoft web browser. Beyond this trivial tidbit, the Internet Properties dialog box doesn't control much.

Internet Protocol Configuration

This is a weirdo tool to find in Windows, mostly because it launches an old command-line utility, *ipconfig*. Don't be alarmed when you choose this item and you see a command prompt window appear, with no other explanation.

The ipconfig utility reports the status of the computer's network adapters and connections. Its list is quite technical, and the details can be found elsewhere in Windows, just not all in one place.

>> Refer to Book 2, Chapter 8 for network troubleshooting.

>> Scroll up the command prompt window to view details that may have scrolled off the window.

>> To close the command prompt window, type **exit** and press the Enter key.

Performance Monitor

This option presents a more direct way to access the performance monitor window. The first is from the Computer Management console and is illustrated earlier, in Figure 3-5.

>> See Book 5, Chapter 1 for full details on the Performance Monitor program.

>> Another type of performance monitor appears on the Performance tab in the Task Manager. See Chapter 6 in this minibook for details on that utility.

Resource Monitor

It seems like the resource monitor and performance monitor would be similar tools, and they are. The Resource Monitor window tracks finite resources in the computer, like memory, processor speed, services, and other items that are related to the PC's performance.

See Book 5, Chapter 1 for more information on using the Resource Monitor.

Task Manager

The Task Manager has evolved from a simple program switcher to an advanced tool for examining running programs, services, and other features. It deserves its own chapter, which is Chapter 6 in this minibook.

TIP

>> The easy way to access the Task Manager is to press the Ctrl+Shift+Esc keyboard shortcut.

>> The Task Manager's Startup tab contains the items that once appeared on the MSCONFIG utility's Startup tab.

>> The Performance tab in the Task Manager is similar to the Performance Monitor program, which is covered in Book 5, Chapter 1.

Command Prompt

Beloved by old-timers, the command prompt can be a useful tool for troubleshooting — but only when you know the commands and their options. Otherwise, this text-mode method of running a computer can be an exercise in frustration.

TIP

>> To manually run the command prompt, press Win+R to summon the Run dialog box. Type **cmd** and press the Enter key to bring up the window.

>> For many troubleshooting tasks, it's necessary to run the command prompt with elevated or administrator-level permissions. To do so, tap the Windows key to pop up the Start menu. Type **command prompt**. When you see the Command Prompt app appear in the search results, from the right side of the menu choose Run As Administrator.

Registry Editor

The Registry Editor modifies the various confusing items stored in the Registry. It's also called *regedit* ("rej-edit"), which is the program name. Most users start the Registry Editor by opening the Run dialog box and typing the Registry Editor command. Here are the specific steps:

1. **Press Win+R.**

   The Run dialog box appears.

2. **Type** regedit **and press the Enter key.**

   The Registry Editor window opens.

Chapter 7 in this minibook covers the Registry Editor and all the fun you can have working in the Windows Registry.

Remote Assistance

Windows Remote Assistance allows you to grant access to another person on the Internet, who can fully control your computer under the pretext of troubleshooting. Yes, it's a tool ripe for abuse.

The problem with Remote Assistance is that you must truly trust the person who is giving the help. Once permission is granted, that person has full control. And yes, fake "help" sites exist on the Internet with people all-too-eager to get into your PC and do mysterious things to make it run better. Avoid the temptation to use such services.

In fact, this book offers you plenty of advice on how to address various PC issues. It's my hope that you never consider getting remote assistance.

TECHNICAL STUFF

» You can disable the Remote Assistance feature in the System Properties dialog box. Refer to Book 1, Chapter 2 for specifics.

» I've used Remote Assistance a few times, both receiving and giving. It's better than troubleshooting over the phone when I'm giving the assistance, but it's difficult for the other person (who is usually not computer literate). My computer manufacturer has used Remote Assistance with me to troubleshoot hardware issues. They didn't resolve anything, yet it was fascinating to watch.

System Restore

The System Restore utility is the Windows wayback machine, allowing you to recover from bad settings or even changes made by malicious software. This vital tool is covered specifically in Chapter 5 of this minibook.

MSCONFIG Startup Options

The primary purpose of the System Configuration utility is to customize how Windows starts. Use the MSCONFIG window's Services tab to enable or disable various startup programs and processes and stuff like that.

Examining the startup services

Windows doesn't just run the programs you tell it to start. A lot of activity takes place before you sign in and before you have a chance to run any programs. These programs that run, started from Windows as well as from your own account, are called *services*. The full lot of them are listed on the Services tab in the System Configuration utility's window.

The list of services is long. If you want to limit it to just your own programs, place a check mark by the item Hide All Microsoft Services. (Refer to Figure 3-3.) Even then, the number of services is lengthy, though you might recognize some of the names as background programs, such as cloud storage synchronization utilities, antivirus, and software update programs.

If you have an issue with any of these startup services, you can disable them. See the following section.

REMEMBER

>> When you disable a service, Windows goes into Selective Startup mode. This mode is shown on the System Configuration utility's General tab.

>> I wouldn't recommend randomly disabling startup services. In fact, some services may start other services automatically, so your efforts might be futile.

>> Some startup services can best be disabled in Safe mode. See Chapter 4 in this minibook.

Disabling a startup service

The best reason to disable a startup service is to determine whether it's the source of your woe. And, keep in mind that these issues may appear before you sign in to Windows or immediately after. That's because startup services run instantly and most of them run all the time.

To disable a startup service, heed these steps:

1. **Open the System Configuration window.**

   Press Win+R on the keyboard. Type **MSCONFIG** and press Enter.

2. **Click the Startup tab.**

3. **Remove the check mark by the startup service in question.**

4. **Click the General tab.**

   The startup selection has changed to Selective Startup, and the option for Load System Services is shaded. These are your clues that the startup process is no longer the same. It's not bad news; you can reverse your choices easily.

5. **Close the MSCONFIG window.**

6. **I recommend clicking the Restart button to test your changes.**

   And the PC restarts.

When the computer comes to life again, you may see a warning, related to the disabled startup service, reminding you of the change. Check the system to ensure that disabling the service fixed the issue. If it didn't, reenable the service and try another troubleshooting technique; disable another service, use Safe mode, and so on. The idea is to work through all startup programs until you find the one that's causing you trouble.

REMEMBER

>> To reenable a service, repeat the steps in this section, but in Step 3 add the check mark.

>> You can also disable a startup service by uninstalling its related program. Less drastic would be to set the program's preferences so that it doesn't run at startup, though not every program offers this feature.

>> The startup services aren't disabled until you restart the PC.

>> After you found the problem program, consider obtaining a software update, which might fix the problem.

Chapter 4

Safe Mode

Things can get so screwy in Windows that Microsoft had to come up with a nonscrewy way of running the PC. I preferred the term *nonscrewy mode,* but the engineers in Redmond came up with "safe mode" instead. You can use this mode to diagnose problems, perform troubleshooting, and run a special utility called System File Checker. The goal is to fix Windows problems in a sane and safe manner.

The Mode Is Safe

Safe mode tells you one thing best: whether the problem is with Windows. In Safe mode, only Windows itself is loaded: the basic parts of the operating system, to varying degrees. Any other software — including device drivers, startup processes, and other programs — aren't loaded in Safe mode. This leads to one immediate, solid conclusion:

When the computer runs fine in Safe mode, the problem you have is not caused by Windows.

As an example, if the computer won't start properly normally but will start in Safe mode, the problem lies with a startup program beyond what Windows loads.

Further, you can use Safe mode to reset various options and settings that might make Windows unusable. For example, if you accidentally set the default window color to green on a green background, you can enter Safe mode to undo that change.

Utilities can be run in Safe mode. For example, you can run System Restore when you otherwise might not be able to access that tool when Windows runs normally.

Truly, Safe mode is a wonderful way to perform diagnostics and troubleshooting in Windows.

» Your duty in Safe mode is to determine which piece of software is causing the problem and to either update that software or disable it to keep the computer running properly.

» The most troublesome device drivers control the PC's video, power management, and networking hardware. All these are disabled when Windows starts in Safe mode.

» I've let a computer sit in Safe mode for a few hours just to ensure that the problem isn't with Windows or the PC's hardware.

» When the problem persists in Safe mode, it's most likely a Windows issue. See the later section "Running the System File Checker (SFC)" for what to do.

Safe Mode to the Rescue

It is my wish that you never need to use Safe mode. First, it's not fun. It reminds me of the old days of low-resolution graphics and limited computer capabilities. Second, using Safe mode implies that something is terribly wrong, which is seldom amusing. Finally, Safe mode itself can be frustrating, with all its options and features.

Understanding Safe mode modes

Safe mode itself comes in varying degrees of, well, "safeness." The three degrees are

Diagnostic mode: The mildest form of Safe mode is Diagnostic mode, which looks the most like Windows usually does.

Safe boot: This setting enters Safe mode.

Safe boot alternate shell (command prompt): This setting activates Safe mode for nerds, which means the computer is operated from a command prompt window. This mode is truly terrifying, but if you know what you're doing, it's quite useful.

Use the System Confirmation, or MSCONFIG, utility to set these modes when Windows operates normally. Otherwise, you can use the Windows Recovery Environment to access Safe mode, as discussed in Chapter 1. Safe mode may also activate automatically on startup when Windows detects various problems.

REMEMBER

>> Safe mode is accessed upon startup, either because you directed the PC to restart in Safe mode or it's started that way due to an error.

>> Startup modes set in the System Configuration (MSCONFIG) utility are "sticky." They remain in effect until you choose Normal and then restart the computer.

>> Some programs also offer a Safe mode for diagnostics and troubleshooting. For example, Microsoft Office applications feature a Safe mode.

Entering Diagnostic mode

For fixing minor issues, I recommend that you restart Windows in Diagnostic mode. In this mode, Windows looks most familiar, but several of its standard drivers as well as other startup programs aren't run.

WARNING

Diagnostic mode requires your Windows password. A PIN or another sign-in option may be ineffective in Diagnostic mode. Therefore, ensure that you know your Windows password before you attempt to use Diagnostic mode.

To restart the PC in Diagnostic mode, heed these steps:

1. **Tap the Windows key.**

2. **Type** system configuration

3. **Choose the top search result, the System Configuration app.**

   The System Configuration utility, MSCONFIG, starts.

4. **On the General tab, choose Diagnostic Startup.**

   Refer to Figure 4-1.

5. **Click OK.**

   A tinier System Configuration window appears with two options: Restart and Exit Without Restart.

6. **Click the Restart button.**

   The computer shuts down and immediately restarts in Diagnostic mode.

Diagnostic Startup Safe mode

Occasionally you'll find this item checked

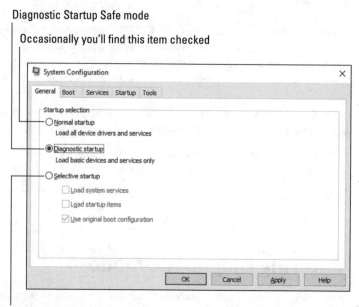

FIGURE 4-1:
Startup options in
MSCONFIG.

This setting shows which startup programs you have disabled

Diagnostic mode looks a lot like the regular mode in which you use Windows. You'll see the desktop, icons, and other familiar features. You'll also note that some services are disabled, such as the network and audio drivers.

While in this special mode, perform your troubleshooting. With certain Windows features disabled (such as networking), you can confirm whether an issue still exists, in which case it's probably not Windows.

To exit Diagnostic mode, repeat the steps in this section, but in Step 4 choose Normal Startup (refer to Figure 4-1). You may notice a few one-time issues after the restart, such as online services losing their automatic sign-in. This effect comes from the disruption caused by starting the system in Diagnostic mode.

Using safe boot for Safe mode

For more aggressive troubleshooting, use the MSCONFIG utility's safe boot option as opposed to Safe mode. Follow these steps:

1. **Open the MSCONFIG utility.**

    Refer to Steps 1 through 3 in the preceding section.

2. **Click the Boot tab.**

3. **Place a check mark by Safe Boot.**

4. **Ensure that the Minimal option is selected.**

    This is the best choice for typical Safe mode troubleshooting.

5. **Click OK.**

6. **Click the Restart button.**

    The computer restarts in Safe mode.

A typical Safe mode screen is shown in Figure 4-2. It's more obvious than starting in Diagnostic mode (covered in the preceding section). I tout this mode — safe boot — as the preferred way to truly troubleshoot your PC.

No desktop background   Windows version info   "Safe Mode" tags (four corners)

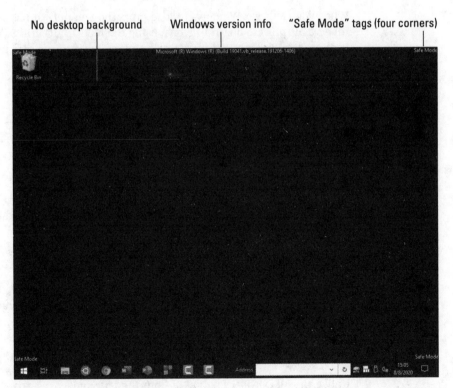

FIGURE 4-2:
Safe mode
(safe boot).

After testing any problems in Safe mode, reconfigure the MSCONFIG utility to start the computer normally. See the later section "Leaving safe boot Safe mode."

>> Unlike in Diagnostic mode, you can use your account PIN or another security method to enter Safe mode.

>> Don't be alarmed when you see startup warning messages in Safe mode. These warnings mean that some programs haven't started. That's the point of Safe mode: to prevent certain programs from starting.

>> Setting the Safe Boot option doesn't affect the settings on the General tab in the MSCONFIG utility.

>> See the later section "Exploring safe boot options" for details on the other boot option items.

Getting into Safe mode at boot-time

When you can't get Windows to load properly, you must direct it to start in Safe mode. This process doesn't involve using the MSCONFIG utility. Your next choice is to use the Windows Recovery Environment, which is covered in Chapter 1.

After starting the Windows Recovery Environment, follow these steps:

1. **Choose Troubleshoot.**

2. **Choose Advanced Options.**

3. **Choose Startup Settings.**

4. **Click the Restart button.**

   The computer restarts, bypassing Windows and the Windows Recovery Environment, to present a list of startup settings.

5. **Enable Safe mode.**

   Press the 4 or F4 key to restart Windows in Safe mode.

REMEMBER

The Windows Recovery Environment must be loaded from a recovery partition on the PC's primary storage device, or you must start the computer from repair media: a bootable thumb drive or media card. Details are offered in Chapter 1 of this minibook.

Unlike the MSCONFIG method of entering Safe mode, restarting your computer is all you need to exit. You don't need to reset any other options; the computer restarts normally — if it can.

Entering Safe mode unexpectedly

When your computer starts in Safe mode unexpectedly, it's telling you that something is wrong. In fact, an onscreen message may explain that a problem requires attention and offer directions. Follow them.

If you don't see a message, ask yourself this essential troubleshooting question: "What has changed?" Did you recently upgrade software? Add new hardware? That change may have caused something that directed Windows to start in Safe mode. Consider removing the new hardware or running the System Restore utility, which is designed to undo recent changes to Windows and software updates.

After you have addressed the issue, restart the computer. If it starts normally, the problem is fixed; otherwise, it restarts in Safe mode again and you must continue to address the issue.

>> Don't try to get work done in Safe mode! Instead, fix the problem. See the later section "Not Safe Mode Duties."

>> System Restore is covered in Chapter 5 of this minibook.

Exploring safe boot options

The System Configuration utility offers a slate of options for entering the safe boot form of Safe mode. These controls are available on the Boot tab, in the Boot Options area, as illustrated in Figure 4-3.

Safe boot has four operating modes, only one of which can be chosen:

Minimal: This is the default choice for starting Windows in Safe mode. It's the option you want unless you need network access.

Alternate Shell: In this mode, Windows boots into Safe mode without a desktop. After signing in, you see a large command prompt window, where you can type troubleshooting commands in Text mode.

Active Directory Repair: Use this option only for enterprise-level Windows installations that use an Active Directory database.

Network: With this option chosen, Safe mode runs with networking active.

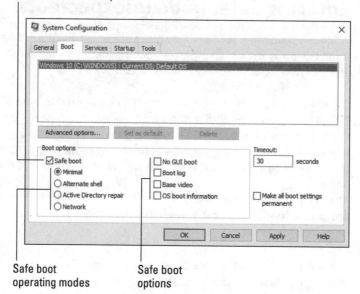

Serious Safe mode option

FIGURE 4-3:
Safe mode options.

Safe boot operating modes

Safe boot options

Each of these modes has up to four options available. You can select these in any combination:

No GUI boot: This mode changes the Windows startup animation. Rumors abound on the Internet that this setting acts as a trick to get your laptop to start faster. This trick is untrue. Don't mess with this option.

Boot log: A file named ntbtlog.txt is created, listing the drivers that are loaded as Windows starts in Safe mode. The log file can be found in the drive C Windows folder, C:\Windows, or wherever Windows is installed.

Base Video: Safe mode starts in low-resolution mode, 640-by-480 pixels, when this option is chosen.

OS Boot Information: This option directs the computer to display detailed text chronicling the boot process as Windows loads.

My advice is to leave each of these items unchecked. The reason is that none of them helps with troubleshooting one way or the other. The only one I've chosen occasionally is Base Video, which is helpful for diagnosing video driver issues that otherwise won't show up when Safe mode is started.

>> If you choose to boot into Safe mode using the alternate shell, press Ctrl+Alt+Delete to suspend the shell. You can then use the commands on the screen to perform other activities, such as restart the system.

REMEMBER

>> The minimal safe boot mode doesn't enable the PC's networking adapter. If you must diagnose the network or access the Internet, you need to activate the network operating mode.

>> The command prompt (Text mode) version of Safe mode requires that you sign in to your Windows account, which takes place at the lock screen. The command prompt then takes over.

>> To exit from Text mode, type **msconfig** at the prompt and press Enter. The System Configuration utility window appears. On the General tab, select Normal Startup, and on the Boot tab, ensure that the Safe Boot item is unchecked. Click OK. Click the Restart button.

>> Some of the more restrictive levels of Safe mode may prevent you from running certain Windows utilities. If so, restart Safe mode with fewer restrictions.

Leaving safe boot Safe mode

When you choose an alternative booting option in the System Configuration (MSCONFIG) utility, you're altering the way that Windows starts. This alternation is in effect until you deactivate it, which is why some beginners may experience Windows restarting only in Safe mode.

To properly exit safe boot, follow these steps whilst in Safe mode:

1. **Press Win+R to bring up the Run dialog box.**

If you're using the alternate shell mode, type **msconfig** at the prompt and skip to Step 3.

2. **Type** msconfig **and press the Enter key.**

The System Configuration utility appears.

3. **On the General tab, ensure that Normal Startup is chosen as the startup mode.**

4. **Click the Boot tab.**

5. **Remove the check mark by Safe Boot.**

6. **Click OK.**

7. **Click the Restart Now button.**

And the computer restarts normally.

See the nearby sidebar, "Safe mode rebooting nightmare recovery," if you ever find yourself unable to restart the PC normally.

TIP

SAFE MODE REBOOTING NIGHTMARE RECOVERY

Sometimes Windows gets stuck in Safe mode. To start the system normally, you must modify settings in the MSCONFIG utility, as covered in the nearby section "Leaving safe boot Safe mode." But if you can't get into Windows or you otherwise can't run the MSCONFIG utility, you end up in a resetting nightmare. There is, happily, a solution.

To force the PC to run the Windows Recovery Environment, you must turn off the computer as soon as you see the Windows startup animation (the circle of dots). When it appears, unplug the PC or remove the battery from a laptop. You must perform this task twice, after which Windows enters a special startup Diagnostic mode; the text *Preparing automatic repair* appears instead of the animated dots.

Wait while Windows diagnoses the problem. Eventually, you can get into the Windows Recovery Environment. Choose the option to run System Restore, and choose a recent restore point to recover the computer.

After the system has been restored, Windows starts normally, though you may have to reinstall some software or Windows updates. See Chapter 5 in this minibook for additional details on System Restore.

Safe Mode Duties

You have only one duty in Safe mode: Fix the problem. After you've completed this task, you restart Windows normally. Troubleshooting is done.

Checking for problems in Safe mode

The best thing you can figure out in Safe mode is whether the problem is related to Windows. If the system runs well in Safe mode, the problem lies with a driver, a startup service, or some other program loaded beyond the Windows basics.

>> The quick-and-easy solution for startup problems is to run System Restore. See Chapter 5 in this minibook for more information.

>> You can uninstall programs in Safe mode as well as roll back driver updates. Refer to Book 2, Chapter 7 for details on uninstalling programs; driver rollbacks are covered in Book 2 all over.

» Sometimes I use Safe mode to install driver updates. Then again, if some other program is preventing an update, you must deal with the conflict: Update the other program, disable it, or uninstall it.

» If the problem persists in Safe mode, it may be a hardware issue.

» I've used Safe mode to uninstall malware that otherwise digs into the system after Windows starts normally. I removed the program from the list of startup services in MSCONFIG as well as in the Registry. Then I uninstalled it using the Programs window (in the Control Panel).

Running the System File Checker (SFC)

One of the most useful yet overlooked tools in Windows is the *System File Checker*, fondly known by its initials: *SFC*. This utility is designed to ensure that Windows is whole. If necessary, it repairs broken parts of Windows and does so without the need to completely reinstall the operating system.

The SFC is a text-mode tool, run at the command prompt. Because you can fix Windows only when using an Administrator command prompt, and because the command prompt in Safe mode is administrator-level anyway (as long as your account is), I recommend using this tool only in Safe mode.

Follow these steps to use the SFC to scan and repair Windows:

1. **In Safe mode, press Win+R.**

The Run dialog box appears.

2. **Type** cmd **and press Enter.**

You see a command prompt (Text mode) window.

3. **Type** sfc /scannow **and press the Enter key.**

The *scannow* switch directs the SFC utility to confirm each part of Windows and replace anything defective or missing. See Table 4-1 for a full list of the SFC command's options.

The program's text output looks like this:

```
Beginning system scan. This process takes some time.

Beginning verification phase of system scan.
Verification n% complete.
```

The percentage value *n* changes over time.

4. **Wait.**

Eventually, verification reaches 100 percent.

TABLE 4-1: ## SFC Command Options

Option	What It Does
/offbootdir	Specifies the location of boot files when they cannot be found on the current PC
/offwindir	Specifies the location of Windows files when they cannot be found on the current PC
/scanfile	Scans and (optional) repairs or replaces the named file
/scannow	Scans all Windows operating system files, repairing or replacing any that are defective or the wrong version
/verifyfile	Scans the named file but doesn't replace the file
/verifyonly	Scans all Windows operating system files but doesn't repair or replace any bad files and saves information in a long, huge log file

The output you see in the command prompt window after verification is complete depends on the results of the SFC utility's operation. When nothing is wrong, you see this text:

```
Windows Resource Protection did not find any integrity
    violations.
```

When problems have been found and repaired, you see something like this:

```
Windows Resource Protection found corrupt files and successfully
    repaired them. Details are included in the CBS.Log windir\
    Logs\CBS\CBS.log. For example C:\Windows\Logs\CBS\CBS.log.
    Note that logging is currently not supported in offline
    services scenarios.
```

When things go awry, you see this text message altered to say that the SFC was "unable to fix some of" the problems. The details are found in the CBS.log file. Most likely in that scenario, your PC is fine. See the next section for information on the CBS.log file.

You can close the command prompt window when you're done running the SFC utility. Exit Safe mode as described elsewhere in this chapter.

TECHNICAL STUFF

>> When SFC cannot fix the problem, you should try additional recovery options. Refer to Chapter 1 in this minibook.

>> Older versions of Windows lacked recovery information preset on the primary storage device. This condition might be echoed on your PC if you've had it for a while and upgraded from an older version of Windows. The bottom line is that the SFC utility may prompt you to input the location of Windows files so that corrupt files can be replaced by proper ones.

Reviewing the CBS.log file

The SFC utility keeps track of its actions in a log file named after a major American television network. The log file reveals some details, if you can find it and are willing to wade through hundreds of lines of text. Follow these steps:

1. **Press Win+E.**

A File Explorer window opens. The first job is to locate the CBS.log file.

2. **Delete the text on the address bar.**

3. **Type** %windir%\logs **and press Enter.**

The environment variable *%windir%* represents the folder in which the Windows operating system is installed. The final percent sign is followed by a backslash and the word *logs*.

4. **Open the CBS folder.**

If you don't see this folder, the System File Checker utility has probably never been run on the PC. Otherwise, you see a folder populated with various log files.

5. **Double-click the CBS.log file.**

If you're prompted to choose a program to view the file, choose Notepad.

6. **Peruse the log file text as if it has deep meaning.**

Gently stroke your chin as you observe the entries.

Seriously, if you want to find any repaired issues in the log file, press Ctrl+F and search for the text *cannot repair*. The file that SFC couldn't fix is listed, along with a technical description of what went wrong. You can't really do anything else at this point, other than continue to gently stroke your chin and perhaps give a knowing nod.

TIP

>> You might also try searching the Microsoft Knowledge Base for information about the filename. Visit support.microsoft.com and type the name of the file that befuddles the SFC.

TECHNICAL
STUFF

>> Supposedly, CBS stands for *component-based servicing*. It's part of the servicing stack feature that supports the Windows Automated Installation Kit (Windows AIK) and blah, blah, blah. All I really know is that CBS is the Columbia Broadcasting System.

Not Safe Mode Duties

Safe mode isn't without its limits. Primarily, it's a troubleshooting and diagnostic tool. It lets you know right away whether the problem lies with Windows.

Safe mode is not designed as a secret way to run your computer when Windows won't start normally. This admonition applies specifically to instances when the PC automatically starts in Safe mode. That means something is wrong. Fix it.

Chapter **5**

System Restore

The first — and best — trick you should try when Windows goes awry is a restart. Simple. Effective. Works most of the time.

When a restart fails to cure the PC's ills, the next instant cure you should try is *System Restore.* This tool has been around since Windows 98, where it was tucked away in a command-line utility. But, starting with Windows XP, System Restore gained full graphical powers to allow recovery from common goofs, such as wrong settings or improperly installed software or hardware.

The System Restore Philosophy

At some point, I believe a Microsoft programmer said, "Whoops." The exclamation had nothing to do with writing code or spilling coffee. It had to do with making a change to some system setting, something that couldn't easily be undone. The programmer said, "If only I had a tool that could unwind Windows to the point where it was before I made this change." And thus, System Restore was born.

TIP

The most drastic form of System Restore is the command to reset the PC. Refer to Chapter 1 in this minibook.

Understanding System Restore

System Restore is a history feature, documenting all Windows settings and configuration options in one handy spot. That spot is called a *restore point*. Its purpose is to sit and wait for disaster. When the peril strikes, the restore point is used to recover those vital system settings and configuration options.

The process works like this:

1. You're about to install new software, update Windows, add new hardware, or perform some other change to the system — or you're just bored.

2. You set a restore point.

   Windows dutifully records the current state of Windows — all the options and settings and other, mysterious things no one knows about.

3. You perform the anticipated action from Step 1.

4. You move on with your digital life.

   If nothing happens, great. But if the system refuses to run or the changes incurred in Step 3 cause issues, you move on to Step 5:

5. You run System Restore to recover the old state of Windows.

   The computer restarts. When it comes back to life, you're informed that System Restore has done its job.

Mostly, System Restore is automatic. A restore point is set whenever you add new software or update windows. You can also manually set a restore point, which I recommend doing before adding hardware or whenever you feel like messing around. Details are offered in the later section "Restore the System, Restore Your Sanity."

>> You can run System Restore directly in Windows. It can also be accessed from the Windows Recovery Environment, which is covered in Chapter 1 of this minibook.

>> System Restore may automatically restore the system if a Windows update fails or the PC cannot start normally.

>> System Restore isn't the same as a backup. A *backup* makes an archival copy of one or more files. System Restore is more focused, backing up and retaining settings and options, not specific files. See Book 4, Chapter 4 for details on backup.

TECHNICAL
STUFF

>> Before System Restore was implemented in Windows 98, the only way to recover from unexpected changes to the system was to restore everything from a backup. Even if you had a recent backup, this process was tedious. It also seemed like overkill, especially if the change you wanted undone was relatively minor.

Accepting System Restore's limitations

System Restore isn't magic. It won't recover a lost document, reset your account password, fix a mass storage error, or remove malware.

Further, System Restore works only when you set a restore point. Windows 10 no longer automatically sets restore points at regular intervals, so the most recent restore point might be a while back. Therefore, it's up to you to remember to set a restore point, especially when changing Windows settings or adding new hardware.

>> System Restore works with Windows and general system settings. It doesn't recover settings you may change in your word processor or email program.

REMEMBER

>> If you have file management problems, use the Undo command in a File Explorer window. Press Ctrl+Z to undo a renaming, moving, deleting, or another file operation. This command works best immediately after you make the mistake.

Activating System Restore

You can't use the System Restore utility until it's activated and a restore point has been set on your PC. To ensure that System Restore is running, follow these steps:

1. **Press Win+Break to summon the System window.**

The Break key may also be labeled Pause.

If your laptop lacks a Break key, pop up the Start button menu and type *system*. Choose the matching item System from the Settings heading.

2. **On the left side of the window, choose the Advanced System Settings link.**

The System Properties dialog box appears.

3. **Click the System Protection tab.**

The tab should be named System Restore because all its options control this feature, as illustrated in Figure 5-1.

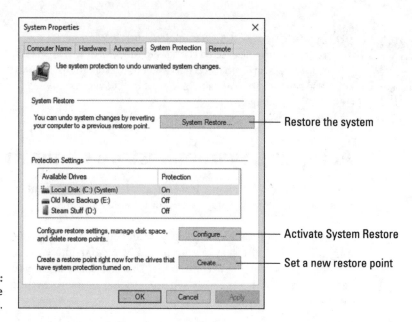

Restore the system

Activate System Restore

Set a new restore point

FIGURE 5-1:
System Restore
controls.

4. **Click the Configure button.**

5. **If the Turn On System Protection option is chosen, you're good. Otherwise:**

6. **Ensure that the Turn On System Protection option is selected.**

7. **Click OK.**

   System Restore is activated.

If you've just activated System Restore, set a restore point at once! See the later section "Setting a restore point."

Restore the System, Restore Your Sanity

It happened. Something weird. A driver update made things worse. New hardware now conflicts with something that's already in your computer, and now *two* things don't work. Or, perhaps your 13-year-old "computer genius" nephew decided to trick out your PC with an unbearable new color scheme and sound profile. Regardless of the foul, you want to recover your PC to The Way Things Were.

Running System Restore

Follow these steps to use System Restore to undo whatever weird thing just happened to your computer:

1. **Save all your stuff — if possible.**

The System Restore operation restarts your computer. If you can still use Windows, save your files; close your programs. Do it now.

TIP

If the changes made to your PC are severe enough, restart Windows in Safe mode to run System Restore. Be aware that you cannot undo the changes System Restore makes when you start it in Safe mode. See Chapter 4 in this minibook for information on Safe mode.

2. **Tap the Windows key.**

3. **Type** system restore

4. **From the list of search results, choose Create a Restore Point (Control Panel).**

System Restore dwells in the System Properties dialog box, on the System Protection tab.

5. **Click the System Restore button.**

The System Restore window appears.

If you just ran System Restore, you may see an Undo option. See the later section "Undoing a system restore" for details.

If you see the Undo option and don't desire to undo a system restore, choose the option Choose a Different Restore Point.

6. **Click the Next button.**

A screen detailing available restore points appears, similar to the one shown in Figure 5-2.

7. **Choose the most recent restore point.**

The most recent (top) item in the list is probably the one you want. I don't recommend choosing an earlier restore point unless you've already tried the top one and it failed. See the later section "Choosing an older restore point."

TIP

If necessary, place a check in the box by Show More Restore Points to see additional items in the list.

8. **Click the Next button.**

A summary screen details what's about to happen. You can click the Scan for Affected Programs link to see the impact the restore operation has. Most people are too impatient to wait for the results.

System Restore

Available restore points

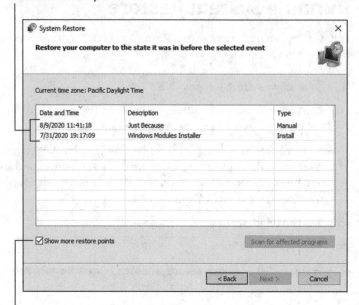

System Restore ✕

Restore your computer to the state it was in before the selected event

Current time zone: Pacific Daylight Time

Date and Time	Description	Type
8/9/2020 11:41:18	Just Because	Manual
7/31/2020 19:17:09	Windows Modules Installer	Install

☑ Show more restore points   Scan for affected programs

< Back   Next >   Cancel

FIGURE 5-2:
Choose a restore
point.

Check to ensure you see all available restore points

9. **Click the Finish button.**

A warning may appear, telling you that you can't interrupt System Restore until after the process has completed. Further, if you're running System Restore in Safe mode, it cannot be undone. Heed this warning!

10. **Click the Yes button to restart Windows.**

Wait while Windows restarts.

After you sign in to Windows, wait a bit more. Eventually, you see a confirmation message, explaining that the system has been restored. Click the Close button.

REMEMBER

» Running System Restore undoes any recent Windows updates. If the problem was the Windows update itself, forestall the update. See Book 4, Chapter 2 for details.

» If you're certain that odd behavior comes from a driver update, you can first attempt to roll back that update. Refer to Chapter 2 for details on what to do with regard to errant devices. You can also disable the device when it's causing woe.

Getting to System Restore from the Windows Recovery Environment

To run System Restore when you can't get Windows to start normally, enter the Windows Recovery Environment. When the menu appears, choose these options:

1. **Troubleshoot.**

2. **Advanced Options.**

   The option to reset the PC is more drastic than System Restore. Do not choose this option unless System Restore fails completely.

REMEMBER

3. **System Restore.**

   The computer restarts and you're prompted to sign in.

The computer runs the System Restore utility in a limited version of Safe mode. Continue following directions on the screen to locate a restore point and bring back your Windows system.

>> Refer to Chapter 1 for more details about the Windows Recovery Environment.

>> See Chapter 4 for details on Safe mode.

Choosing an older restore point

If you acted quickly enough, choosing the most recent system restore point is your best bet. Sometimes, however, you may want a less-recent restore point. For example, I recently managed to botch a system upgrade *and* a software addition, so I needed to restore my computer to a point from several days earlier.

The System Restore screen lists only a handful of recent restore points. To see more, look for an option titled Show More Restore Points (refer to Figure 5-2). Place a check mark in this box to review all available restore points.

WARNING

>> Choosing an older restore point increases the likelihood that the restoration won't be successful. If possible, you can try to restore the system incrementally: Choose a recent restore point, and then run System Restore again with the next-oldest restore point.

REMEMBER

>> When you restore to an older restore point, you remove any software and hardware updates installed in the between-time. You may have to reinstall software to rerun updates after restoring the system.

System Restore

Setting a restore point

System restore points are set automatically when Windows updates or new software is installed. Beyond these instances, you can set a manual restore point — for example, right before you add or upgrade hardware or perhaps before you attempt to reconfigure the network.

To manually set a restore point, follow these directions:

1. Tap the Windows key to pop up the Start menu.

2. Type system restore **or as much of this text as required to see a matching "system restore" item in the search results.**

3. Choose the item Create a Restore Point (Control Panel) from the list.

The System Properties dialog box appears, System Protection tab forward.

4. Click the Create button.

5. Type a descriptive name for the restore point.

Reference the restore point in terms of the item you're installing or changing on the computer — for example, *Configuring new Wi-Fi router* or *Changing desktop themes.*

6. Click the Create button.

Eventually, the System Protection dialog box appears, confirming that the restore point was created.

7. Click the Close button.

The restore point is created.

8. Click the OK button to dismiss the System Properties dialog box.

After the restore point is created, proceed with whatever activity you were about to do. You now have peace of mind, knowing that a restore point looms in the past, in case you need it.

TIP

You can confirm that the restore point was created, by attempting to run the System Restore process. In the list of available restore points (refer to Figure 5-2), look for the top item to match the one just created.

Undoing a system restore

If you didn't run System Restore from Safe mode or from the Windows Recovery Environment, you can undo a recent restore. This option is presented when you click the System Restore button in the System Properties dialog box. The first screen in the System Restore window looks like Figure 5-3.

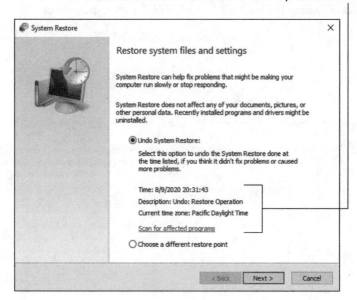

FIGURE 5-3:
The System
Restore undo
option.

Choose the option Undo System Restore, and then click the Next button and follow the directions on the screen to undo what was undone by running System Restore.

Rare is the time when you need to undo a system restore. In fact, if restoring the system made things worse, you might consider resetting Windows. Refer to Chapter 1 in this minibook.

System Restore on Schedule

Restore points are created automatically whenever you install or update software. Windows may also create points on a schedule. To confirm that the schedule is active, or to create it yourself, you use the Task Scheduler.

The Task Scheduler is the Windows utility that runs various programs and services based on certain conditions occurring in the PC. To set an automatic restore point, a time trigger is used. For example, every Sunday at midnight, the Task Scheduler directs the System Restore utility to create a new restore point.

To create a System Restore task, or to confirm that it's already set up and running properly, obey these directions:

1. Tap the Windows key.

2. Type Task Scheduler

3. Choose the top search result, the Task Scheduler app.

The Task Scheduler window appears, as illustrated in Figure 5-4.

Next scheduled run time

Task Library tree   Task is ready   Task ran successfully

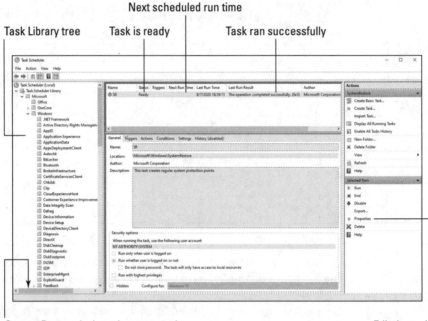

FIGURE 5-4:
The Task
Scheduler.

System Restore is down here somewhere   Edit the task

4. Open the Task Scheduler Library and choose Windows and then System Restore.

You see a screen that lists the System Restore (SR) task. The event details should show that its status is Ready, that triggers are available, and that it is scheduled to run again soon and has run successfully before. Figure 5-4 illustrates these points.

5. If everything looks good, close the Task Scheduler window. If it doesn't, you can edit the task to ensure that Windows creates restore points for you automatically.

The rest of these steps configure System Restore to run weekly. These steps are unnecessary if System Restore is already operating on a regular schedule.

6. Click Properties in the Action list.

The SR Properties (Local Computer) dialog box appears.

7. Click the Triggers tab.

If you see that no triggers are present, the task never runs.

8. Click the New button.

The New Trigger dialog box appears.

9. Choose Weekly to set a new restore point every week.

You can choose Daily if you find that item more comforting. Restore points don't occupy a huge amount of storage, yet disaster doesn't strike often enough for me to justify a daily restore point.

10. Set the trigger time.

I choose midnight, though if you don't leave your PC on all the time, choose a time when you know that you'll be using the system.

11. Choose the day of the week.

12. Click OK to close the New Trigger dialog box.

The trigger you set appears in the list of triggers, and the details reflect the chosen day and time.

13. Click OK to close the SR Properties (Local Control) dialog box.

The task is now set with a trigger, and its status in the Task Scheduler window reflects the trigger settings and next run time.

14. Close the Task Scheduler window.

At this point, you must wait for the event to trigger to confirm that the Task Scheduler is running System Restore and setting a restore point.

TECHNICAL STUFF

>> You can use the Task Scheduler to have Windows run programs on a given schedule or for whatever trigger is available: shutdown, upon completion of another event, when idle, and so on. In the Actions pane (refer to Figure 5-4), choose Create Basic Task and work with the wizard to build your task.

>> Windows uses the Task Scheduler to perform various services. These are listed in the System Configuration (MSCONFIG) utility on the Services tab. Some of the services run all the time, but others wait for triggers and are set in motion thanks to the Task Scheduler.

Chapter **6**

The Task Manager

A s a multitasking operating system, Windows can do many things at once. Even when you aren't running a specific program, internally Windows is abuzz with activity. To view all the stuff that's going on, from your applications to whatever-the-heck Windows is up to, you use the Task Manager. It provides tools for managing programs, monitoring performance, and controlling services and tasks.

Task Control Central

The ancient version of Windows didn't offer true multitasking. Instead, it was a task sharing environment. Yet it still required a way for a user to switch between running programs. Because this early release of Windows lacked a taskbar, the Task List window was used, as shown in Figure 6-1.

The Windows 10 Task Manager has its roots in the simple origins of the Task List. Yes, you can still use the window to switch tasks, but it's far more potent than that.

> » Every program that runs in Windows is referred to as a *task;* hence, the term *multitasking* and the name *Task Manager*.

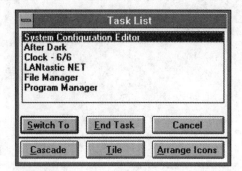

FIGURE 6-1:
Windows
version 3.1
Task List.

**TECHNICAL
STUFF**

>> The Task List was superseded by the Task Manager in Windows 95, which also
introduced the taskbar as a more direct way to switch programs.

Summoning the Task Manager

To view the Task Manager, press the Ctrl+Shift+Esc keyboard shortcut. It's not
that difficult to do: Press the left Ctrl key and then Shift and then Esc. You see the
Task Manager window, as shown in Figure 6-2.

If you see the minimal Task Manager, shown on the left in Figure 6-2, click the
More Details chevron to reveal its full window. This chapter assumes that the full
window is shown.

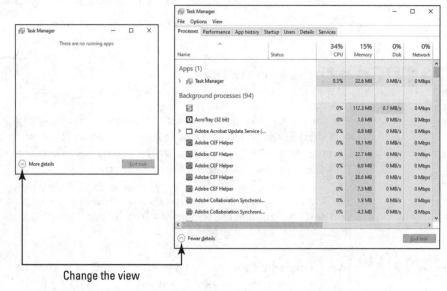

FIGURE 6-2:
The Windows 10
Task Manager.

Change the view

To dismiss the Task Manager window, press Esc.

>> You can also get to the Task Manager from the Ctrl+Alt+Delete menu: Press Ctrl+Alt+Delete and choose Task Manager. This shortcut comes in handy when other methods of bringing up the Task Manager may not work.

>> You can configure the Task Manager window to float over every other window on the screen: Choose Options⇨Always On Top from the Task Manager's menu bar. If you prefer that the Task Manager behave like other windows, choose Options⇨Minimize on Use.

>> The nerdy way to open the Task Manager is to type **taskmgr** in the Run dialog box. Press Win+R to summon the Run dialog box.

TECHNICAL STUFF

>> In Windows XP, the Ctrl+Alt+Delete command brought up the Task Manager window. And, as long as I'm being nostalgic, in MS-DOS, pressing Ctrl+Alt+Delete restarted the computer.

Switching tasks

The Task Manager's oldest function, dating back to the original Task List, is to switch programs. It can still perform this operation. Follow these steps:

1. **Press Ctrl+Shift+Esc to bring up the Task Manager window.**

If you see the minimal Task Manager window, click the More Details button.

2. **Ensure that the Processes tab is forward.**

The Processes tab divides the things that Windows does *(processes)* into two groups: Apps and Background Processes (refer to Figure 6-2). Programs you run are listed in the Apps category. Programs with multiple open windows are categorized by program name.

3. **Double-click a program's item in the list to switch to it.**

For programs with multiple open windows, expand the program's group and then double-click to switch to a specific window.

Of course, better ways exist in Windows to switch programs, such as pressing the Alt+Tab key combination or choosing a button from the taskbar.

TIP

The Task Manager window may minimize after you switch to another program. This behavior is set on the Options menu.

Exploring the Task Manager window

The Task Manager features seven tabs, each of which deals with some aspect of programs running in the PC or the use of resources. Here's the list:

Processes: Running programs appear on this tab in two parts: Apps (your programs) and Background Processes. The Background Processes list includes both programs run from your account as well as Windows processes.

Performance: This tab shows charts that update based on the PC's resource load. It's an echo of items available in the Performance Monitor window, which is covered in Book 5, Chapter 1.

App History: As with the Performance tab, this tab shows resource usage for specific apps you've used over a given period.

Startup: Once found in the System Configuration (MSCONFIG) window, this tab lists program that start automatically when you sign in to Windows.

Users: Also related to the Performance tab, this tab shows resource consumption by user. Typically, only your account is shown in the list, though other people can share the same PC.

Details: This tab shows the individual tasks related to the programs listed on the Process tab. See the later section "Connecting programs to processes."

Services: On this tab you find the individual activities carried out by many of the Windows background processes. See the later section "Enjoying the services" for more information.

In the Big Picture, the Task Manager window is frequently used in combination with the System Configuration (MSCONFIG) utility as well as the Performance Monitor and Resource Monitor to diagnose and troubleshoot Windows problems.

>> Refer to Chapter 3 in this minibook for information on MSCONFIG.

>> The Performance Monitor and Resource Monitor are covered in Book 5, Chapter 1.

TECHNICAL STUFF

>> As the Task Manager window has transformed over the years, so have its tabs. The Processes tab was formerly called Applications. The Details tab in the Windows 10 Task Manager is similar to the Windows 7 Processes tab. And, as I mention in this section, the Startup tab was once found in the MSCONFIG utility window.

Connecting programs to processes

A connection exists between the items on the Task Manager's Processes and Details tabs. Each item listed as a process is connected to one or more items listed as details. You can view the relationship yourself, as illustrated in Figure 6-3.

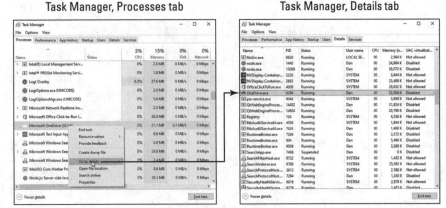

Task Manager, Processes tab   Task Manager, Details tab

FIGURE 6-3:
How a program relates to a process.

To explore the connections on your PC, follow these steps in the Task Manager window:

1. **Right-click on an item listed on the Processes tab.**

   You can choose one of your programs or one of the myriad things Windows does. If the item expands, choose a subitem. And you can't choose the Task Manager itself, for some reason, though it too has a related entry on the Details tab.

2. **Choose Go to Details from the shortcut menu.**

   The Task Manager window switches to the Details tab, highlighting the program that started the program or process. For example, from Figure 6-3, the Microsoft OneDrive cloud storage utility is named OneDrive.exe.

I use the Go to Details command in several ways. First, when I want to know a program's real name, showing its details is a nifty trick. That's because programs don't always use their actual program names; Microsoft Word is called WINWORD. EXE. Second, I believe that it's a more direct way to end a process than to end a program, especially for stubborn programs that won't die. See the later section "Halting a process on the Details tab."

TECHNICAL STUFF

Technically speaking, a single program is capable of running multiple processes. The Task Manager's Processes tab is misnamed in that respect. What you see listed as a "process" is really a program or an application. Items shown on the Details tab are really processes. I have no idea why Microsoft is messing with the nomenclature, other than they seem to want to rename desktop computer "programs" to be similar to mobile "apps," which is nonsense.

Examining all the processes

Windows runs a lot of *processes*. These are individual programs that perform tasks for Windows in the background, as well as for programs you run in both the foreground and background. The messy lot is shown on the Details tab in the Task Manager window.

The list of processes acts as a large table: Click a column head to sort the list: Name for the process name (its program name), User Name for the user who owns or started the process, CPU for the number of CPU cycles the process consumes, and other items.

Here are some interesting things you can do when examining the processes listed on the Task Manager's Details tab:

>> To see what's making the PC run slowly, use the CPU column to sort the Details list. Ensure that items consuming CPU time appear at the top of the list. One of them may be the culprit that's consuming all the PC's power.

>> Don't freak out when the System Idle Process uses a vast amount of the CPU's time — sometimes, up to 99 percent. That's normal. Running the System Idle process is what the computer does when it's not doing anything else. That's probably because the computer doesn't have its own Facebook account.

>> Duplicate entries in the Details list might indicate the presence of malware. Though be aware that some Windows processes (such as svchost.exe) have multiple entries. By themselves, multiple entries aren't a sign of trouble.

>> See Book 4, Chapter 3 for more information on fighting and removing malware.

>> Sort the list by username to view which processes were started by Windows (or SYSTEM), which are owned by your account, and which belong to other owners.

WARNING

>> Yes, the End Task button is used to kill off a selected process. Don't use this button randomly, because it adversely affects Windows.

FRIEND OR FOE: SVCHOST.EXE AND RUNDLL32.EXE

Two processes that lurk on the Task Manager's Details tab are often a source of confusion for budding Windows troubleshooters. They are the RuntimeBroker.exe and svchost.exe programs. Both are single programs (or processes) that provide a plethora of services in Windows. Yes, a plethora.

The RuntimeBroker.exe process deals with app permissions. It plays a role in the bigger picture of security and privacy, so it shouldn't be disabled.

The svchost.exe process runs multiple copies (or instances) of itself in Windows. Therefore, you find several svchost.exe entries listed on the Task Manager's Details tab.

The big issue with both services is that many of the Bad Guys like to name their malware RuntimeBroker.exe or svchost.exe just to confuse and anger you. See Book 4, Chapter 3 for details on hunting down malware.

Enjoying the services

The Services tab in the Task Manager window details *running services.* These are duties carried out by the various processes shown on the Details tab. Some processes may have only one duty, but many of Windows processes carry out several services. These services work to create the Windows computer environment, and do things for you without requiring much attention.

For example, a service updates network folders to reflect their current contents. This service runs constantly, though some services start on demand and others might run manually or when requested.

The job of the Services tab in the Task Manager is to list services. You can see the service name, a description, and whether the service is running or stopped. More information, however, is available in the Services console: Click the Open Service link near the bottom of the Task Manager window to view the console and control the various services directly.

The Services console is shown in Figure 6-4. I consider it a look-only location; you don't want to arbitrarily shut down or start up services when you don't really know what they do.

Service name   Useful description

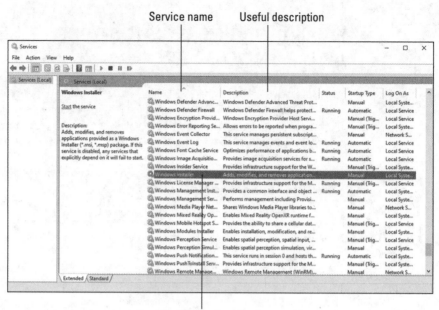

FIGURE 6-4:
The Services
console.

Double-click to view details

To examine a service, double-click its entry in the console window. You see a Properties dialog box for the service, where you can stop it, start it, or edit its contents.

>> The Description column is quite useful, helping you discover what a
service does.

>> Some nerds go to the trouble of disabling services not required by their PCs;
for example, deactivating the touch-input service on a desktop PC without a
touchscreen monitor. This procedure *might* improve performance, but a
Windows Update or System Restore can undo the changes, which are tedious
to make. I've never experienced any system boost from disabling services.

>> The command to run the Services console directly is

TECHNICAL
STUFF

```
mmc services.msc
```

mmc is the program name of the management console, and *services.msc* is the
name of the Services plug-in for the console.

Here a Task, There a Task

Beyond all the gussied-up graphics and features, the core purpose of the Task
Manager window is to manage your programs — specifically, to deal with some
programs that may become stubbornly stuck or otherwise obstinate.

Ending a stuck program

In a victory for hardware engineers, it happens often that computer programs die. Of course, the software factions can gleefully point out that when certain software dies, other software can help remedy the situation. (When hardware dies, the other hardware doesn't offer help.)

A variety of terms are used to describe the act of a program biting the digital dust: *crash, hang, torque, die,* and others too foul to mention. The term used by the Task Manager is *not responding,* which appears next to a program on the Processes tab when the program has crashed, hanged, torqued, or died.

To help evict a nonresponsive program, follow these steps:

1. **Summon the Task Manager window.**

Press Ctrl+Shift+Esc.

2. **On the Processes tab, select the nonresponsive program.**

3. **Click the End Task button.**

You may see a dialog box, questioning your desire. If so, click the End Now button.

No evil lies beneath the End Now button. It merely sends the "quit" signal to the program. It's more of a direct line of communication, especially when a program's window is nonresponsive.

TIP

>> You can use the End Now button in the Task Manager window to quit any program, whether the program is responsive or not.

>> Avoid using the End Now button to halt background processes and Windows programs listed on the Task Manager's Processes tab. Instead, disable those tasks on the Startup tab. See the later section "Disabling startup programs."

>> If the End Now button fails, sign out of Windows. You don't need to restart the PC, but by signing out, you halt most processes anyway. If signing out doesn't work, restart the PC.

>> Programs can also get stuck when Windows shuts down. Refer to Book 2, Chapter 9.

Halting a process on the Details tab

Programs on the Task Manager's Processes tab have a direct relation to processes (my term) on the Details tab. Refer to the earlier section "Connecting programs to processes" for more grousing, but my point is that the Details tab lists running programs, and it sports an End Task button just like the Processes tab, covered in the preceding section.

Sometimes, when I'm desperate to terminate a program, I obey these steps:

1. **Right-click the pesky program entry on the Processes tab.**

2. **Choose Go to Details from the shortcut menu.**

The program's specific process is highlighted on the Details tab.

3. **Click the End Task button.**

A warning dialog box may appear, reminding you that ending a process isn't to be taken lightly.

4. **Click the End Process button.**

The process is slain.

WARNING

Randomly killing processes can render your PC inoperable. It's not a Terrible Thing, but you need to restart Windows (or reset the computer) to regain control.

Disabling startup programs

A good way to disable consistent problem programs is to prevent them from starting in the first place. This technique is necessary for *background* programs and processes — those that start automatically when Windows runs or after you sign in to your account.

To review the startup and background programs, click the Startup tab in the Task Manager window. You see a list of the background programs that are started after you sign in to your account, similar to the list shown in Figure 6-5.

To disable a startup program, follow these steps:

1. **Select the program on the Task Manager's Startup tab.**

2. **Click the Disable button.**

The program's Status column changes to read *Disabled*.

Selected startup program

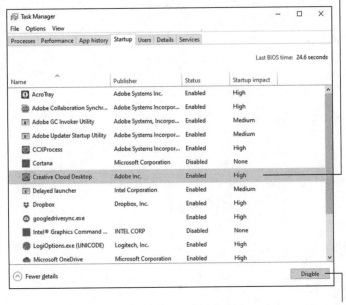

FIGURE 6-5:
Startup
programs.

Disable selected startup program

Disabling the startup program doesn't kill it off; the program won't start the next time you sign in to Windows. To prove that you were successful, sign out of Windows and sign back in again.

REMEMBER

>> Startup programs provide background services for your Windows session. Some, such as PC security and antivirus programs, are required.

>> In Figure 6-5, you see the Cortana utility disabled. This feat can be accomplished from the taskbar's shortcut menu.

>> If the startup program is bothering you, check for an update after you disable it. The newer version may have fixed the program that irks you.

>> If the startup program is preventing other programs from running, boot Windows in Safe mode. In this mode, disable the startup program and then start Windows normally. Refer to Chapter 4 in this minibook for details on Safe mode.

>> Many startup programs also appear as icons in the taskbar's notification area. It's possible to stop some of these programs by clicking on the notification icon and choosing a Close or Exit command. Not every taskbar notification icon offers this feature and, of course, not every startup program appears as a notification icon.

Chapter **7**

The Windows Registry

T he Registry isn't a troubleshooting tool as much as it can be a pain in the rump. It helps to know about the Registry, how to make modifications, and what to avoid. Beyond that, and if you're in a hurry, just read the last section in this chapter, which covers so-called Registry "cleaners."

Behold the Registry

Microsoft created the Registry to solve several problems. Number one was to provide a central location for all the options, settings, and configurations for Windows, your user account, and all your programs. This massive berg of information is jammed into a single unit, called the *Registry*.

More importantly, Microsoft created the Registry to thwart attempts by enthusiasts and hackers to discover secrets and surreptitiously modify Windows settings. One reason that using the Registry is obtuse is that Microsoft's efforts were successful: The Registry is a foreboding, twisted knot of confusion and technology.

REMEMBER

The bottom line is that the Registry doesn't hold secrets. Settings made in the Registry can just as easily be viewed or changed by using Windows itself. A few items hidden in the Registry, however, require you to delve into its depths. Just don't expect anything to overwhelm or thrill you.

>> The Registry contains information used by Windows and your programs. It helps the operating system manage the computer and programs to use the computer's resources.

>> A program may use the Registry to keep options, settings, and a list of recently opened files.

TECHNICAL STUFF

>> The Registry took over the role of the INI (initialization) files that once thrived in Windows. Over time, the INI (say "innie") files grew cumbersome and slowed down the operating system. The Registry provided a solution as a consistent location for Windows and program settings.

Understanding the Registry

The Registry is essentially a database. Its information is stored in various secret locations, though *dynamic* information is kept in the computer's memory. All the data is organized by using a structure similar to folders in the file storage system.

The top level of the Registry contains *hives,* each of which starts with the curious word *HKEY.* Table 7-1 describes the visible hives in the Registry. (The Registry has other hives that are used internally and are not of significance, despite your disbelief. Honestly, you should get it out of your head that secret things dwell in the Registry!)

TABLE 7-1: **Registry Hives**

Name	Abbreviation	Contents
HKEY_CLASSES_ROOT	HKCR	Information used by programs for file association and for sharing information
HKEY_CURRENT_USER	HKCU	Settings and configuration for the current user
HKEY_LOCAL_MACHINE	HKLM	Settings and configuration for all users
HKEY_USERS	HKU	Settings and configuration for all users on the computer; the information in HKCU is copied from this hive when the user logs in
HKEY_CURRENT_CONFIG	N/A	Hardware information about the PC's resources and configuration

Beneath the hives are folders, or *keys*. Keys can also have *subkeys*, just as folders have subfolders. The object is organization.

Keys contain *values*. Every value has a name and data, which can be numeric, binary, or text. You can find several values in a single key, or a key can be empty or contain only subkeys.

As with files and folders, you locate keys and their values in the Registry by following a *pathname*. For example, the following pathname leads to the key where Windows stores all its Registry information:

```
HKCU\Software\Microsoft\Windows\CurrentVersion
```

I used the abbreviation HKCU for HKEY_CURRENT_USER in the preceding line. It's followed by the subkeys *Software*, *Microsoft*, *Windows*, and, finally, *Current-Version*. The subkeys at that location detail all Windows settings, plus details for Windows' own programs, apps, and colorful whatnot.

Keys, like pathnames to files, can get long. Sometimes, a key name that's too long to fit on a single line must be wrapped, such as

```
HKCU\Software\Microsoft\Windows\CurrentVersion\Explorer\
    VisualEffects\CursorShadow
```

This key contains a binary value that determines whether Windows displays a shadow on the mouse pointer. The line is too long to fit on the page, so it wraps.

Incidentally, the CursorShadow key helps demonstrate a point I continue to drive home: You can easily turn the mouse pointer shadow on or off by using the Pointers tab in the Mouse Properties dialog box. You need not delve into the Registry, nor is there any benefit to do so.

>> To view or modify the Registry, the Registry Editor program is used, as covered in the next section.

>> Some keys are empty, though they still contain a *Default* value. That's because all keys must contain a value or a subkey.

TECHNICAL
STUFF

>> The Registry concept exists in all modern computer operating systems. In Unix, for example, custom settings are kept in the /etc directory. In Mac OS X, settings dwell in a Library folder.

Using the Registry Editor

To view, modify, or create information in the Registry, you use the Registry Editor utility. It's also known by its filename, regedit.

To run the Registry Editor, follow these steps:

1. **Press Win+R to summon the Run dialog box.**

2. **Type** regedit **and press Enter.**

3. **Click the Yes button or type the administrator's password to continue.**

    Behold the Registry Editor window on the screen, as shown in Figure 7-1.

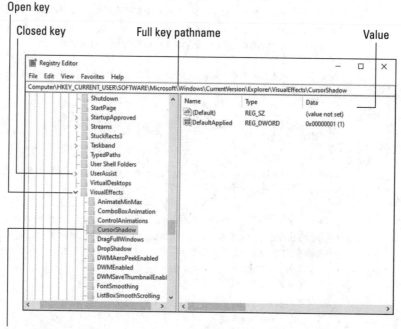

FIGURE 7-1:
Registry Editor.

The Registry Editor window uses a tree structure to display the various keys: To open a key, click the triangle next to it. Values appear on the right side of the window, as shown in Figure 7-1.

Close the Registry Editor window when you're done messing around.

TIP

>> A pathname appears on the Registry Editor window's status bar (refer to Figure 7-1), which helps you better determine which key is selected. You can use this status bar to type a key directly.

>> You can explore the Registry, view things, waste time there. But don't view the Registry as a playground or an opportunity to discover more about your computer. Use the Registry only when you must, such as when directed to do something by documentation or technical support people.

WARNING

>> All the information organized into keys and values is vitally important to Windows. Don't experiment with the Registry by modifying values to see what happens. Doing so can have adverse effects on your computer.

Backing up the Registry

A healthy thing that any sane user does before messing with the Registry is to back it up. Back up! Back up! Back up! I shan't be sick of screaming this mantra!

Follow these steps to back up the Registry:

1. In the Registry Editor, choose File ⇨ Export.

The Export Registry File window appears. It works like a typical Save As dialog box.

2. Choose a location for the backup.

If you're troubleshooting, choose the desktop as a good, temporary location for the backup. Otherwise, pick a folder where you can find the backup, should you need it.

3. Type a name for the backup.

I name the backup based on the reason for backing up — for example, Removing Files from MRU Lists.

4. Click the Save button to save.

5. Proceed with whatever you plan on doing in the Registry.

6. Close the Registry Editor window when you're done.

To restore a Registry backup, choose File ⇨ Import in the Registry Editor.

>> A backup of the Registry is made when you set a restore point in Windows. See Chapter 5 in this minibook for more information on System Restore.

>> If your Registry misadventures cause severe problems, start the PC in Safe mode for recovery. See Chapter 4 in this minibook.

Modifying the Registry

You can do several things with the Registry:

>> Add a new key.

>> Add a new value.

>> Rename a key or value.

>> Change an existing value.

>> Delete a key or value.

I strongly recommend that you take any of these actions only upon direction from some authority, such as tech support or valid documentation. Avoid hacks or tricks presented at nontechnical sources, such as social networking sites. The Registry isn't a playground or a place to experiment — even on your spouse's laptop.

Here are the general steps you take to modify the Registry:

1. **Start the Registry Editor.**

   Refer to the directions found earlier in this chapter.

2. **Back up the Registry.**

   Refer to the earlier section "Backing up the Registry."

3. **Open the key containing the item you want to modify.**

   The authority tells you the key's pathname; for example:

   ```
   HKCU\Software\Microsoft\Windows\CurrentVersion\Explorer\
      Advanced
   ```

   Start at the top level, the *hive*. Then open successive folders until you find the key you're looking for. The key just mentioned contains numerous Windows settings.

The changes you make to the Registry may or may not take effect right away. Sometimes, you need to restart Windows to test the changes. Sometimes, you can get away with simply restarting a given program.

WARNING

» The Registry Editor window remembers which keys were open the last time it was used. Because of this memory, you may have to scroll to the top part of the left pane and close the top-level hives to better maneuver around the various keys.

» You must be precise when creating or renaming a key or value! A misnamed key or value may not harm Windows, but then again it has no effect whatsoever.

» I don't consider web pages or advice from an Internet chat room a "higher authority" for modifying the Registry.

» Only when you can confirm directions from two separate sources on the Internet should you consider following those directions to modify the Registry. Even then, be sure to check that the two sources aren't just duplicate copies of the same information.

» One of the best sources of Registry information is the Microsoft support site: support.microsoft.com.

Making specific Registry changes

You can perform several activities inside the Registry after you arrive at the proper key:

Create a new key

To add a new key (folder) to an existing key:

1. **Select the parent key.**

2. **Choose Edit ⇨ New ⇨ Key from the menu.**

   The new key appears, with its name (New Key #1) selected for editing.

3. **Type the key's name and press Enter.**

The key is created, but it's empty; it contains no values. The next step is probably to create a value for the key.

Add a new value

To add a new value to an existing key or a new key:

1. Ensure that the key (folder) is selected.

The value is added to the right side of the window, which displays the key's contents.

2. Choose Edit ➪ New.

3. Select the data type from the New menu.

The authority you're referencing should specify which data type to choose. After you choose the data type, the new value appears in the key. Its name is selected, ready for renaming.

4. Type the value's name.

Creating a value doesn't set the value's data. (Well, it sets the data to zero.)

5. Double-click in the Data column next to the new key.

An Edit dialog box appears with the value name listed.

6. Type the value and click OK.

The value is assigned to the key.

The only scary value is Binary, which involves typing hexadecimal (base 16) digits. Again, the reference you're using tells you what to type.

Rename a key or value

It's possible to rename a key or value, mostly to preserve an existing key as a backup. To do so:

1. Select the key or value to rename.

2. Press the F2 key.

F2 is the Rename keyboard shortcut in Windows; specifically, in the File Explorer program.

3. Type the new name and press Enter.

The key or value has a new name, though keep in mind that Windows and your programs look for the old name. In some cases, when the old name isn't present, the key is re-created.

Change a value

Perhaps the most common Registry chore is changing a value:

1. Double-click the value to summon an editing dialog box.

The Edit dialog box is customized for the type of data the value stores.

2. Type the new data.

3. Click OK.

The value is updated.

Delete a key or value

To remove a key or value:

1. Select the key or value.

2. Press the Delete key on the keyboard.

Deleting a key deletes all the key's values and all the subkeys and all their values.

WARNING

3. Click the Yes button to confirm.

Depending on the item, Windows or a program may re-create the key.

Finding stuff in the Registry

Occasionally, you know that something exists in the Registry but you don't know *where* it exists. In these instances, you summon the power of the Registry Editor's Find command to help you locate the text or information tidbit you desire. Here's how:

1. Start the Registry Editor.

2. Back up the Registry.

"Oh, but I'm just finding something." Sure you are. Back up anyway. Directions are found earlier in this chapter, in the section "Backing up the Registry."

3. Scroll to the top of the left side of the window and click the word *Computer*.

When Computer is selected, you ensure that your search starts at the beginning of the Registry.

4. **Press Ctrl+F.**

   The Find dialog box appears.

5. **Enter the text you want to find.**

   For example, enter the name of a file that appears in a most recently used (MRU) list.

6. **Click the Find Next button.**

7. **Review the key or value to ensure that it's the one you're looking for.**

   Depending on how detailed you were, some false positives might occur in the search.

8. **Click the Find Next button, if necessary, to locate the next tidbit in the Registry.**

9. **Do whatever task needs completing when you find what you're looking for.**

Indeed, the Registry is huge. Sometimes, a search can take a long time to complete. Yet that's why the Find command exists.

>> I close the Find dialog box after the first found result. You don't have to close the dialog box, but it does get in the way.

>> Use the F3 key to repeat the last Find command. The F3 shortcut is handy because it lets you repeat a search without reopening the Find dialog box.

TIP

Registry Cleaning

Oh, how many times do I need to say that you don't need to mess with the Registry? I shouldn't even bother repeating myself, but I do. To bring the message home, I'd like to address the issue of cleaning the Registry. In a word: Don't.

Some third-party utilities claim that they can somehow miraculously scour the Registry and remove redundant entries and unused keys and values or purge the rotting remnants of nasty things.

Though cleaning out dead Registry entries might make sense, it's not anything you should concern yourself with. If the Registry has any such issues, Microsoft would have developed a Registry defragmenter type of utility a long time ago.

They haven't. That says a lot. Therefore, I don't recommend getting or using a Registry cleaner or even attempting to do so on your own.

WARNING

>> Many of those free Registry cleaners that you download from the Internet are really spyware or some other form of malware. They serve only to slow down your computer, making the problem worse.

>> Honestly, it would be impossible for any third-party program to know which Registry keys are useless and whether they can be deleted. To assume that any program would know that information is ridiculous.

>> Cleaning the Registry may do more damage than good.

>> No evidence exists that any Registry cleaning utility provides any improvement in performance.

>> See Book 4 for important information on PC security.

Chapter **8**

Events and Diagnostics

There's no point in asking a child, or a politician on the witness stand, why they did something. The answer is either "I don't know" or "I don't remember." That's because children, as well as politicians, don't like to be held accountable. Your computer is neither a child nor a politician. As such, it dutifully keeps records of what it does, when it does it, and the outcome. The computer is also brutally honest about reporting its activities. You can use that information to help troubleshoot and maintain your PC if you follow the advice and information presented in this chapter. Honestly!

What Has Gone On Here?

Sophisticated operating systems keep track of all activities in *log files.* Just about anything that goes on in the computer — from a user logging in (get it?) to programs crashing to routine tasks being scheduled — is noted in a log somewhere.

> » Even with a log file, troubleshooting can be difficult. Often, an event or program that crashes the system is too quick for a note to be made in a log file.

TIP

>> The best way to use the logs is to confirm an error after the fact. So, when the computer randomly restarts or an update fails, you can review the logs to see whether any errors or warnings occurred before the event. If so, you can better pinpoint the cause.

>> You don't really "log" in to Windows 10 — you sign in. The original term was *log in* or *log on*.

TECHNICAL STUFF

>> Windows wasn't always as sophisticated as it is today. Early versions lacked a log file.

Reviewing events

Many activities carried out in Windows create entries in a log file. These activities are related to the various services and processes Windows runs in the background, though some activities are triggered by your actions.

Rather than keep a single log file, Windows keeps several logs or journals of its activities. The program that lets you access the logs is called the Event Viewer. Obey these steps to access this program:

1. Tap the Windows key on the keyboard.

2. Type Event Viewer

3. Choose the top search result, Event Viewer app.

The Event Viewer console appears. It categorizes items by their source and the type of event.

4. Open the Windows Logs folder.

5. Choose the System log.

A list of events populates the center of the window.

6. Choose an event to display details in the window.

In Figure 8-1, the Event Viewer shows an event in the Windows System log. You see the three types of events: information, warning, and error.

Most events are routine, classified as informational. Even those events that show a warning or an error might be routine. The only way to know for certain is to review the information associated with the event.

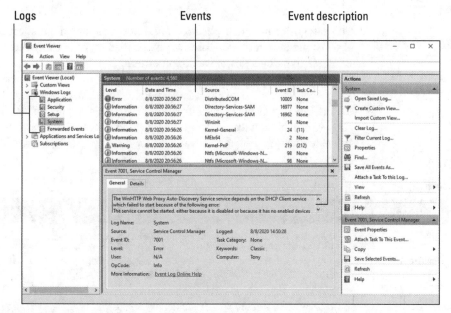

Logs   Events   Event description

FIGURE 8-1:
The Event Viewer.

Understanding events

Events, also known as "all those things that happen inside your computer," are classified in the Event Viewer. Each event is associated with a specific log based on the event category. Overall, two folders hold the various categories:

Windows Logs: These logs contain events belonging to Windows or the programs included with Windows, such as Windows Defender.

Applications and Services Logs: These logs list events associated with specific programs, though not every program has a log item in this folder.

Table 8-1 describes the logs located in the Windows Logs folder.

TABLE 8-1:   **Event Categories**

Windows Log	Type of Events That Are Monitored
Application	Windows programs that are not specifically the operating system itself
Security	Items pertaining to system security
Setup	Events relating to application installation and configuration
System	Things that go on in Windows itself, such as startup events and device driver use
Forwarded Events	Events on network computers (with a subscription set up in order to see these types of events)

Events and Diagnostics

The categories in the Applications and Services logs depend on which programs are installed on your PC. Common categories include Hardware Events, Internet Explorer, Windows PowerShell, and others.

Each event listed in a log has a specific type. Most are informational, which means the entry says something like, "Hey! This happened." Others might indicate warnings or failures. Icons flag each event, and the various types are listed in Table 8-2.

TABLE 8-2:   **Event Types**

Type	What Happened
Error	Something bad happened, such as a service failed or data was lost.
Failure Audit	Something was attempted that didn't work, such as an illegal log-in or an attempt by a non-administrator to access administrator-level features.
Information	Something happened successfully.
Success Audit	Something was attempted and worked out, such as signing in to a remote PC; the opposite of a failure audit.
Warning	An event occurred that is worth noting but isn't specifically an error.

Warnings and errors may not indicate any trouble. Instead, they may imply that something didn't go as expected. Details are offered in the Event Viewer window. You can examine the description (refer to Figure 8-1) or click the Details tab for more information. Not everything presented is human-readable, or, even if you can read it, it might not be obvious what's going on.

Filtering and searching events

The true power of the Event Viewer is its capability to quickly present the information you need. You use filters to create a summary of log entries you're interested in — items that can best tell you what's happened in the computer.

A *filter* is like a search through the logs, though it's more sophisticated than a typical search: You specify the log, event type, time, and other information. This way, you see what you want without having to wade through the entire, boring log.

As an example, the following steps create a filter that shows only warnings and errors in the Windows logs:

1. **From the list of actions on the right side of the Event Viewer window, choose Create Custom View.**

   The Create Custom View dialog box appears.

   The difference between the Create Custom View and Filter Current Log actions is that Custom View is permanent; it becomes part of the Event Viewer window.

2. **Choose the event levels Critical, Warning, and Error.**

   Place check marks in those three boxes.

3. **Ensure that By Log is chosen.**

4. **On the Event Logs menu, choose Windows Logs.**

   Place a check mark in the box to select all Windows logs.

5. **Click the OK button.**

   Another dialog box appears.

6. **Give the log a name.**

   In this example, I use the name All the Bad Things.

7. **Click OK.**

   The custom view appears in the Custom Views folder, showing up with the name you assigned in Step 6.

Don't be alarmed when you see all the errors, warnings, and critical flags. These steps are created to show a summary of warnings and errors in all the system logs. Many of these events don't mean that anything is wrong with the computer — just that some task or activity didn't turn out as planned.

REMEMBER

Reviewing the logs is done mostly *after* something weird happens. The log files themselves always show some events with warnings or errors. But when you're tracking down a known issue, these warnings and errors may help you locate the source.

Diagnostics to the Rescue

Contrary to popular belief, a diagnostic isn't someone who doesn't believe in two gods. Nope, a *diagnostic* is a computer tool you can use to help diagnose (get it?) something that happened in your PC. It's a type of test that can confirm how or where something isn't running correctly.

Understanding diagnostics

Next to *plasma inducer* and *phase inhibiter, diagnostic* was one of the most common terms used in the TV series *Star Trek: The Next Generation.* But unlike those other terms, *diagnostic* is a real word that applies to a real computer tool that you can use for troubleshooting.

A diagnostic comes in two flavors: report and check.

A *report* type of diagnostic simply inventories what's available. For example, the System Information window presents an inventory type of diagnostic report. Its value lies in telling you what's up with the computer. Oftentimes, an internal hardware conflict or a malfunctioning device is obvious on this type of diagnostic report.

The *check* type of diagnostic is to computer hardware what a physical examination is to a human being: The hardware is tested. For a video display, it might mean that colors are displayed and various graphics modes reviewed. For a hard drive, information may be written to and read from the hard drive repeatedly to ensure reliability. This type of testing is a check type of diagnostic.

Star Trek, of course, showed various diagnostic "levels." Supposedly, the Level 1 diagnostic was the most intense, apparently forcing such introspective self-examination that the starship itself struggled with the process. The Level 3 diagnostic was more casual. All this is silliness when compared to the realistic diagnostics you can perform on your PC for troubleshooting purposes.

Viewing system information

The System Information window displays a summary of your PC's current hardware and software state. It's the type of diagnostic that offers a report, as opposed to probing and testing hardware or software.

To view the System Information window, follow these steps:

1. **Tap the Windows key.**

2. **Type** System Information

3. **Choose the top search result, System Information app.**

   The System Information window is shown in Figure 8-2.

The System Summary window, shown in Figure 8-2, lists an overview of your PC's hardware and software status. For more details, choose a specific item from the System Summary tree: Click the + button to expand a category.

Expand and collapse categories   Details

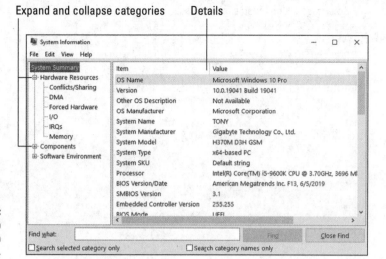

FIGURE 8-2:
The System
Information
window.

A lot of the details in the System Information window are quite technical. For example, the Memory category doesn't list installed memory; that detail is found in the System Summary window. Instead, you see memory addresses and how specific chunks of RAM are allocated in the system. This info is nifty, but boring.

Diagnosing DirectX

Microsoft introduced DirectX in the 1990s to help game programmers better use the PC's hardware muscle. The results are positive: Today, the PC remains a superior gaming platform. By allowing game programmers access to components such as memory, video, sound, and input devices, DirectX is a proven success.

You can use the DirectX diagnostic tool to check on not only how the DirectX system is working but also whether the PC has problems with video, sound, and other vital resources. Here's how:

1. **Press Win+R to bring forth the Run dialog box.**

2. **Type** dxdiag **and press Enter.**

3. **If prompted to check digitally signed drivers, click the Yes button.**

   Behold the DirectX Diagnostic Tool as it peruses your PC's system, as shown in Figure 8-3. It may take a few moments to run through its paces, so wait until it's done before you proceed.

4. **Click the Next Page button.**

   You want to see the text *No Problems Found* in the notes for each of the tabs.

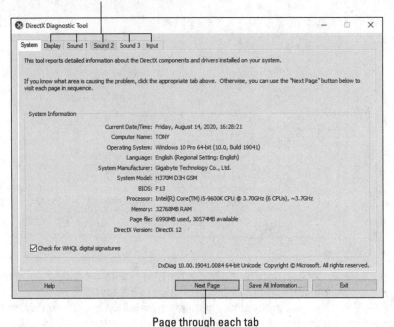

Don't miss out on these exciting tabs

Page through each tab

FIGURE 8-3:
The DirectX
Diagnostic Tool.

The pause taken by the DirectX Diagnostic Tool is caused by the diagnostic routines that are running. When these routines are complete, the tool displays its results on several tabs. Click the Next Page button to view information about each different part of your PC, those various things controlled by the DirectX software.

>> Like many diagnostic utilities, the DirectX Diagnostic Tool works best to confirm that a known problem exists. If you use the tool to check on the PC in general, pay attention to the Notes text box found at the bottom of some of the window's tabs. This text box lists any known problems or issues.

>> Your PC most likely has the best version of DirectX for whatever software you use. The only time you need a DirectX update is when you install new software that requires it. For example, when installing a new game, you may be prompted to upgrade to the latest version of DirectX. Do so at that time.

>> DirectX is smart enough that an older version cannot overwrite a more current version.

Running the Windows Memory Diagnostic tool

The Windows Memory Diagnostic tool scrubs and scours the PC's RAM to find problems or defects. It's not a solid diagnostic in that, well, it must run in memory to test memory. So there's a thin chance that it may not catch some problems, but it's a good tool to use when you suspect computer memory issues.

To run the Windows Memory Diagnostic tool, obey these steps:

1. **Save everything.**

The diagnostic procedure restarts your computer, so save your stuff, close windows, and get ready for a restart.

2. **Tap the Windows key on the keyboard.**

3. **Type** Windows Memory Diagnostic

4. **Choose the top result, Windows Memory Diagnostic app.**

5. **Choose the option Restart Now and Check for Problems.**

Wait until the computer restarts. When it does, the Memory Diagnostic Tool screen appears almost immediately. Wait while memory is checked thoroughly. Don't get bored; the display entertains you, as illustrated in Figure 8-4.

When the test is over, the PC restarts again.

6. **Sign in to Windows.**

The test results are displayed as a notification pop-up, which looks like Figure 8-5 when the diagnostic finds no errors.

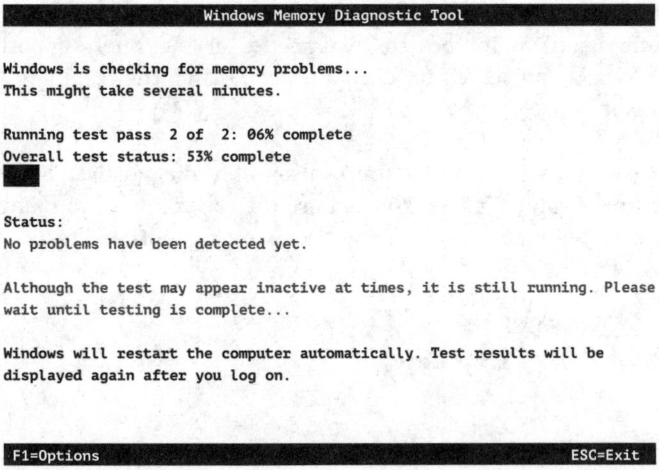

```
                        Windows Memory Diagnostic Tool

Windows is checking for memory problems...
This might take several minutes.

Running test pass  2 of  2: 06% complete
Overall test status: 53% complete


Status:
No problems have been detected yet.

Although the test may appear inactive at times, it is still running. Please
wait until testing is complete...

Windows will restart the computer automatically. Test results will be
displayed again after you log on.


 F1=Options                                                     ESC=Exit
```

FIGURE 8-4: The Windows Memory Diagnostic tool in action.

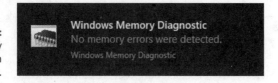

FIGURE 8-5:
The memory
diagnostic ran
successfully.

When a problem is detected with memory, the only solution is to find and replace that bad memory. In this circumstance, I recommend replacing all the PC's RAM. In fact, upgrade to more memory, which not only fixes the issue but also gives your PC a performance boost.

>> Adding more memory to a PC is the least expensive and most productive way to improve its performance.

>> Refer to Book 2, Chapter 4 for additional information on the PC's memory. Book 5, Chapter 3 also covers the advantages of adding more RAM.

WARNING

>> The Windows Memory Diagnostic tool isn't perfect. My most arduous trouble-shooting adventure involved the gradual replacement of every single computer component. Nothing seemed to fix the problem. Despite the Windows Memory Diagnostic reporting that memory was good, only when I fully replaced the PC's RAM (and upgraded to a larger capacity) did the hardware problem vanish.

Using other diagnostic tools

Windows is rather limited when it comes to diagnostic tools, which makes sense because Microsoft sells an operating system, not PC hardware. That hardware can vary from system to system, so when it comes time to look for diagnostic tools, you must hunt in the domain of the hardware manufacturer.

For example, Intel makes a slew of hardware diagnostic tools. You can find both motherboard and processor diagnostics at the Intel support web page: Visit `intel.com` and search for *diagnostic tool*. Match the results to the specific hardware on your PC.

Display adapter manufacturers also offer diagnostics. For example, NVIDIA features a control panel. You can use the control panel to manipulate the display adapter, but it also offers diagnostic reporting tools and tests.

Likewise, the network adapter may have its own diagnostic tool or a suite of tools available. These programs may have come with the hardware or be available online at the developer's support site.

>> Video diagnostics can be something to behold: The colors are fascinating. Watching the display adapter change between various text and graphics modes can be fun to behold. But mostly the diagnostic performs repeated tests that have no effect on the display.

TECHNICAL STUFF

>> The best diagnostics usually come on bootable discs. The reason is to ensure that the hardware is being examined without interference from Windows or other startup programs. Therefore, the program must run by itself and have direct access to the PC's guts. Even so, few diagnostic tools available to the public take the boot disc approach. Only professional diagnostic tools come on boot discs. Even then, few PC technicians use them, because it's cheaper to replace parts than it is to undertake a true, deep level of troubleshooting.

Events and Diagnostics

4

PC Privacy and Security

Contents at a Glance

Chapter **1**

PC Privacy

Who would think that connecting your personal computer — with all your private information, photos, banking data, and passwords — and connecting it to the Internet could somehow compromise your privacy? Not just the Bad Guys, but also online advertisers and marketing trackers want to know your every detail. With all that goes on in a Windows 10 PC, protecting your privacy has become an important part of keeping your PC secure.

» In this chapter, *app* refers to programs you run on the computer. Microsoft is following the mobile paradigm by renaming programs as apps. *App* is short for *app*lication, which is a fancy way to say "program."

On
» Many items in the Settings app feature an on–off master control, similar to what's shown in the margin. This graphical goober acts like a toggle: Click it to activate or deactivate a setting, placing the switch in the On or Off position, the opposite of its current position.

App Permissions

Modern PCs come with a variety of input devices, including a camera and microphone. These devices enrich the computing experience, providing for video chat and other useful and fun activities. Ensure that they look at you and listen into conversations only when you direct them to do so.

Setting general privacy options

To view the main privacy settings in the Settings app, follow these steps:

1. **Pop up the Start menu.**

   Press the Windows key on the keyboard.

2. **Click the Settings icon.**

   The icon is shown in the margin. Clicking it opens the Settings app.

3. **Choose Privacy.**

The General category lists overall privacy settings for the computer. If you prefer to keep everything to yourself, set all the master controls to the Off position.

TIP

>> I recommend deactivating the top item, which deals with advertising IDs. I leave the other items in the General category active.

>> Disabling advertising tracking doesn't do much to thwart the advertisers. These sneaks use multiple methods to discover who you are and what you do on the Internet.

Reviewing the permissions

To confirm which apps or programs have access to sensitive PC hardware, heed these directions:

1. **Press the Windows+I keyboard shortcut.**

   The Settings app appears.

2. **Choose the aptly named item Privacy.**

3. **Scroll down to view the App Permissions list on the left side of the window.**

   You see multiple items shown: Microphone, Voice Activation, and so on, as illustrated in Figure 1-1.

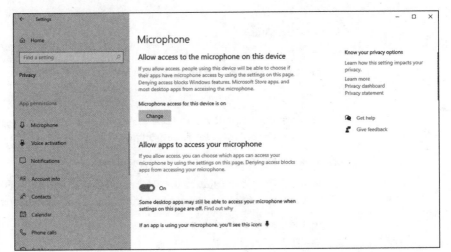

FIGURE 1-1:
Checking app
permissions.

4. **Choose an item in the list to view settings on the right side of the screen.**

   Later sections in this chapter cover specifics for some sensitive items.

For each hardware item, you find a Change button at the top of its settings, as shown in Figure 1-1. Use this button to allow or deny access to a device. For example, you could disable the computer's microphone, meaning no app has access.

To allow an app access, click the Change button and ensure that the master control is on (activated). Further, activate the switch by the option to allow apps to access the device.

Once the switch is active, you can peruse the list of apps to enable or disable access for each app, as covered in the next section.

Allowing camera and microphone access

With regard to security, perhaps the two most sensitive pieces of hardware on a computer are its camera and microphone. Follow these steps to confirm which apps have access to these hardware features:

1. **Tap the Windows key on the keyboard to pop up the Start menu.**

2. **Type** microphone

3. **Choose the item Microphone Privacy Settings.**

   The Settings app opens into the Privacy area, with the Microphone item highlighted.

4. Click the Change button.

5. If you want to have programs use the computer's microphone, set the master control to the On position.

Disabling the microphone means that no apps will use it or even know it exists.

6. Beneath the heading Allow Apps to Access Your Microphone, ensure that the master control is set to the On position.

By activating this option, you can choose which apps have access.

7. Scroll down the window to browse the apps that can access the microphone; activate or deactivate an individual app's permissions.

Set the master control to On or Off to allow or deny an app access to the microphone, as shown in Figure 1-2.

For example, if you don't see why a game would need access to the microphone, disable its access: Locate the game in the list (similar to Figure 1-2), and set its master control to the Off position.

To control access to the computer's camera, continue with these steps:

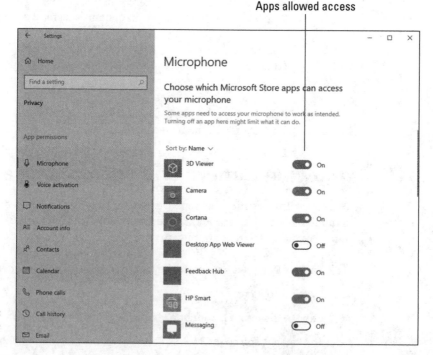

FIGURE 1-2:
Microphone permissions.

8. **From the list of app permissions on the left side of the Settings app window, choose Camera.**

   Not every PC has a camera; none is listed in Figure 1-2.

9. **Repeat Steps 4 through 7 to control which apps have access to the camera.**

Ideally, you want to grant access only to apps that truly need it. This admonition holds true for other hardware listed in the Settings app: To deny access to a hardware feature, choose the item from the left side of the window and then work through the list of apps presented in the window.

TIP

WARNING

>> Even if you disable microphone or camera access (refer to Step 5), some apps may prompt for access or — worse — won't run properly.

>> When an app is using the computer's microphone, the Microphone icon appears on the taskbar in the notification area, as shown in the margin.

>> If you're seriously concerned about the microphone picking up idle conversation or the camera capturing a raw moment, disable the hardware: Place opaque tape over the camera or, if the camera features a lens cap, close the lens cap. You can also disconnect an external microphone by unplugging it from the pink audio input connector.

>> Some programs may ignore the privacy settings regarding the microphone and camera. Don't blame me! Microsoft announces this warning at the bottom of the app's permission list in the Settings app. Further, it lists the apps that may bypass the Windows privacy settings. These apps access the PC's hardware directly.

Disclosing your location

Some laptops and practically no desktop PCs feature a GPS radio. This gizmo divulges the computer's location on Planet Earth to programs eager to use (and abuse) such information. Even if your computer lacks such sophistication, you can set a specific location to assist various programs that desire such details.

To review, set, or limit access to the computer's location, heed these directions:

1. **Open the Settings app.**

   Press the Windows+I keyboard shortcut.

2. **Choose Privacy.**

3. **Choose Location from the list of items on the left side of the window.**

4. Click the Change button.

5. Ensure that the master control is on so that location access is activated for the computer.

Location access is used by the Maps app as well as the Night Light feature's automatic sundown-to-sunrise setting. If you want to use these features, activate location access.

6. Beneath the heading Allow Apps to Access Your Location, set the master control to the On position.

With this setting active, you can choose which apps use the location settings.

7. To manually set your location, click the Set Default button.

The Maps app appears, allowing you to set your computer's current location.

8. Click the Set Default Location button.

If a default location appears, such as Home or Work, choose it, or choose the option Choose Location to use the Maps app to find a specific spot.

9. Close the Maps app when you've completed setting a location.

10. Scroll down in the Settings app to set which apps have permission to access your location.

The Maps and Weather apps make good choices to allow access to the computer's location information.

For a desktop computer, location data isn't a big deal. It helps apps such as Weather as well as the Night Light feature work properly. For a device with a GPS, consider disabling location services if you desire to keep your location private.

» GPS stands for *global positioning system*. It's a wireless radio that communicates with satellites to determine your current latitude and longitude. Mobile devices use this technology for navigation, but specific apps (such as weather apps) use it as well.

» When a program accesses the computer's location details, a Location icon appears on the taskbar in the notifications area, as shown in the margin.

» The Set Default button (refer to Step 7) may not appear on devices that use a GPS radio to determine the computer's location. (I have no such device available for testing.)

» It's rather silly to repeatedly set your laptop's location whenever you change locations. On my laptop, I set my home location and wherever the laptop ends up, I deal with it.

WARNING

» Though you may disable location access (refer to Step 5), your computer's IP address can still be used to guess your location to a certain degree. IP addresses aren't assigned geographically, yet enough web pages ask for location information that an informal location database has been constructed over time. It's fairly accurate.

Disabling Cortana

Windows 10 features a digital assistant named Cortana. She (and I'm assuming a gender here) is similar to Amazon's Alexa, Apple's Siri, and Google's whatever-it's-called services, responding to voice commands and performing various artificial intelligence tricks.

It's possible to banish Cortana from the taskbar as well as disable her helpful features. Heed these steps:

1. Right-click the taskbar.

2. Choose the Show Cortana Button option.

   If this item features a check mark, choosing it removes Cortana from the taskbar. This step doesn't disable Cortana, however. Continue:

3. Press the Windows key on the keyboard.

   Up pops the Start menu.

4. Type cortana and ensure that the Cortana app appears in the search results.

5. From the left side of the search results, choose the App Settings item.

   The Cortana app's Settings screen appears. If not, Cortana is already disabled and you're done.

6. Below the heading Runs at Log-In, deactivate the master control.

7. If it makes you feel better, disable the Microphone setting as well.

   This item may already be disabled if you worked through the earlier section "Allowing camera and microphone access."

Similar to Siri and Google Assistant, Cortana is constantly monitoring your utterances. Microsoft claims not to save this data, but so did Amazon, though they admitted to using random audio data for testing purposes. Whatever. If you feel better, deactivate Cortana.

On the Interwebs

The term *Interweb* was coined by writer J. Michael Straczynski, creator of the *Babylon 5* TV series. It was later picked up, inadvertently, by a US Senator who attempted to describe the Internet as a series of tubes. Today it's a humorous term for the Internet — specifically, websites. Like other scary things, it's important to guard your privacy when you use the Internet to visit a website — the Interweb.

Dealing with activity history

Despite your best efforts, you may find that Windows keeps track of your online comings and goings, which programs you run in Windows, and other activities that may seem innocent to you. Even so, better check. Follow these steps:

1. **Open the Settings app.**

   Press the Windows+I keyboard shortcut.

2. **Choose Privacy.**

3. **From the categories on the left side of the screen, choose Activity History.**

   Look what you've been up to! Well, nothing yet. But you see items listed that describe which activities are monitored.

4. **To prevent snooping, uncheck all the boxes and deactivate the master control.**

   That's it.

To view what Windows has been up to, click the link Manage My Microsoft Account Activity Data. The web browser opens and you're forced to sign in to your Microsoft account. Eventually you see a screen detailing which activities are tracked and stored. Yes, you're given an opportunity to clear each one, but be aware that the data has already been digested.

The link to view your Microsoft account activity data doesn't appear when you don't use a Microsoft account to sign in to Windows.

Guarding against web page tracking IDs

To guard your privacy while browsing the web, you must make settings in the web browser app. In this section, I cover the most popular web browser, Google Chrome, and Microsoft Edge.

Privacy settings in Google Chrome

To access Chrome's settings, follow these steps:

1. Click the 3-dot icon in the upper right corner of Chrome's window.
2. Choose Settings.
3. On the left side of the window, choose the category Privacy and Security.
4. In the Privacy and Security area, choose Security.
5. Select the Enhanced Protection option.

TECHNICAL
STUFF

If you're a nerd, you can access Chrome's security settings screen by typing **chrome://settings/security** on the address bar.

Microsoft Edge privacy settings

In Microsoft Edge, follow these steps to check on or update the current privacy settings:

1. Click the 3-dot icon in the upper right corner of Edge's window.
2. Choose Settings.
3. From the categories on the left side of the window, choose Privacy and Services.
4. On the right side of the window, select Strict.

   The Strict category employs the highest level of privacy settings.

TECHNICAL
STUFF

Nerds may rejoice by typing the following command on Edge's address bar to quickly access the privacy settings screen: **edge://settings/privacy**

» Installing an update

» Seeing what the updates do

» Updating applications

» Doing a BIOS upgrade

» Removing an update

» Restarting a stuck update

Chapter **2**

Keeping Software Current

S oftware is never truly "done." Programmers continue to hone their code, fixing bugs and adding features. For them, the process is an addiction, and as with most addicts, no end is in sight. Still, software updates offer improvements, plug holes, and deal with security issues, which makes them a necessary part of computer security as well as troubleshooting.

Windows Updates, Doesn't It?

It may not seem like a security issue, but keeping Windows up-to-date is perhaps the first and most important thing you can do to thwart the Bad Guys. It's also a good thing to do for your sanity, because the various updates and patches fix bugs and address other issues you might have with the operating system. The tool that makes it all possible is Windows Update.

Understanding Windows Update

Windows Update is a program, but it's also a service. It runs all the time, checking in with the Microsoft mothership to see whether anything new is available. If so, updates are installed automatically, often restarting Windows along the way.

To check the status of Windows Update, obey these steps:

1. **Press the Windows+I keyboard shortcut to open the Settings app.**

2. **Choose Update and Security.**

You see the Windows Update screen, illustrated in Figure 2-1.

Any pending updates would appear here

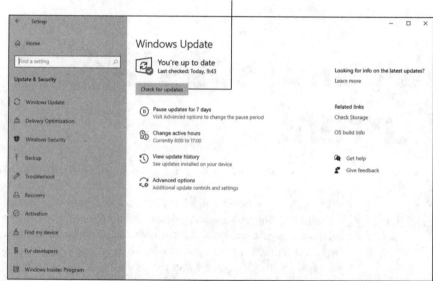

FIGURE 2-1:
Windows
Update in the
Settings app.

In Figure 2-1, no updates are looming. You can click the Check for Updates button to see whether anything is available; otherwise, all is hunky-dory.

When an update is available that requires you to restart Windows, a Restart button appears in place of the Check for Updates button. (Refer to Figure 2-1.) Your options are to restart at once; click the Restart button to proceed. Or you can wait and Windows restarts automatically at a preset time. A notification also appears, reminding you that a restart looms in your future.

>> Pending updates might be flagged directly on the main Settings app screen. If so, click the graphic to run Windows Update.

354   BOOK 4 **PC Privacy and Security**

REMEMBER

» Unlike in older versions of Windows Update, you cannot defer updates in Windows 10. In fact, some security updates fly in (usually, early Tuesday mornings) and force your computer to restart automatically. The only way to avoid this restart is to turn off your computer at the end of the day.

» A pending restart generates a notification. If you don't catch the pop-up notification, press the Windows+A keyboard shortcut to look for pending restarts and updates in the Action Center.

» Other programs run their own update services. For example, Adobe may pester you about updates, as does most third-party security software. See the later section "Other Software Updates."

Configuring Windows Update

Windows Update sports only a few configuration options. You can't skip an update, nor can you indefinitely postpone one, but you do have options. To review them, follow these steps:

1. **Press the Windows+I keyboard shortcut.**

The Settings app appears.

2. **Choose Update and Security.**

The following items are listed below the Check for Updates heading (or they appear under the list of pending updates):

Pause Updates for 7 Days: Choose this item to suspend any update restarts for seven days. The Check for Updates button changes to read Resume Updates. Click the Resume Updates button to end the 7-day suspension and immediately check for fresh updates.

Change Active Hours: This option lets you set a time range when Windows won't automatically restart your PC. For example, if you work 8 A.M. to 5 P.M., you can set these hours so that Windows Update doesn't interrupt you to beg for a restart.

View Update History: See the next section for details on this option.

Advanced Options: These options set items related to Windows Update, including update notifications. An item is available to pause updates for 35 days, though due to the frequency of security updates, I don't recommend using this option.

The angst of not knowing when your PC will reset overnight is quelled when you pay attention to the notifications: Press the Windows+A keyboard shortcut to view the Action Center and review any pending restarts. If you see one looming, visit Windows Update in the Settings app and click the Restart button to get it over and done.

TIP

I recommend pausing updates for your laptop if you're going to be on the road for a while with intermittent Internet access.

Reviewing updates

Windows dutifully records a log of all recent updates. This information is good to have to review an update's purpose, should you wish to unwind an update. To view the update log, obey these directions:

1. Press the Windows+I keyboard shortcut to open the Settings app.

2. Choose the Update and Security option.

3. Click the View Update History button.

You see a categorized list of recent updates, each specifying its date and whether it was successfully installed, as shown in Figure 2-2.

Update categories/types

Roll back an update

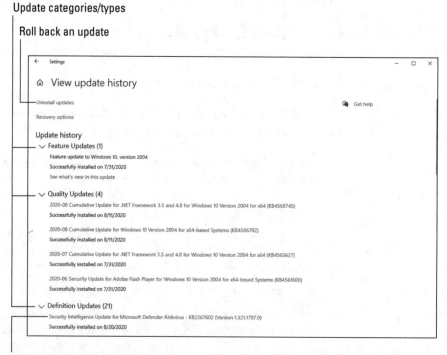

FIGURE 2-2:
Windows Update history.

View update details on the web

To see a description of the update, click the link. The web browser opens to display update details from the Microsoft support website.

The Uninstall Updates link is vital for when an update doesn't play well with your PC. See the later section "Undoing an update."

Updating drivers

The Windows Update service may or may not update *drivers* — these are the control programs that run specific software, such as the printer driver, display adapter driver, and network driver. In my travels, I've seen Windows Update add some of these drivers, but the practice is inconsistent.

To ensure that hardware drivers are updated, use the Device Manager as described in Book 3, Chapter 2. Confirm that the hardware is using the best possible driver, as described in that chapter.

Other Software Updates

Windows is the most important software in your computer, but it's not the only software. Other programs offer updates just as Windows does and for identical reasons. With a broadband Internet connection always on and ready, ensure that all your software is up-to-date to address bugs, security, and other issues.

Installing a program update

Programs update in one of three ways:

>> Automatically

>> By prompting you

>> Not at all

Most modern software — specifically, programs that come with a subscription, like Microsoft 365 and various antivirus utilities — update automatically. The updates may be prompted for, or you can check manually, as illustrated in Figure 2-3. Regardless, the update flies in and a new version is installed, or you're prompted to save your work and quit so that the update can be applied.

Check for updates

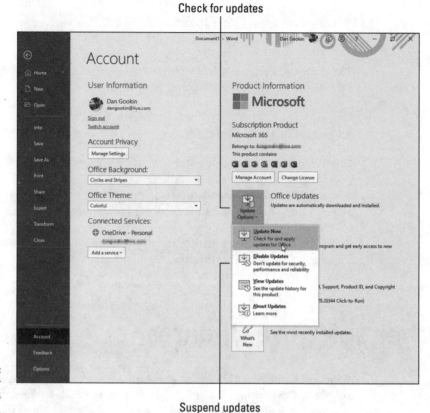

FIGURE 2-3:
Checking for
Microsoft 365
updates.

Suspend updates

Programs that don't automatically update are still good; it's often said that software never expires. Even so, newer versions may become available over time, offering bug fixes, better features, and security updates. When a program isn't updated automatically, the only way to know whether a newer version is available is to visit the developer's website. Often a command on the File or Help menu is available to check for an update.

>> Most software updates replace any currently installed version, even for a manual update. You don't need to uninstall the older version to install the new one. Further, none of your settings and associated files is removed during the upgrade process.

>> Automatic updates for subscription software continue as long as you keep the subscription current.

TECHNICAL
STUFF

>> The magic that makes automatic updates happen occurs either when the program starts (it peeks out on the Internet to check for a new version) or from a hidden program that checks for updates at regular intervals. These hidden programs, called *processes,* can be viewed in the Task Manager window. Refer to Book 3, Chapter 6.

Updating the firmware (BIOS)

The firmware dwells in silicon, swaddled in a chip on the computer's motherboard. Still, the contents of the silicon are software. Like other software, the firmware — also known as the *BIOS* — occasionally requires an update.

BIOS updates address everything you'd expect from a software update: improved features, bug fixes, and security concerns. Unlike other software, however, the computer can't start without a BIOS. This update may cause anxiety, but rarely does the process screw things up.

A BIOS update is provided by your computer's motherboard manufacturer. Most systems feature a utility that runs in the background (a *process*) that checks with the manufacturer's website for updates. When one is available, you see a notification alerting you to the pending update — perhaps with driver updates as well, if the manufacturer is exceedingly nice.

When you receive a BIOS update notification, carry it out: Follow the onscreen directions and then sit back and watch. The process takes a few minutes.

REMEMBER

>> The update process for the computer's BIOS involves restarting the computer. Therefore, save your stuff and close your programs before proceeding with the update.

>> Most BIOS updates take place on the Text mode screen. Welcome to 1987.

>> Modern PC firmware is smart enough to recognize when a BIOS update fails. If so, recovery options appear when the computer restarts. I've seen such a message once. It terrified me, but the computer was okay and survived until the next update.

TECHNICAL STUFF

>> A BIOS update occasionally uses the verb *flash*. This term describes the technology behind the process: The BIOS sits on a memory chip that uses flash RAM, similar to a thumb drive or media card. So you often hear the nerds say, "Flash the BIOS," which has nothing to do with taking pictures or wearing a trench coat.

Update Hiccups

Like everything with the computer, updating Windows or any other program may not go as well as you had hoped. Some updates cause problems. Sometimes, updating gets stuck. Solutions are available, but keep in mind that updating Windows is an important part of computer maintenance. It must be done.

Undoing an update

When an update doesn't go as planned, roll it back. You can do so within Windows, or, under dire circumstances, you can roll back an update from Safe mode or when using the Windows Recovery Environment.

First, if you can get into Windows, follow these steps to roll back an update:

1. **Press the Windows+I keyboard shortcut to open the Settings app.**

2. **Choose Update and Security.**

3. **On the right side of the window, choose the View Update History item.**

Refer to the earlier section "Reviewing updates" for an explanation of the Update History screen.

4. **Click the Uninstall Updates link.**

The Control Panel's Installed Updates window appears. It lists all updates that Windows monitors, which includes Windows updates as well as updates to third-party programs.

5. **Choose the update you want to undo.**

The updates are categorized by program and then by date. Choose the top item in the Microsoft Windows category to remove the most recent Windows update.

6. **Click the Uninstall button that appears on the toolbar.**

The toolbar appears above the list of recently updated programs.

Not every update features the Uninstall button. The button may not appear for a minor update.

7. **Follow the directions provided on the screen.**

If prompted to restart Windows, do so.

The update should be removed successfully and your system restored. If not, or when the computer won't start, boot the system into the Windows Recovery Environment and enter Safe mode, as described in Book 3, Chapter 4.

You can use System Restore to recover from a bad Windows update. If you can't access System Restore in Windows or in Safe mode, use the Windows Recovery Environment. Refer to Book 3, Chapter 1 for details.

Fixing a stuck Windows update

I have one laptop that keeps getting stuck when updating Windows. The progress bar doesn't move, and restarting Windows doesn't fix the bad update. The solution is to purge the temporary update files, or *cache*, which clears the pipes and allows the update to proceed.

If you have difficulty getting a Windows update to process, follow these steps:

1. **Pop up the Start button menu.**

2. **Type** command **to find the Command Prompt app.**

3. **From the list of actions on the right side of the search results, choose Run As Administrator.**

4. **Click the Yes button when prompted by the UAC.**

   Or, in the unlikely event that you don't have an Administrator account, type the Administrator's password to continue.

5. **Type this command:**

   ```
   net stop wuauserv
   ```

   Type the three words shown here, separated by spaces. Press the Enter key when you're done.

   The name of the Windows Update service is *wuauserv*. Upon success, you see the text

   ```
   The Windows Update service is stopping.
   The Windows Update service was stopped successfully.
   ```

   If you see a message claiming that the service isn't started, the problem isn't with Windows Update. More troubleshooting is required.

   If the service is running but can't be stopped, you must boot into Safe mode and try again.

6. **Type the command** cd %windir% **at the prompt.**

   It's the command **cd**, a space, and then **windir** surrounded by percent characters.

   The command prompt changes to reflect the Windows directory *(folder)*.

7. **Type the command**

   ```
   cd SoftwareDistribution
   ```

   Don't put a space between *Software* and *Distribution!* The SoftwareDistribution folder is where Windows updates lurk.

8. Type the command

```
del /F /S /Q Download
```

This command purges the files that Windows uses to update the system. It's okay to delete them, because the update has failed; Windows downloads them again when you're done.

With the files purged, the final step is to restart the Windows Update service.

9. Type this command:

```
net start wuauserv
```

The following text confirms success:

```
The Windows Update service is starting.
The Windows Update service was started successfully.
```

10. Close the Administrator Command Prompt window.

The cool kids type the **exit** command.

These steps should resolve the issue: The files that Windows couldn't use for the update are removed. Fresh files are downloaded automatically and then installed.

Chapter **3**

Keep Mr. PC Safe

Evil plots bubble and brew to dethrone you from your seat of power at the PC. Wicked software oozes into your computer from the Internet, invited or not. Once inside, it grows roots tangled and deep. Only skilled software can fully extract the infection. And, like any medieval fantasy plot, it's best to stop the Bad Guys before they cross the moat.

Malicious + Software = Malware

The jargon used to refer to evil software is no longer a diverse buffet of amusing, confusing terms. While nerds quibbled over the technical differences between a *virus* and a *worm*, some clever rogue combined the words *malicious* and *software* to come up with *malware*. It's the preferred term to describe all nasty software.

Protecting your PC

Despite its new name, malware is an ancient software category. Programs that do bad things are as old as programming itself. I'm sure some nerd, back in the 1960s, upon being terminated, wrote a program that ejected every sheet of paper from the teletype machine. As time passed, these programs grew more malevolent and, thanks to the Internet, more pervasive.

The first, best thing you can do to protect yourself from malware is to *learn more about your computer*. Honestly, you can't tell when something is wrong when you're unable to determine exactly what "right" is.

The second thing you can do is to not be a fool. Modern operating systems are sophisticated and always on the defensive. The way malware succeeds is by preying on human weakness. Computers become infected these days because people drop their guard and do stupid things. It happens to everyone, thanks to a psychological concept called social engineering.

MALWARE MALCONTENTS

phishing: The phishing scam involves a legitimate-looking email message or website. The goal is to fool you into signing in to your account — say, on a phony banking site — which gives the Bad Guys your account name and password. Pushy phishing sites may even ask for your account number, social security number, and other personal details.

spyware: This evil software monitors your movements on the Internet, sending information back to a central computer that then targets you with advertising. The worst part is that such software becomes nearly impossible to remove.

hijack: To redirect traffic on the web browser, sending you to advertising sites or redirecting all your searches. Hijacking infections typically masquerade as web page helpers or shopping assistants.

Trojan horse: This type of malware pretends to be a legitimate program. The program's ulterior motives are to delete data, compromise security, relay spam or porn, and otherwise infect your computer.

virus: Like its living counterpart, a computer virus infects your computer, taking control over some or all of its functions. The virus destroys data or looks for things like passwords, credit card numbers, or other sensitive data. This information is sent to another computer. A virus can also "own" your computer, turning it into a zombie box on the Internet. The *zombie box* is used to relay spam email or pornography or to coordinate attacks against websites on the Internet.

worm: This type of malware is a special form of virus. A worm replicates itself over a network. In addition to compromising your PC's security, the worm sends out a copy of itself to everyone in your email address book or to other computers on the local network.

Social engineering is the art of making people do things that they otherwise wouldn't. For example, you're fooled into opening an email attachment because the message claims that it contains a payment due to you, a receipt for an item ordered, or a compromising picture of a celebrity. Despite the warnings, you open the attachment. Your computer is infected. The Bad Guys win.

The final thing you can do to protect yourself from the malware tsunami is to use software tools to ensure that your computer hasn't been compromised, and to repair any damage done. These tools include an antivirus program, antispyware, and a firewall. The good news is that Windows comes with all these tools.

Obtaining malware (accidentally)

I knew a computer nerd who collected viruses. I did, too! I kept a copy of the old Melissa virus on my PC, just for test purposes. Then one day the Windows Defender program found it and killed it off. So much for experiments.

You probably don't set out to find malware. It happens. Sometimes you're aware of it right after it happens, but mostly you have no idea. Still, malware has only a limited selection of infection vectors:

Download from a web page: Even if your web browser watches for suspicious sites, you can still click a link to download malware. More frequently, malware piggybacks as an "extra" for legitimate software you obtain. Always read everything before you click the Download button.

An email attachment: Malware arriving as an email attachment is the same bad stuff that comes from a web page. The difference is primarily in social engineering: The malware is most likely disguised as a message from a friend or has another tempting aspect that entices you to open it.

Infected media: Back when floppy disks were popular, most malware arrived on infected media. This threat is far lower today because the Internet is the most common infection vector. Still, be on the lookout for infected thumb drives and media cards.

REMEMBER

The key to avoiding infection is to pay attention. Even if you run antivirus software, some people diligently disable it just so that they can open that email attachment claiming they inherited $10,000,000 from the former prime minister of Wambooli.

Surviving the malware scourge

You have two tools to keep your PC safe from the Bad Guys. The first tool is your own brain. For more details on using this tool, see the book *Your Brain For Dummies*. The second tool is a central location for all security in Windows, the Windows Security Center. To access this tool, heed these steps:

1. **Pop up the Start button menu.**

2. **Type** Windows Security **or as much of it as necessary until the Windows Security app item appears in the list.**

3. **Choose the Windows Security App item.**

You see the Windows Security Center window, delightfully illustrated in Figure 3-1.

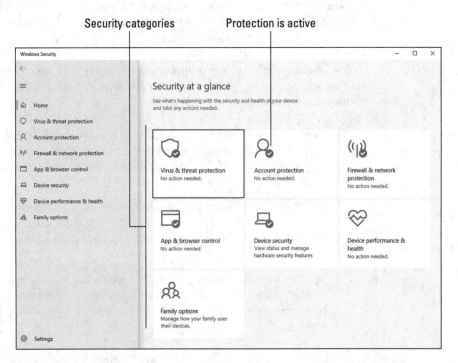

FIGURE 3-1:
The Windows
Security Center
window.

The Windows Security Center gives you an overall view of your PC's security status. Each tile in the window represents protection against a given threat: viruses, account, or firewall, for example. Click a tile to investigate an item further.

In Figure 3-1, you see green check marks by various items. This icon indicates that the item is operating normally. Yellow warning icons appear by items that need attention. Further, the Windows Security Center provides notifications on the taskbar when something requires your attention.

Defending Against Viruses and Malware

It took a long time, but eventually the Windows operating system was updated to include its own antivirus tool. Originally named Windows Defender, virus protection is now part of the Windows Security Center (refer to the preceding section). This protection is offered in both active and passive modes, and its definitions are regularly updated, thanks to the Windows Update process.

>> Refer to Chapter 2 in this minibook for details on Windows Update, which must be active to keep current the Windows Defender malware definitions.

>> Yes, the malware landscape changes so often that weekly updates are necessary.

>> You can use Windows Security in addition to third-party antivirus software. You don't really need to run two antivirus programs, but if doubling up makes you feel better, use both tools.

>> The term *computer virus* originates from the 1973 movie *Westworld,* written and directed by Michael Crichton.

TECHNICAL STUFF

>> The first computer virus was created back in the 1970s. Curiously enough, the second computer virus was created to track down and delete copies of the first computer virus. As the personal computer revolution caught fire in the mid-1980s, computer viruses broke out all over. It was the perfect storm of people who failed to understand their computers, pirated software, the Internet, and human weakness.

Understanding malware protection

An antivirus utility, such as the Virus & Threat Protection offered in Windows, features two modes of operation:

Passive: In this mode, the program lurks in the background and monitors the computer's activity, looking for malware.

Active: In this mode, the antivirus program probes all parts of the computer's memory and storage system, looking for signs of infection. Active scans can be done manually, or they take place on a schedule.

When a sign of infection is found, the antivirus software alerts you to its presence. The virus may be destroyed or the file quarantined for later examination. Later sections in this chapter describe how to deal with this situation.

Scanning for malware

Virus protection is on by default in Windows 10. To confirm, check the Windows Security Center, as covered in the earlier section "Surviving the malware scourge." If protection is deactivated, click the Virus & Threat Protection tile and follow the directions to activate it.

The Virus & Threat Protection tool runs in the background; you need to do nothing unless it finds an infection. You may, however, be notified to run a quick scan, especially if the computer or laptop has been turned off for some time. If so, follow these steps to perform a quick scan:

1. **Open the Windows Security Center.**

    Refer to the steps in the earlier section "Surviving the malware scourge."

    If it's been a while since a scan was done, you see a yellow flag on the Virus & Threat Protection tile. Click the Scan Now button just below the tile. Otherwise, continue:

2. **Click the Virus & Threat Protection tile.**

3. **Click the Quick Scan button.**

    The antivirus tool reviews sensitive locations and various files on your PC, scanning for signs of infection.

The scan takes time, even though the word *Quick* appears on the button. If a suspect item is located, you'll be alerted. See the next section for what to do.

TIP

>> To perform a more rigorous scan, click the Scan Options link. Select the Full Scan option. Click the Scan Now button.

>> If you suspect that a specific file or folder is infected, click the Scan Options link and select the Custom Scan option. Click the Scan Now button and then browse to the folder you want to scan, such as the Downloads folder if you suspect that a file you downloaded might not be what it claims.

Dealing with an infection

When the Virus & Threat Protection tool locates a suspected infection, the questionable file is immediately placed into quarantine. Yes, you can freak out at this point, but don't: Any damage has been thwarted. In the quarantine state, the file can do no harm, but you still must decide what to do with it.

To review any suspected infections, follow these steps:

1. **Open the Windows Security Center.**

Pop up the Start button menu and type **Windows Security** to search for and choose the Windows Security App item.

2. **Click the Virus & Threat Protection tile.**

3. **Choose the Protection History option.**

4. **Ensure that Quarantined Items is selected.**

5. **Click the View Details button.**

Quarantine items appear in a list. These are suspect files, and they can include some false positives.

You can deal with the quarantined items in three ways.

First, you can ignore the items. Your PC is safe, and the quarantined items stay that way.

Second, you can remove the suspected infections: Select an item and click the Remove button. Or click the Remove All button to purge the lot. The files are obliterated and won't bother you again.

Third, you can restore a false positive. For example, a file that you know is safe was found by Windows Defender as suspect. If so — and providing you *know* the file is safe — select it and click the Restore button. Further, you might consider setting this file as an allowed item so that it isn't falsely quarantined again.

➤➤ You don't need to perform an active scan to find an infection. Windows Defender works all the time.

➤➤ Items you remove from quarantine and set as allowed appear in the Allowed Items list. You can remove an item if you later discover that it is indeed malware.

Life Behind the Firewall

Think of the Internet as an open door, through which the rest of the world — everyone and every computer on the Internet — can stop by and visit your computer. In its gentle, knowledge-sharing beginnings, that's how the Internet worked: The free flow of information between scientists was more important than closed doors. Everyone was welcome.

The sad reality today is that every nasty computer on the planet is at the door between your computer and the Internet. Every minute of every day, visitors of questionable intent knock on this door. Do you let them in? Or do you leave the task of monitoring that traffic to a special piece of software called a firewall?

>> Windows comes with its own firewall program, conveniently named Windows Firewall. Like malware protection, it's on all the time. It works to monitor Internet traffic to ensure that visitors are welcome and guests are permitted to leave.

>> You need both antimalware and firewall protection on your PC. A firewall alone doesn't stop malware, especially when you're tricked into welcoming it in; Windows antimalware protection monitors network traffic.

Understanding the firewall

In construction, a *firewall* is designed to impede a fire from traveling from one place to another. Firewalls are rated by time, so a 1-hour firewall theoretically stands for one hour before the flames lick into the next room. Computer firewalls also prevent disaster from spreading, though they work immediately and don't wear down with time.

What the firewall does is monitor both incoming and outgoing Internet traffic. When a firewall is properly configured, only the information you request from the Internet is allowed in. Outgoing information can also be filtered.

When unrequested information tries to get in or out, the firewall instantly blocks it. If it's a new request, you're prompted to allow or block. So you have the final say-so: You can direct the firewall to allow known types of access and deny anything questionable. The firewall warns you only once; otherwise, you must use the Windows Firewall app to review a mistaken decision.

>> To keep your computer system secure while it's connected to the Internet, you need a firewall.

>> Firewalls come in both hardware and software versions. Windows Firewall is a software version. The broadband gateway (or router) may also feature a firewall, though I recommend using both.

>> You can test your computer's firewall by visiting the Gibson Research website. Visit grc.com and run the ShieldsUp! web app.

Using the Windows Firewall

Windows Firewall is on all the time — or it should be. Check the Windows Security Center window, as described in the earlier section "Surviving the malware scourge." If this window says that the firewall is off, follow the onscreen directions to activate it.

Normally, you don't visit the Windows Firewall program as it runs in the background. The only time you notice it is when an alert appears, as covered in the next section.

To witness the Windows Firewall and behold its interface, follow these steps:

1. **Tap the Windows key.**

2. **Type** Windows Firewall

3. **Choose the item Windows Defender Firewall Control Panel from the search results.**

   The Windows Firewall window is illustrated in Figure 3-2.

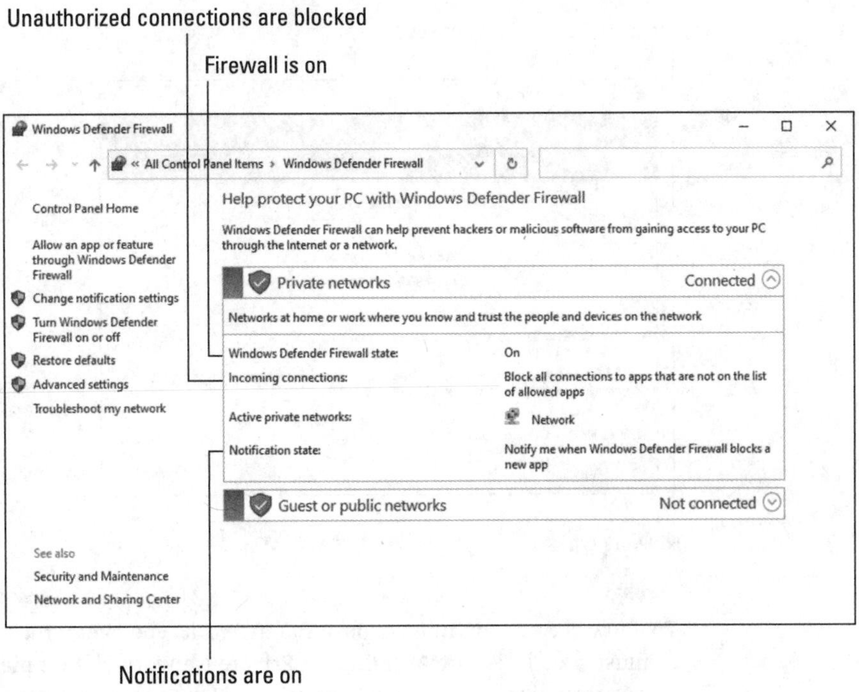

Unauthorized connections are blocked

Firewall is on

FIGURE 3-2:
Windows Firewall.

Notifications are on

The Windows Firewall window is boring, but it tells you three important facts: The firewall is on, unauthorized incoming connections are blocked, and you'll be notified of any unexpected access. These are good things to know.

At this point, you're pretty much done with the window. You can use the links on the left side of the window to change some of the settings, though if your window looks like the one shown in Figure 3-2, you have nothing else to do.

Dealing with a firewall alert

You see firewall warnings during one of three situations:

You're using a new program that accesses the Internet for the first time.

Something sneaky is trying to access the Internet.

Something sneaky is trying to get into your computer from the Internet.

In each situation, the firewall is unfamiliar with what's going on, so you're warned, similar to what's shown in Figure 3-3.

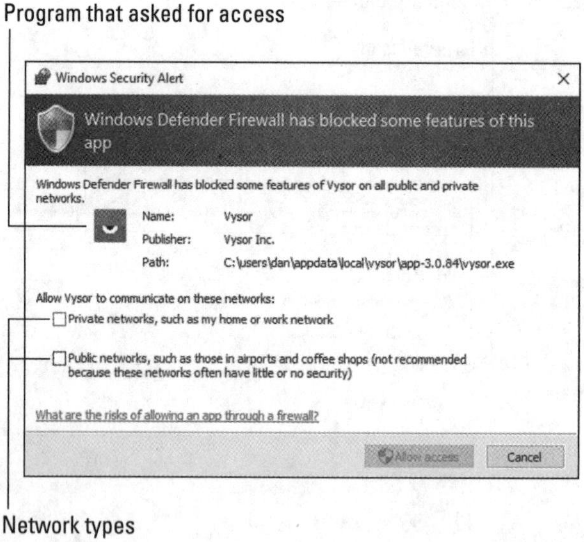

Program that asked for access

FIGURE 3-3: A firewall warning.

Network types

To allow access, you must choose the network type over which access is allowed, as illustrated in Figure 3-3. Choose Private Networks if you plan to use the software only at work or home, where you trust the network. Choose Public Networks if you trust the program and plan to use it in a public place — a coffee shop or an airport, for example. After selecting the network type(s), click the Allow Access button.

TIP

>> When you see the warning, ask yourself whether you just started the named program asking for access. If so, allow the access, as is shown in Figure 3-3 when I first ran the Vysor application. If not, deny access.

>> Many online games trigger a firewall warning the first time they're run. This type of access should be allowed through the firewall over the local (private) network.

>> Choosing the Public Networks option (refer to Figure 3-3) is reserved only for when you absolutely trust the software *and* the public network you're using. Otherwise, your online activity can wait until you connect to a secure network.

REMEMBER

>> After you allow a program through the firewall, it won't ask again. That's because you created a new firewall rule that allows the program Internet access.

>> You can unblock a program if you learn later that it's legitimate. See the next section.

Reviewing firewall rules

When you allow or block a program through the firewall, you create a firewall *rule.* Windows presets a bunch of firewall rules, and some programs create rules when they're installed. To view the list of rules, follow these steps:

1. **Tap the Windows key and type** Windows Firewall

2. **Choose Windows Defender Firewall Control Panel from the search results.**

   The Windows Firewall window appears, drearily illustrated earlier, in Figure 3-2.

3. **On the left side of the window, click the Advanced Settings link.**

   The Windows Firewall with Advanced Security console appears.

The center part of the console window lists basic firewall actions. These actions say the same thing: Disallowed inbound or outbound connections are blocked. To see more specifics, choose a category such as Inbound Rules from the left side of the window. You see more details, as illustrated in Figure 3-4.

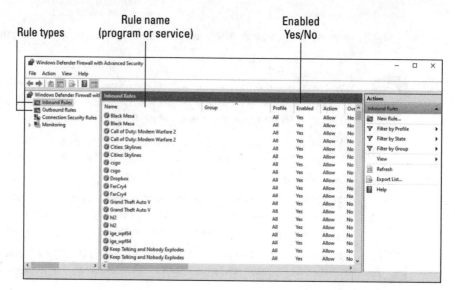

FIGURE 3-4:
Firewall rules.

Each program or service features an inbound rule, an outbound rule, or both. The rule can be enabled or disabled, or it can be deleted to remove the rule and have the firewall prompt again for access.

The details shown in the Windows Firewall with Advanced Security Console are nerdy. Yet it's a useful location if you mistakenly allow a program and want to block it again: Select the program's rule and press the Delete key to remove it.

Chapter **4**

Backup and Restore

Backup isn't something you do to thwart a malware attack. The backup process doesn't check each file for infection, but it does keep around a safety copy of all your PC's files. This copy is important because, should the worst thing happen to your computer and you lose everything, the backup copy can help restore your system. As such, backup plays a key role in keeping your PC secure.

An Emergency Copy

Backup is perhaps the most ancient of computer utilities. It's been around, formally or not, as long as the computer file has existed. I assume that at some point an early computer scientist lost a clutch of files. Wanting them back, the scientist invented the safety copy, or *backup.* Smart computer users have been backing up their files ever since.

Windows comes with backup software, though it's not really a separate program. Instead, backup is a feature called File History. You activate this feature and it performs the same actions as a traditional backup program: It makes safety copies of all your files.

To make backup work, you need external storage on your PC; you cannot back up the PC's primary mass storage device to itself — not even to another partition on the same drive. It's best to use an external drive, network storage, or cloud storage.

The backup program, File History, runs automatically. Once it's configured, you don't have to do a thing — that is, unless something happens to one or more of your computer's files. Then you use File History to restore the files.

REMEMBER

You have no reason in the 21st century not to keep with you copies of your digital life — pictures, videos, music, and documents. You will never lose this stuff if you use the Windows File History feature as described in this chapter.

>> The process of backing up files is referred to as *archiving*. A backup copy of a file is also known as an *archive*.

>> In ancient times, computer users had to manually run a backup. If you forgot, over time the backup copy would be useless because it was too old. Today's backups are automatic.

>> Online or cloud backup involves a subscription, either to the cloud storage utility or an online backup host. You can use this type of service in addition to File History, though I don't cover online backup services in this book.

>> You can back up files to cloud storage — if you have enough storage on that service. File History doesn't recognize cloud storage as a suitable source for backup, so you'd have to perform a manual backup (copy the files). The Microsoft OneDrive service can be used for cloud backup. If you subscribe to the service, it bugs you relentlessly to try cloud backup.

>> The second half of the backup operation is called *restore*. With File History, you can restore a single file or all files in the backup. Hopefully, you rarely, if ever, need to restore from a backup.

Prepare for Backup!

Don't waste any more time: Get your PC ready for backup. The software comes with Windows 10, but you also need a place to store the backup. You can use an external hard drive or network storage. Once you've obtained the storage location, configure and set up Windows 10 File History, and then backing up your data is easy.

Getting external storage

TIP

The most common storage device to use for backup is an external mass storage device. Here are the criteria for you to look for:

Capacity: The storage device must have a capacity equal to or greater than the PC's primary mass storage device. After all, you must store all your files, programs, and even Windows on this drive.

Connection: If your PC has USB 3.0 or eSATA, get a drive with that type of interface. Standard USB connections are fine, but not fast.

Media type: A solid-state drive (SSD) is faster than a traditional hard disk drive (HDD) but more expensive. Speed isn't really an issue for backup, but capacity is an issue. Large-capacity HDDs or even hybrid drives are a good choice.

Cost: You pay more for an SSD with high capacity, but do the math: Calculate cost as dollars per gigabyte. You may find that the higher-capacity drives are cheaper on a cost-per-gigabyte scale.

The external storage device doesn't need to be dedicated to backup, though that's what I do. If I need additional external drives, they're in addition to the backup drive.

>> For more information on external hard drives, see Book 2, Chapter 2.

>> Feel free to delete any "bonus" programs installed on the external hard drive. After all, it's *your* hard drive. You may have to reformat the drive to remove the programs.

>> I recommend that you connect the drive directly to the PC case for most efficient file transfer.

>> External storage for a laptop is yet another thing you must lug around. For my laptop, I use an external hard drive that I keep in the office. On the road, I receive warnings that the backup drive isn't available. That's okay: The laptop backs up after I return to the office and reconnect its external backup drive.

TIP

>> You can also use the external storage for the Windows system image. See the later section "The System Image."

Using network storage

If your computer network offers network storage, you can use it for backup and File History. The best way to make this storage work is to map external storage to a drive letter in Windows. That way, the storage is consistently available.

REMEMBER

>> Refer to Book 2, Chapter 8 for details on mapping network storage to a drive letter in Windows.

>> Ensure that the network storage location offers enough capacity for the backup.

Configuring File History

To enjoy the goodness of backing up, you must activate the File History feature — or ensure that it's already on. Follow these steps:

1. **Press the Windows+I keyboard shortcut.**

   The Settings app appears.

2. **Choose Update & Security.**

   Obviously, backing up is important if Microsoft classifies it in the Update & Security category.

3. **From the list on the left side of the window, choose Backup.**

4. **Ensure that the toggle by Automatically Back Up My Files is set to the On position.**

   If the toggle is already in the On position, you're done. Otherwise, the next step is to choose a drive and set folders for backup:

5. **Click the Add a Drive button.**

   Windows generates a list of qualified storage devices — primarily, external drives and available (shared) network storage. If the list is empty, review the preceding two sections.

6. **Choose the backup drive.**

   The next step is to select folders for backup, which is covered in the next section.

After you activate File History, it begins to work. Files are backed up on a regular schedule, which you can check; see the later section "Modifying the backup routine."

TIP

The Backup screen in the Settings app may show an entry for using OneDrive to back up files. If this is an option you're interested in, click the Back Up Files link located below the OneDrive heading.

Selecting folders for backup

The File History feature automatically selects your user account's folders for inclusion in the backup. All files in the listed folders, as well as files in subfolders, are backed up. To check the list, and change the list of folders, obey these steps:

1. **Press the Windows+I keyboard shortcut to visit the Settings app.**

2. **Choose Update & Security.**

3. **Choose Backup from the list on the left side of the window.**

4. **Choose More Options.**

You see the Backup Options screen, illustrated in Figure 4-1.

Below the heading Back Up These Folders (toward the bottom), you see a list of folders monitored for inclusion in the File History feature. Refer to Figure 4-1 for the specific location.

The list of folders is pretty much identical to the folders in your user account (or user profile) folder.

I recommend that you add two folders to the list:

```
C:\Program Files
C:\Program Files (x86)
```

These folders hold your programs. Should anything bad happen to the hard drive, you want to restore those programs as well, which is why I recommend adding them to the list.

To add folders to the list, click the Add a Folder button and use the Select Folder dialog box to locate each folder. Open the Drive C icon to find both program file folders.

You can add other folders as well, if you don't see them in the list. Review the list carefully to ensure that the folders you use are all there; not every folder in your account's folder is listed. For example, cloud storage folders aren't listed, which is normal because these folders are backed up on the cloud.

Backup and Restore

Perform an immediate backup

Proof that the last backup was successful

Backup drive location (network drive)

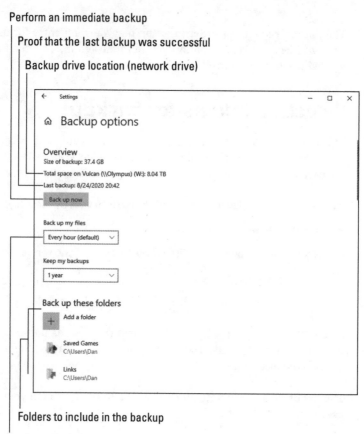

Overview
Size of backup: 37.4 GB
Total space on Vulcan (\\Olympus) (W:): 8.04 TB
Last backup: 8/24/2020 20:42

Back up now

Back up my files

Every hour (default)

Keep my backups

1 year

Back up these folders

+ Add a folder

Saved Games
C:\Users\Dan

Links
C:\Users\Dan

FIGURE 4-1:
The Backup
Options screen.

Folders to include in the backup

Backup schedule

Modifying the backup routine

The File History feature runs on a regular schedule, noting which files have changed or have been added since the last backup. Those modified or new files are added to the backup hourly, unless you set another schedule. And the backup files are kept for the longest time possible — unless you direct the program to purge old backups after a spell.

To modify the backup routine, use the Backup Options window, as shown in Figure 4-1. Refer to the steps in the preceding section for how to muster this window. In the Backup Options window, use the Back Up My Files menu to choose an interval.

A 1-hour interval for backup is more than good. If you find that you need to recover files more frequently, choose a tighter interval, such as ten minutes. On my laptop, I use a Daily item because the laptop isn't regularly connected to its backup drive.

Changes you make in the Backup Options window are set instantly. You don't need to click a Save button or an OK button to confirm.

Making an immediate backup

No matter how you set the backup schedule, you can always direct the File History feature to perform an immediate backup. For example, after I haven't backed up my laptop for a while, I can connect it to the backup drive and demand that it perform a backup right away.

To direct Windows to back up at once, obey these directions:

1. **Press the Windows+I keyboard shortcut.**

   The Settings app appears.

2. **Choose Update & Security.**

3. **Choose Backup.**

   The Backup Using File History window appears.

4. **Choose More Options.**

5. **Click the Back Up Now button.**

   Windows performs a backup, archiving new and changed files to the backup drive.

The backup takes anywhere from a few seconds to several minutes, depending on how much information needs to be archived.

Confirming that the backup worked

When you doubt whether a backup has taken place, rest your furrowed brow by visiting the Backup Options screen. (Refer to Figure 4-1.) Look for the Last Backup entry, which should be recent enough to ease your mind.

If a backup fails, text appears on the Backup Options screen to explain why. The most common reason is that the backup drive is unavailable. Otherwise, the text in the window explains what the problem is so that you can take corrective steps.

File Time-Travel

You can use File History in two ways. First, you can restore previous versions of individual files. So, if you accidentally overwrite a file or delete a file's contents, a recent version can be recovered. Second, you can restore all files from the backup, which might happen after a hard drive disaster.

Recovering an older version of a file

The File History utility gets its name from its capability to recover older versions of a file. This feature is part of all backup programs, though it's often called Restore. The idea is the same: From the backup archive, you pluck an older version of a file. The File History feature makes it easy.

To restore an older version of a file from the backup drive, follow these steps:

1. **Right-click the file.**

   You can also right-click a folder to recover all its contents.

2. **Choose Restore Previous Versions from the shortcut menu.**

   The file or folder's Properties dialog box appears, with the Previous Versions tab upfront, as shown in Figure 4-2. If this tab is empty, File History is not enabled for the drive. Refer to the earlier section "Configuring File History."

3. **Choose a previous version from the list.**

   Ideally, you should select the most recent version, though if you're after an ancient version of the file or folder, you can pluck it from the list instead.

   Your next step depends on what you want to do with the older version of the file:

   - *To replace the current version:* Choose Restore and then choose Replace the File in the Destination. The current file is replaced with the backup.

   - *To keep both the current version and restored backup:* Click the Restore button's menu and choose Restore To. Select a destination folder for the recovered file.

   - *To preview the archived copy:* Click the Open button. The file isn't restored, but you can peruse its contents to see whether it contains the information you need.

4. **Close the file or folder's Properties dialog box when you're done.**

File in question

— Older versions of the file

— Restore button's menu

FIGURE 4-2:
Previous versions
of a file.

When no previous versions exist, you see the message There Are No Previous Versions Available after Step 2. This means the file is new and hasn't been backed up, that the file hasn't changed, or that a backup copy doesn't exist.

>> The File History utility isn't a substitute for recovering a file from the Recycle Bin; if you delete a file, you need to recover it from the Recycle Bin.

>> File History works only on files in folders you've selected when configuring the utility. Refer to the section "Configuring File History," earlier in this chapter.

Browsing File History

For a full view of files and folders that are backed up, you can use the File History browser. You might find this file recovery method better than hunting down files and folders and right-clicking on them. The File History browser window is shown in Figure 4-3.

Backup and Restore

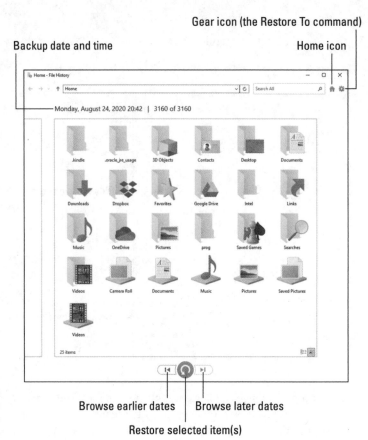

Backup date and time

Gear icon (the Restore To command)

Home icon

Monday, August 24, 2020 20:42 | 3160 of 3160

Browse earlier dates   Browse later dates

Restore selected item(s)

FIGURE 4-3:
Browsing for files
and folders to
recover.

To visit the File History window, follow these directions:

1. **Tap the Windows key.**

2. **Type** File History

3. **Choose the item Restore Your Files with File History.**

It probably won't be the top item in the search results.

This list of items you see in the File History window match those folders you selected for backup when File History was configured. (Refer to the earlier section "Configuring File History.")

To restore an item, select it and then click the big green Restore button, illustrated in Figure 4-3. As with restoring individual files, you'll be prompted about whether you want to replace the original file.

If you want to restore a file, folder, or group to a specific folder, click the Gear icon (refer to Figure 4-3) and choose the Restore To command. Select a folder for the backup files.

Use the left and right arrows to browse your file history. The backup date and time are shown at the top of the window.

Restoring all your personal files

If you have the misfortune to lose all your personal files, you can use File History to restore everything. If you can start Windows, follow these steps:

1. **Run File History as described in the preceding section.**

   You need to access the File History browser window.

2. **Ensure that you're viewing your account's main (home) folder and that the window shows the most recent date.**

   Click the Home icon, illustrated in Figure 4-3.

3. **Press Ctrl+A to select all files and folders.**

4. **Click the big green Restore button.**

5. **Continue following the directions on the screen as the restore operation progresses.**

If you can't get into Windows (say the hard drive is damaged), you must first restore Windows before you can run File History. You can use the Windows Recovery Environment to begin the process of restoring Windows.

Also see the section "Restoring a system image," later in this chapter.

The System Image

The File History feature doesn't back up Windows. In fact, I don't recommend that you attempt to use it to back up Windows or any files in the Windows folder. Instead, you must create something called a system image, which is used to restore Windows in times of dire woe.

Creating the system image

If you haven't already, create a *system image* for your Windows computer — it's a backup copy of Windows that you can use to rebuild the system if disaster strikes the PC's primary storage device. Follow these steps:

1. **Press the Windows+E keyboard shortcut to summon a File Explorer window.**

2. **In the Address bar, click the menu on the far left and choose Control Panel.**

The ancient Control Panel appears. Many of its features have moved into the Windows 10 Settings app — but not the System Image utility.

3. **Below the System and Security heading, click the link Backup and Restore (Windows 7).**

4. **On the left side of the window, choose Create a System Image.**

The Create a System Image Wizard runs.

5. **Choose a location for the system image.**

TIP

I recommend that you use the same external hard drive that you use for File History. You can use network storage, but Windows displays a warning. If you're certain that the network storage is secure, you can use it.

6. **Click the Next button.**

The wizard lists drives (partitions) to save with the system image. If your PC features UEFI and Recovery volumes, they're automatically included in the list along with drive C, the PC's primary storage device.

7. **Add other drives to the items included in the system image backup.**

I don't recommend adding any other drives, unless you're certain that they're not otherwise being backed up.

8. **Click the Next button.**

Review the system image backup details on the screen.

9. **Click the Start Backup button to create the system image.**

Windows creates the system image file on the media you selected. The amount of time this process takes depends on the quantity of data backed up and the connection speed.

When the process is complete, you may see a prompt asking whether you want to create a system repair disk. The repair disk, or *Recovery volume,* is what makes the system image useful. If you don't already have a repair disk, create one: Click Yes and follow the directions on the screen. Refer to Book 3, Chapter 1 for more details on the repair disk.

REMEMBER

» You need only one copy of the system image. This process isn't something you must repeat every so often. When you have the system image, you can restore it later, should you need to. See the next section.

» Beyond security, another limitation of using network storage is that the computer must have network access if you plan to rebuild the system. If you must boot into Safe mode to restore the system, ensure that you enable networking.

» You can use the Windows 7 Backup and Restore program to restore files from an older Windows computer. In the Backup and Restore (Windows 7) window, click the link Select Another Backup to Restore Files From, and then browse for the older computer's backup files.

Restoring a system image

The only time you need to restore a system image is when the computer's primary mass storage device is dead, missing, or replaced with a cheese sandwich. With all that data gone, you have to rely upon three items:

A Recovery volume: Use this media to start the PC and access the Windows Recovery Environment. The tools presented help you navigate through recovery, as detailed in Book 3, Chapter 1.

The system image: Use this information to restore Windows and other partitions as a base to rebuild your computer system. Tools on the Recovery volume help you use the system image information.

File History: Finally, with Windows restored, you run the File History program to recover your PC's lost files and programs. Details are offered earlier in this chapter; refer to the earlier section "Restoring all your personal files."

You don't need to restore a system image if you merely need to recover from a Windows disaster. The first thing you should try is System Restore; refer to Book 3, Chapter 5. Second, you can try to reset the PC, which is covered in Book 3, Chapter 1. Otherwise, the process of using the system image works like this:

1. **Start the PC by using the Windows Recovery Environment.**

2. **Choose Troubleshoot.**

3. **Choose Advanced Options.**

4. Choose the See More Recovery Options item.

5. Choose System Image Recovery.

This item may appear after Step 3 on some computers.

Point the system image recovery tool at the location of the system image files, created when you follow the steps from the preceding section. Then sit back and wait as the system is rebuilt.

Yes, the complete process is more complex than four simple steps. For example, you may need to purchase and install a replacement primary storage device, a new hard drive or SSD. The good news is that you have the system image when you need it. Along with a recent backup, you can fully restore your system no matter what happens to the computer.

5

This Old PC

Contents at a Glance

Chapter **1**

Performance and Resources

Think about the differences between your current computer and a brand-new, top-of-the-line model. Don't consider price. Instead, the items you use for comparison include a better processor, more memory, larger and faster primary storage, and the latest software. These items are collectively known as *resources*, and a newer PC has better resources than your current computer.

Sorry, I didn't mean to depress you. Your computer is a worthy machine, but it might be acting slow because it just doesn't have the resources it once did. Those resources — the processor, memory, storage, and other items — all play a direct role in the computer's performance. Windows lets you monitor these resources to ensure that they're being used to the best of your PC's capabilities.

The Relationship Between Performance and Resources

Performance and resources are related. Resources include processing power, storage, and other hardware capabilities. The amount of performance you squeeze out of a computer directly relates to the resources available. You may not be able to swap out hardware, but you can do what it takes to eke out the best possible performance from the hardware your PC currently has.

The tools Windows offers to monitor performance and resources are

>> The Performance Monitor

>> The Performance tab in the Task Manager window

>> The Resource Monitor

These tools demonstrate that Microsoft has an uncanny knack of not assigning tools unique and descriptive names. All these utilities do basically the same thing: Present charts and graphs illustrating how resources inside the computer are used. Each has differing degrees of complexity, and some are better suited for specific tasks, which is why each is covered in this chapter.

>> Of all the tools, the Performance Monitor is the oldest, introduced for Windows NT back in the 1990s. It's also the most complex of the trio. See the later section "Viewing the Performance Monitor."

>> The Resource Monitor was introduced with Windows Vista. It's the most useful of the three, especially for tracking down issues with specific programs. See the later section "Monitoring system resources."

>> The Task Manager's Performance tab once dwelled in the System Configuration Utility (MSCONFIG) window. It's a bit friendlier than the Performance Monitor — plus, it's easier to access. See the later section "Checking the Performance tab."

>> Yes, overlap exists between all three tools. You need not use them all.

>> Performance and resources play a role in troubleshooting with regard to software. For example, a bug may cause a program to consume more and more resources over time. Known as a *memory leak,* it's easy to spot such a program based on how it's using resources and how the PC's performance degrades over time. See the later section "Using the monitors as troubleshooting tools."

How Ya Doin', PC?

To measure the PC's performance, or how well it's utilizing available resources, you summon a tool called the Performance Monitor. You can also check PC performance from the Task Manager, though the Performance Monitor is more thorough in its presentation.

Viewing the Performance Monitor

The Performance Monitor console is the most sophisticated of the Windows resource graphing tools. It's also the most difficult to use, probably due to its origin as a Windows NT program.

To bring up the Performance Monitor console window, obey these steps:

1. **Tap the Windows key on the keyboard.**

2. **Type** performance

3. **Choose the Performance Monitor app from the list of search results.**

    The Performance Monitor appears in a console window.

4. **From the left side of the console window, choose Performance Monitor.**

    This item is located in the Monitoring Tools folder, as illustrated in Figure 1-1.

The Performance Monitor window is rather barren at first; you need to add items to the monitor to view the graph, especially one as detailed as the one shown in Figure 1-1.

To add an item, click the Add (green plus) button. In the Add Counters dialog box, click to select a counter and then click the Add>> button. Click OK to view the results.

The display in the Performance Monitor can get rather hectic, which makes it my least favorite monitoring tool. Still, it offers plenty of details. If you need to get specific in monitoring an activity, this is the tool to use.

For example, to monitor network traffic, add the Network Adapter counter to the display. Choose a specific counter to monitor by unchecking the other counters. For example, uncheck everything but Bytes Received to check on incoming network traffic.

TIP

>> To clean up the display, select a counter and click the X (Cancel) button. You can Shift+click to select multiple counters and remove them all at once.

Performance and Resources

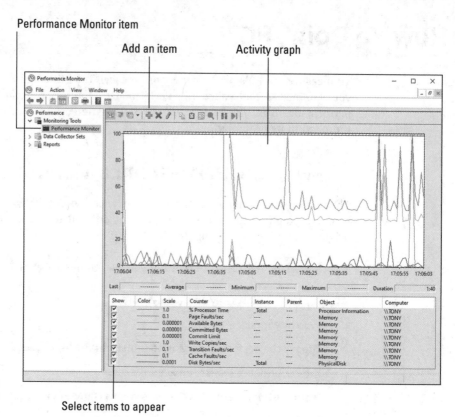

Performance Monitor item

Add an item

Activity graph

FIGURE 1-1:
The Performance
Monitor.

Select items to appear

>> The difference between removing a counter and unchecking it is that you can more easily recheck a counter to again review its status.

Checking the Performance tab

The easiest monitoring tool to use is found in the Task Manager window. To view this item, follow these steps:

1. **Press Ctrl+Esc to bring up the Task Manager window.**

2. **Click the Performance tab.**

The Performance tab is illustrated in Figure 1-2.

The Performance tab lists key resources as thumbnails on the left side of the window. In Figure 1-2, you see entries for the CPU, memory, mass storage devices, the network, and the graphics processing unit (GPU) with more items in a scrolling list.

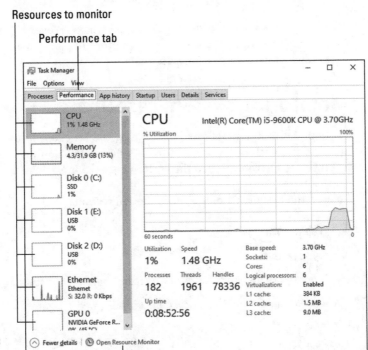

FIGURE 1-2:
The Task
Manager's
Performance tab.

To view a different category's performance graph, choose its thumbnail from the left side of the window. The graph changes over time, scrolling from right to left. The higher the line on the graph, the more the chosen resource is in use or being consumed.

The CPU meter tells you how much processing horsepower is in use. In Figure 1-2, the values are low until a spike happens. The low values indicate that Windows isn't doing much; the spike occurred when I opened another program. If the figure were high, or suddenly spiked, that means more activity is taking place, such as a background task or service.

The Memory meter tracks how much memory is in use. This item fluctuates as you use programs. For example, running a photo editor may consume a huge amount of memory, but the Performance tab would show that amount of memory freed after you exit the program.

Disk items show storage activity. Ethernet shows network activity. If a Bluetooth adapter is available, you may see an entry for it as well.

TIP

For further details, use the Resource Monitor, which is covered in the next section. As a shortcut, click the Open Resource Monitor link, located at the bottom of the Task Manager window's Performance tab.

Monitoring system resources

To monitor specific programs or activities, the best tool to use is the Resource Monitor. It's far less complicated than Performance Monitor, and it offers more information and control than the Performance tab in Task Manager.

To open the Resource Monitor, heed these directions:

1. **Tap the Windows key.**

2. **Type** resource

3. **Choose the Resource Monitor app from the search results.**

The Resource Monitor window appears, illustrated in Figure 1-3.

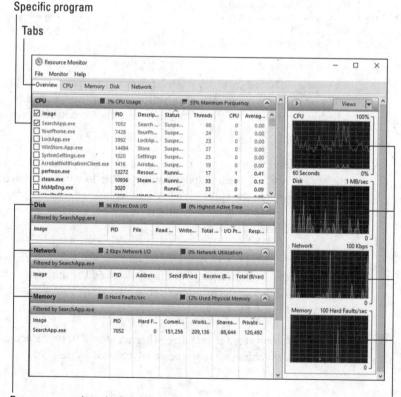

Specific program

Tabs

FIGURE 1-3:
The Resource
Monitor.

Resources monitored related to program

Program's charts

The Resource Monitor's Overview tab, shown in Figure 1-3, shows the big picture on system resources: CPU (processor), Memory, Disk, and Network, along with charts for each.

The various tabs (refer to Figure 1-3) show more details and even more charts.

What's interesting about the Resource Monitor is that you can examine the effects of specific programs on resources. For example, in Figure 1-3, the service SearchApp.exe is selected. Its effect on resources is shown in each category (click the chevron to expand a category) as well as highlighted in each of the graphs. When you choose a program in this manner, you can spy on its effects on all resources. See the next section for details on using this technique.

Using the monitors as troubleshooting tools

All the performance- and resource-monitoring tools provide good feedback, but the details are trivial. Activity always abounds inside a computer. The concern is whether that activity is causing the system to slow down.

Whenever the PC starts acting slowly, pop up Task Manager and click the Processes tab. Click the CPU column header to sort the list of running programs by processor use. (If necessary, click the header twice so that the programs using the CPU the most appear at the top of the list.) The program using the most CPU time is probably the one slowing your PC.

You can also click Task Manager's Performance tab to check on memory and other resources. But to confirm that the single program is consuming too many resources, use Resource Manager: In the Resource Manager window, choose the suspect program from the list on the Overview tab. Then select all resources.

What you're looking for is increased consumption of resources over time. In some cases, the program may busy itself for a short span, and then regular activity resumes. When a program continues to consume resources, you might consider terminating it to see whether the PC's performance improves.

>> If a single program is to blame, consider getting an update for the program.

>> If the program is a background task that gobbles too many resources, consider rescheduling the task for a time when you're not using the computer.

>> A program that continues to use resources after it quits, especially memory, has a memory leak. You should stop using the program and see whether an update or a replacement is available.

>> Some web page plug-ins may cause problems. These plug-ins might appear as issues with the web browser program itself, but they're not. The way to fix this issue is to check the web browser's settings or preferences and disable the plug-in.

>> Malware also consumes resources at a rabid pace. You can attempt to halt the run-amok program, but it's best to run a scan and have Windows Defender remove it. See Book 4, Chapter 3 for details.

Chapter **2**

More Mass Storage

This chapter is brought to you by the word *capacity*. It's a great word, especially when applied to mass storage on a computer. The greater the media's capacity, the more room for storing your stuff — not just programs and your documents but also massive files, such as your music collection, movies, and grocery lists. You need the storage space!

The Mass Storage Pie

A new mass storage device is full of potential. That's because it's empty. This condition doesn't last long. Eventually the storage device becomes home to files and programs. Like all human stuff, these items accumulate, and over time the once-empty and full-of-potential hard drive is filled and, well, you have a problem.

Looking at the storage situation

To take a quick glance at storage capacity on all your PC's mass media devices, open File Explorer and wander over to the This PC window. Follow these steps:

1. Press the Windows+E keyboard shortcut.

A File Explorer window appears.

2. Choose This PC from the items listed on the left side of the window.

You see an overview of storage available to the computer, similar to what's illustrated in Figure 2-1.

Local storage devices   Capacity thermometers

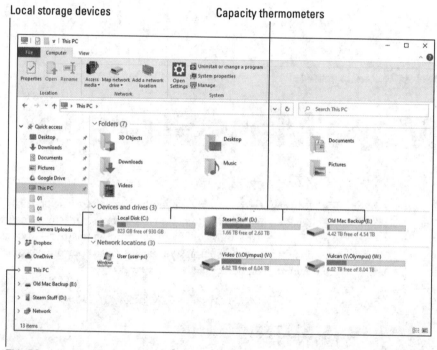

FIGURE 2-1: The PC's storage overview.

This PC

At a glance, you can determine the capacity for your PC's storage. The blue part of the thermometer is used space; the gray part represents available space.

When available space gets too low, the used part of the thermometer graph is colored red, which helps you quickly identify full hard drives. You must deal with this situation if you want to continue to use the drive.

For more details on storage, right-click the drive and choose Properties. You see the storage device's Properties dialog box. On the General tab, detailed information about the drive's used and free space is shown, as illustrated in Figure 2-2.

Hmmm, disk pie!

Storage capacity specifics   Total drive capacity

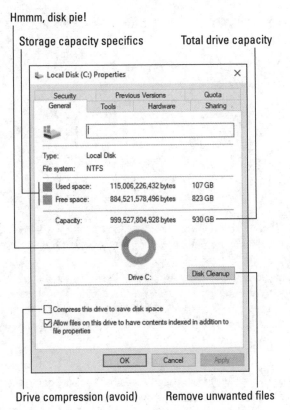

FIGURE 2-2:
Storage details
for Drive C.

Drive compression (avoid)   Remove unwanted files

In Figure 2-2, you see that the drive's total capacity is 930GB. It's a 1TB drive, but the actual storage capacity of the media is less due to overhead and a given number of bytes taken by the government for tax purposes. The more important figure is Free Space, which in Figure 2-2 is generous.

>> When free space falls below 10 percent, Windows displays a warning message regarding free capacity. When you see this message, act immediately. See the later section "Get Yourself More Mass Storage Capacity."

>> If you use a thumb drive for the Windows ReadyBoost feature, it also appears full in the This PC window. See Chapter 3 for more information on ReadyBoost.

THE OBLIGATORY BYTE CAPACITY REFERENCE

As with computer memory, all storage media capacity is measured in bytes. A byte is a character of information, capable of storing a single letter, number, jot, or tittle. By itself, a byte is useless, so computer nerds have special terms to describe mass quantities of bytes:

Kilobyte (KB) is about 1,000 bytes, or enough storage for a single page of text. And that's plain text — no fancy formatting or graphics.

Megabyte (MB) is about a million (1,000,000) bytes. That's enough storage for a minute of digital audio.

Gigabyte (GB) is about a billion bytes. That's enough storage for an hour of video. Most media cards and thumb drives measure their capacity in gigabytes.

Terabyte (TB) is about a trillion bytes, or 1,000GB. Mass storage devices, HDDs and SSDs, measure their capacity in terabytes.

Beyond the terabyte is the petabyte, which is 1,000TB. Then come the exabyte, the zettabyte, and (my favorite) the yottabyte, which would be a great name for a candy bar. If I'm still writing technology books in 100 years, I'll be writing about yottabyte storage.

>> Optical discs are always full. They show a red capacity bar in the This PC window. This condition holds true even for writeable discs.

>> I dislike the name This PC. In older versions of Windows, it was called My Computer, which seems more descriptive. O, Microsoft!

Measuring bulky things

Of all the files that come to roost on your PC's hard drive, some occupy more space than others. These bulky beasts of bytes singularly or collectively are the cause of capacity concern. You can't avoid some of them, but you can manage the lot.

The PC's primary mass storage device is home to three groups of files:

>> The computer's operating system, Windows

>> The software — programs and applications — that let you do things with your computer

>> Your stuff: files, documents, media, and other things you create or collect

The ideal situation is to have a hard drive that boasts a capacity to hold all three types of files, not only for now but also for as long as you plan to own your computer.

For the operating system, you can't really reduce its size. Windows is as a big as Microsoft makes it.

You can manage software. Older programs can be uninstalled, and you have the option to install newer programs on secondary storage when primary storage gets full.

For your own stuff, you can afford to be most cruel. Purging older files improves storage capacity in a positive way, but I recommend instead that you consider archiving files to secondary or removable storage. You can also hunt down specifically large files and remove them.

Get Yourself More Mass Storage Capacity

The hard drive squeeze was on in the early 1990s. Back then, programs and files were growing in size while hard drive capacity remained static. Computer users ran out of room to store their stuff. Various solutions were devised: Archive large files, remove unneeded files and programs, add a second or third hard drive, and compress both individual files and entire hard drives. These tools, all still available today, provide a healing balm for dwindling mass storage capacity woe.

Dealing with large files

A quick way to improve dwindling storage media capacity is to hunt down those items that consume the most storage space. These are large files, some of which you might not be aware of. For example, I purged from my PC's hard drive a movie I downloaded. Ta-da! I gained 4GB of storage.

To locate bloated files on your computer, use the Windows Search command. Follow these steps:

1. **Press the Windows+E keyboard shortcut to bring forth File Explorer.**

File Explorer opens, displaying the Quick Access items.

2. **Click the address bar and choose your account name from the menu.**

Click the right-pointing chevron (>) on the left end of the address bar. Your account name appears in the list. On my PC, it's my name (Dan Gookin). It might be called "User."

3. **Click the Search text box, located near the upper right corner of the File Explorer window, and type the text** size:gigantic

Type **size**, no space, a colon, no space, and **gigantic** This cryptic text directs Windows to search for files greater than 4GB in size in your personal account area.

The list of matching files may be empty. If not, you can peruse the list to see whether any of these hefty byte bytes can be removed. Otherwise, use the Size menu on the Search Tools Search tab, illustrated in Figure 2-3, to look for huge files, and then medium files, as shown in the figure.

Size command

Menu chevron   Search Tools Search tab   Search text box

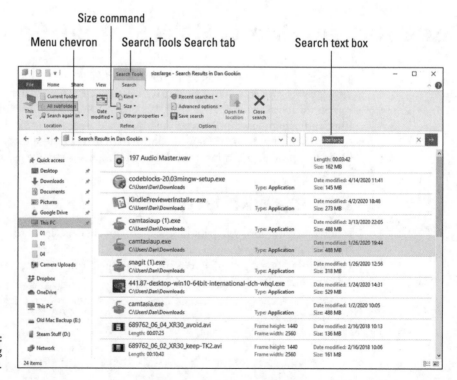

FIGURE 2-3:
Locating
large files.

You can gawk at the list, but the point is to find larger files that you can remove to free up the space they occupy. You may see files you downloaded or created ages ago — something you needed once but no longer. If so, great: You can delete or archive the file.

To delete a file, select it in the Search Results window and then press the Delete key on the keyboard. This action sends the file to the Recycle Bin, which doesn't really delete it. Only when you empty the Recycle Bin is the file's storage space freed.

Archiving is best when you may still need the file but don't need to have it handy. To archive a file, you can move it to external storage or compress it. To move the file, select it and press Ctrl+X to cut it. Then open a folder window on an external drive or a media card. Press Ctrl+V to paste the file, moving it to the media. To compress the file, see the later section "Compressing single files."

TIP

>> You can press Shift+Delete to instantly delete a file and recover the storage space it used. The Shift+Delete operation isn't reversible, however. Use it with care.

>> You may find some compressed (Zip) folders when perusing the list. Be careful! You want to confirm the compressed folder's contents before you banish it into oblivion.

>> See the nearby sidebar, "Things that gobble storage space," for tips on what types of files consume the most storage.

Using Disk Cleanup

Windows offers a tool to help you purge files you may no longer need and might not otherwise be able to locate. The Disk Cleanup utility locates files that can easily be removed to free up some disk space. To run it, obey these directions:

1. **Tap the Windows key.**

2. **Type** disk cleanup

3. **Choose the Disk Cleanup app from the search results.**

4. **Select the mass storage device that you want to clean up.**

   This prompt appears only when you have multiple storage media on your PC. You probably want to choose Drive C, the main storage device, which is already selected for you.

THINGS THAT GOBBLE STORAGE SPACE

As the PC's capabilities have grown, so have the size and type of files you find on mass storage devices. The larger files are typically the most sophisticated, storing media and other fancy items that would have choked the IBM PC/XT's puny 10MB hard drive into a catatonic state. Here are the bulkiest types of files you find on a typical PC:

Video: The most space-consuming file you can add to your computer is a movie. Feature films eat up several gigabytes. Even regular video files are very large; a 2-minute video can be 30MB or more. My recommendation is to send video files to external storage after you're done with them.

Music: Expect to use about 1MB of disk storage for each minute of music you store on your PC.

Pictures: Image files can be small, such as those you find on the Internet or exchange by email. But Raw image files — those you want to keep so that you can print a 4-x-5 enlargement (or larger) — can occupy several megabytes of storage.

Programs: Most programs don't use a lot of space, but some can be ginormous. Computer games especially can consume gigabytes of storage. But that value is *static:* After you install the program, it doesn't continue to consume more space. See the later section "Uninstalling programs" for details on removing large programs you no longer need.

Documents: The documents you create on your computer take up the least amount of space. A word processing document uses 100K or so, which is 0.1MB — just a thin slice of the media pie.

The Disk Cleanup utility scans the media, looking for useless files. When it's done, you see the Disk Cleanup dialog box, as shown in Figure 2-4.

5. **Place check marks by all the items.**

    Seriously, nothing listed in the dialog box is of any consequence to you, yet the Disk Cleanup utility leaves several items unchecked, probably just to give you something to do.

6. **Click OK.**

7. **Click the Delete Files button to confirm and begin the cleanup process.**

    Wait while the files are removed. When the process is complete, the window goes away.

Check all the items

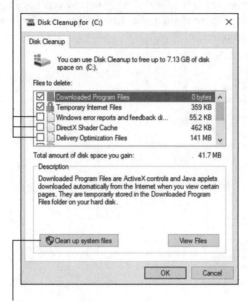

FIGURE 2-4:
The Disk Cleanup
dialog box.

More aggressive purging

For even more aggressive file purging, click the Clean Up System Files button (refer to Figure 2-4). The Disk Cleanup utility starts over again, but this time it lists various unneeded bits and pieces of Windows.

TIP

» Check the media's before-and-after size when you run the Disk Cleanup utility. This is the best way to gauge how successful you are in increasing media capacity.

» You can also access the Disk Cleanup utility from a drive's Properties dialog box: Click the Disk Cleanup button on the General tab. Refer to Figure 2-2.

» The Disk Cleanup utility is nifty, but its results don't show the kind of massive cleanup effort you may expect. Rarely in my experience has it fully fixed the problem of a crowded hard drive. Use this tool in combination with other suggestions in this chapter to help improve storage capacity.

Uninstalling programs

Programs can occupy a lot of storage real estate. You may have programs installed on your PC that fit the humongous category — specifically, programs that you may not have run in a while. If so, feel free to remove their bloated bytes from the primary storage device.

In Figure 2-5, you see the list of installed programs on my PC, as sorted by file size. If a program appears in the list that I no longer use, I can easily remove it to free the storage it occupies.

Click to sort by size

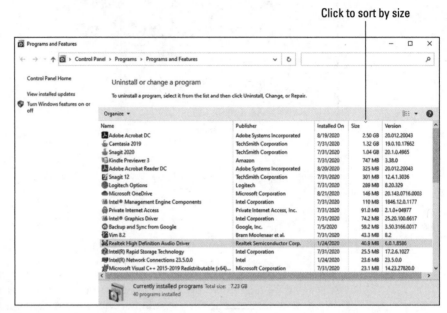

FIGURE 2-5:
Large programs,
sorted by size.

To view large programs installed on your PC, follow these steps:

1. **Tap the Windows key.**

2. **Type** control panel

3. **With the Control Panel app chosen from the search results, choose the Programs and Features item on the right side of the search panel.**

   The Control Panel opens, showing the Programs and Features item.

4. **Click the Size column heading to sort the list of programs by their size.**

   You may have to click the column heading twice so that the list is presented from largest to smallest.

To uninstall a program you no longer use, select the program and then click the Uninstall button that appears. Continue following the onscreen directions.

>> Refer to Book 2, Chapter 7 for more details on uninstalling programs.

>> The later section "Adding mass storage" covers adding a second mass storage device to the PC, which can be used to install software.

>> In this book's previous edition, the list of programs in old Figure 2-5 showed substantially more storage occupied. Most of them were games. To alleviate the storage crunch on Drive C, I moved these games to an external drive. This is the archiving solution mentioned elsewhere in this chapter — specifically, in the later section "Relocating programs."

Compressing single files

Windows comes with a file compression feature. It's not the same as creating a Zip file archive. This type of compression is done on the fly: When you open the compressed file, it's decompressed to its original size. So, as a user, you don't notice the compression in any way other than that your files consume less storage space — a wee bit more overhead is required to open and decompress the files.

To compress a single file, heed these directions:

1. **Right-click the file or folder icon to compress.**

When you compress a folder, you compress all files and folders held in that folder. It's a simple way to compress a slew of files all at once.

2. **Choose Properties from the shortcut menu.**

3. **On the General tab of the Properties dialog box, click the Advanced button.**

The Advanced Attributes dialog box appears.

4. **Place a check mark by the option Compress Contents to Save Disk Space.**

5. **Click OK to close the Advanced Attributes dialog box.**

Nothing happens yet.

6. **Click OK again to dismiss the Properties dialog box.**

If you're compressing a folder, you see a further confirmation, asking whether you want to compress only the folder or all its files and contents.

7. **For folders, choose the default option: Apply Changes to This Folder, Subfolders and Files. Click OK.**

The file or folder is compressed.

 Compressed files and folders are superimposed with blue pinchy arrows, as shown in the margin. That's your only visual clue that a file is compressed. Otherwise, you can interact with the file as you always have. Windows handles the decompression for you.

TECHNICAL
STUFF

COMPRESSION ISN'T ALWAYS THE ANSWER

File compression works because the typical file has a lot of redundant informa-tion in it — lots of bytes and chunks that repeat over and over or just empty space. Compression software takes advantage of this redundancy by removing repeating chunks of data. Using magic I can't begin to explain (or understand), a file that once sucked up 1MB of disk space can suddenly consume only 64KB or so. This savings is significant.

Compression, however, isn't a magic lozenge for curing a cramped hard drive. That's because only certain files compress well.

For example, text files can be smooshed down to become quite small. Windows Bitmap files (BMP) compress well. Most of the files on your hard drive, however, are probably already in a compressed state. Therefore, they don't benefit from additional compres-sion. In fact, by compressing them, you might make your computer run slower because of all the overhead required to decompress the file on the fly.

To remove compression from a file or folder, repeat the steps in this section, but in Step 4 remove the check mark by the item Compress Contents to Save Disk Space.

>> Also see the nearby sidebar, "Compression isn't always the answer."

>> This type of file compression works well for files you plan to keep around, but for files you don't need often, consider *archiving* (copying) them to external media.

>> Single-file compression offered by Windows is done on the fly, which is faster than extracting files from a Zip archive.

Compressing every dang doodle file on a drive

Windows offers a single command that sifts through every file on a drive and applies the compression attribute to them all. The result is that the entire storage device is compressed so that files occupy less space. This strategy isn't a surefire solution to a cramped hard drive, but it can be done.

To compress an entire storage device, follow these steps, though I recommend that you read this entire section before you begin:

1. **In the File Explorer program, display the This PC window.**

   Press the Windows+E keyboard shortcut to start File Explorer, and then choose This PC from the locations listed on the left side of the window.

2. **Right-click a drive icon and choose Properties from the shortcut menu.**

3. **Place a check mark by the item Compress This Drive to Save Disk Space.**

4. **Click the Apply button.**

5. **Ensure that the second option is selected in the Confirm Attribute Changes dialog box: Apply Changes to Drive X:\, Subfolders and Files.**

6. **Click OK.**

   If you encounter file errors during this process, click the Ignore All button. Files get busy and are in use by other processes, for example. There's no way to compress them all.

7. **Wait.**

8. **Close the drive's Properties window.**

   No confirmation dialog box appears when the operation is over, which is kind of a letdown.

Now that you've read the directions but haven't actually performed them (see my recommendation in the paragraph preceding the steps), I don't recommend that you follow this procedure. Yes, it works, but it's not the best solution. Like the users back in the early 1990s who were faced with cramped hard drives, compression is only a stopgap solution. The real solution is to get a higher-capacity hard drive and use it instead. See the next section.

REMEMBER

>> The compression feature may not be available for all types of storage media.

>> All file and folder icons on the compressed mass storage device sport the blue pinchy arrows, indicating that the files and folders are compressed.

>> A compressed file or folder may not occupy less disk space because not all files compress well. See the earlier sidebar "Compression isn't always the answer."

>> To decompress the drive, repeat the preceding steps but remove the check mark in Step 3.

Even More Storage

The true solution to a nearly full drive is to augment its storage capacity. The easy way to do that is to add another mass storage device to your PC. The best way to augment primary storage is to replace Drive C with another drive of a higher capacity. That method is rather complex and scary, which is why I cover it last.

Adding mass storage

A basic computer upgrade is to add more mass storage. You can add a drive internally (if room is available) or externally. Either way, the key to adding more storage is to remember to use it!

>> Refer to Book 2, Chapter 2 for more information on adding mass storage to your PC.

REMEMBER

>> When you install a new program, choose the advanced options so that you can direct the setup procedure to choose the secondary mass storage device for the program. This trick keeps the programs from clogging up a smaller primary hard drive, but it works only when you remember to choose the secondary hard drive.

>> To resolve my issue with games hogging up Drive C, I directed Steam (my game management program) to install new games on the external drive by default. This setting saved Drive C over 1TB of storage occupied by all those games. Putting them on the external drive doesn't slow down the games' load time or performance.

TIP

>> If you do elect to use secondary storage for installing programs, I recommend that you create a Program Files folder on that drive, similar to the Program Files folder on the primary hard drive. Install programs in that folder.

Relocating programs

One way to improve storage capacity is to uninstall programs you no longer use. The question then arises: Why not just move those programs to another storage device?

The short answer is that you can't easily move installed programs. That's because programs aren't single files. They may not even be installed in a single folder. Further, the program's location is recorded in various places so that the program itself can find its pieces. The operation to move the program's files fails unless you know how to update all the details.

If possible, you can uninstall the program and then reinstall it to the secondary storage. This process is time consuming, which is why most people avoid it. Also, some software licenses and keys don't let you reinstall software without paying for it a second time.

Getting a larger Drive C

You made the mistake when you bought your computer. You were excited, you didn't know better, or you were looking at the price and not your needs. The bottom line is that the PC's primary storage device is too tiny. You need 2TB of storage, and your computer has a relatively puny 500GB hard drive.

Without knowing anything about computers, you may think that you can just swap out the old hard drive for a newer one with more capacity. The problem with this technique is that Drive C is more than just a hard drive. It's where Windows dwells, along with all the configuration files, drives, programs, and whatnot for your computer. You must be careful with this drive and its contents.

One technique is to replace the drive and then rebuild it using common troubleshooting tools: Treat the event as a disk disaster. Follow these general steps:

1. **Ensure that you have a fresh backup available, a Windows recovery disk, and a system image.**

2. **Install the new hard drive in the console, replacing the old Drive C.**

3. **Start the PC with the recovery disk.**

4. **Use the Windows Recovery Environment to prepare the disk for use, applying a file system and formatting the media.**

    Refer to Book 2, Chapter 2.

5. **Recover the system image to the new drive.**

    Details are offered in Book 4, Chapter 4.

6. **Restore your files from a recent backup.**

This technique recovers all the original information from the old Drive C to the new drive. The huge drawback is that it's very time-consuming.

Another technique is to install a second, larger drive in the console and then clone the contents of the original drive to the second drive. Follow these general steps:

1. **Add the second drive to the PC's case.**

It must be an internal drive, so the case needs room for the second drive. Keep the original Drive C in place.

2. **Use a disk cloning utility to duplicate the contents of Drive C to the newer drive.**

The cloning utility moves over all files to Drive C, duplicating it on the second drive. You might also confirm that any Recovery and UEFI volumes are cloned as well.

3. **Open the PC's case again and swap the drives.**

Set the new drive as the PC's boot drive, which may involve swapping cables and resetting a switch on the drive.

4. **Restart the PC.**

The system now uses the cloned drive, which has a higher capacity.

This technique involves both hardware and software acumen, but it's faster and safer than replacing a drive and rebuilding.

>> Windows lacks disk cloning software. This software is available commercially, such as Norton Ghost, which also serves as a backup utility. Freeware cloning programs are available. I've used CloneZilla with success.

>> You don't have to physically swap drives inside a computer. Keep both drives internal, but just switch the cables. You might need to modify the boot order by changing the UEFI program. Refer to Book 3, Chapter 1 for details on the UEFI.

>> Refer to Book 3, Chapter 1 for details on using the Recovery volume. Book 4, Chapter 4 covers creating a system image.

>> I wish I could be more specific about how the process works, but this is one hardware operation where the details rely upon specific hardware. As long as you have the proper backups as described in this section, the operation can move forward.

TIP

>> I recommend St. John's Wort for anxiety.

Chapter **3**

Boost PC Performance

Your PC is no longer a puppy. It lacks that zip, that endless energy. Now your computer system acts more like an old, droopy dog. You don't take it for a walk — you take it for a drag. The pep and vigor are gone. Yes, it happens to both pets and PCs. In modern culture, we seem to admire things that are snappy, upbeat, and full of life. When your computer starts to lack those qualities, it's time for some reinvigoration.

Man, Your PC Is Slow!

Do computers run more slowly over time? The answer is no. Performance can suffer, but electronically, a computer out of the box runs just as fast as the same computer years later. What changes, however, is the computer's *experience*. As Indiana Jones once said, "It's not the years, honey — it's the mileage."

» No secrets exist to boost PC performance. For example, your PC lacks a Fast mode or secret hyperdrive switch. All the components are designed to work well together, so even if you could speed up some aspect of the computer, it may not affect overall performance.

TECHNICAL
STUFF

» A trick the nerds use to speed up their computers is something called *overclocking:* They modify the PC's firmware to increase the processor's speed. In some cases, the speed boost does affect performance, but it can cause other problems, including burning out the processor. I don't believe overclocking to be a valid solution for an older, slower PC.

Understanding slow

Your computer is a busy beast. Even when you're not doing anything and it appears that Windows is sitting idle, lots of activity takes place. Add in some updates, new software, new hardware, and more updates, and over time these activities tax the system's performance. It's natural and expected.

Even if you never changed a thing in your computer, it would seem slower over time. That's because new computers come out with better hardware, faster processors, and more memory. Relatively speaking, your once-powerful beast is now a humdrum machine.

Yet, whereas a computer slowing over time is anticipated, what's alarming is the onset of *suddenly slow.* I call it this-stupid-thing-wasn't-this-slow-last-week syndrome. It's a situation that needs to be addressed because it spotlights a problem you can fix. You can also check for the usual suspects, such as spyware and a memory leak. Refer to the next two sections.

REMEMBER

» Old computers are slow. It's expected.

» Most PCs last a good four to six years. If you perform regular maintenance and replace a few parts (hard drive, memory), you can make Mr. Computer last a few years longer. Eventually, you need a new computer.

» Another issue with older computers is software. After a time, Microsoft stops supporting the older versions of Windows. Security patches are no longer sent out, which is a risk. And your old programs may not be compatible with newer versions. These issues also prompt the need to buy a new computer.

TIP

» One place where you'll notice performance lagging is when you switch between running programs. If you detect a slight pause as the next program takes over the screen, memory has become sluggish. A solution is to install more memory. See the later section "Adding more RAM."

Unclogging the spyware

One of the villains in the slow-PC melodrama is spyware. It may not make your PC suddenly slow, but if you notice a decrease in performance over a short span of time, you probably have a system riddled with unwanted programs.

>> The Windows Security app is designed to hunt down and remove spyware. It should be on all the time in Windows 10. Refer to Book 4, Chapter 3 for details on accessing the Windows Security app and running its Virus & Threat Protection feature.

>> You can also run third-party antispyware programs. These may find ugly programs that Windows overlooks.

>> A telltale sign of spyware infection can be found by monitoring resources in the Task Manager and Resource Manager windows. In the Task Manager window, on the Processes tab, use the CPU column to sort the list of programs. Spyware populates the top part of that list, crippling your PC's power. The Resource Manager window can also be used to monitor specific programs that bring your PC's pace to a crawl. See Chapter 1 of this minibook for details.

Finding a memory leak

Don't bother putting a pan behind the PC; a memory leak causes no external mess. Instead, a memory leak consumes memory available inside the computer. It's a software thing: A program, either malware or a regular program with a bug, just keeps gobbling up RAM. The solution is to kill the program and stop using it until an upgrade or a replacement is found.

The best resource for finding memory leaks is the Resource Monitor tool, covered in Chapter 1 of this minibook. The Memory tab in Resource Monitor shows memory consumption increasing over time. That's one sign of a memory leak.

Speed Up Your PC

The old joke goes that you can greatly increase your PC's speed by plugging it into a power source with a higher voltage. Ha-ha. Of course, this trick doesn't work and you'd be silly to attempt it. That's because more realistic methods exist to improve PC performance and to address older, slower computer issues.

Performing regular maintenance

In Windows 10, most system maintenance is done for you, automatically. These chores include

>> Backing up

>> Installing system upgrades

>> Running antimalware software (Windows Security)

>> Optimizing the mass storage device

>> Checking the mass storage device for errors

You can ensure that each item is taken care of; each of these topics is covered elsewhere in this hefty tome. Pay heed that a lot of these issues deal with the mass storage device. That's because other parts of the computer don't really need cleaning. Well, you can wipe down the monitor every so often and take a vacuum to the air vents, but that's about it.

WARNING

>> If your computer, especially a laptop or tablet, features a touchscreen, ensure that you use the proper cleaning solution on the monitor. Avoid using abrasive chemicals, such as ammonia or alcohol.

>> Vacuuming out the PC's vents is a noble thing to do, helping air circulation and keeping the case cool. Especially if you have pets, vacuum the vents every month or so.

>> You can also clean inside the case, but it's not a routine thing to do. I take a small vacuum or a can of compressed air and clean the dust inside a PC console maybe once a year or whenever I perform an internal upgrade.

Upgrading the hard drive

A hard drive is a spinning disk. It rotates. It has moving parts. Because it's in motion, a hard drive is perhaps the most likely thing inside a PC to go bad and need replacement. You don't need to regularly replace a hard drive, but doing so eventually can give your computer more storage capacity as well as faster media.

>> Can you hear the hard drive? I'm not referring to the squirrel-chasing noise that most hard drives make when they're accessing information. Instead, be aware of squeaking sounds — like old brakes on a car. This noise means that the hard drive bearings might be ready to go.

>> Especially if Windows reports disk read errors, consider upgrading the hard drive.

>> Your best insurance against hard drive disaster is to back up your stuff. Refer to Book 4, Chapter 4.

>> Also see Chapter 2 of this minibook for details on replacing hard drives.

>> The hard drive issues covered in this section do not apply to an SSD (solid-state drive).

Adding more RAM

The best, fastest, and least expensive way to upgrade your PC is to add more memory. While you're at it, replace the installed memory with faster memory. Often, both activities are the same.

Your PC came with a given amount of RAM — say, 4GB. If you increase this amount, you give Windows and your programs more elbow room to do their magic. Trust me: Computers *love* more memory.

The upgrade from 4GB to 8GB or even 16GB is relatively easy to do. You replace the existing memory cards with newer cards. Book 2, Chapter 4 offers details. You can do the job yourself or hire someone else.

Book 2, Chapter 4 also covers accessing online memory merchants to purchase your PC's RAM upgrade. These websites feature scanning software that can determine which type of memory is best for your PC and provide you with a list of upgrade options.

AN UPGRADE TO AVOID

It's possible to replace a hard drive and upgrade memory, but what about the PC's processor? Can you just plug in a faster processor and be done with it? The answer is unclear.

The processor is married to the PC's motherboard as well as to other electronics in the system. You may be able to replace the processor without replacing the motherboard, which adds great expense to the process. If you can find a faster, compatible processor, the price won't be cheap. I would recommend comparing the price of the upgrade to a more effective memory upgrade.

Because a new processor is expensive, I strongly recommend that you have an experienced professional install it for you. Again, the reason is code: These chips ain't cheap. You don't want to risk messing up anything.

Putting ReadyBoost to work

A less expensive hardware upgrade that's still quite effective is to use Windows ReadyBoost technology to improve hard drive performance. ReadyBoost works by supplementing system memory and mass storage access with a portion of fast flash memory from a USB thumb drive.

To make ReadyBoost work, you need a thumb drive or media card with a capacity between 256MB and 32GB. Further, I recommend that you use a USB 3.0 thumb drive and attach it to a USB 3.0 port on the back of your PC. It's best to use the back because this thumb drive is dedicated to ReadyBoost; you won't use it for anything else.

After you have the thumb drive, follow these steps to use ReadyBoost on your PC:

1. **Plug the thumb drive into a USB port on your PC.**

You may see an AutoPlay notification appear. Dismiss the notification, though if you see a ReadyBoost option, choose it as a shortcut.

2. **Press the Windows+E keyboard shortcut to open a File Explorer window.**

3. **Choose This PC from the items listed on the left side of the window.**

You see an overview of all storage available to your computer. One of the items listed is the thumb drive you just inserted.

4. **Right-click on the thumb drive's icon in the This PC window.**

5. **Choose the Properties command.**

6. **In the drive's Properties dialog box, click the ReadyBoost tab.**

If you don't see the ReadyBoost tab, the thumb drive's technology isn't compatible with ReadyBoost. If the text on the ReadyBoost tab announces that your device is too sophisticated to use ReadyBoost, you're done. Otherwise, you see settings similar to the one shown in Figure 3-1.

7. **Choose the Use This Device option.**

Other settings presented need no further modification.

8. **Click OK.**

Your PC immediately starts using the thumb drive to improve performance. Don't be alarmed if its Capacity graphic in the This PC window turns red. That's the setup you want; nearly all the thumb drive's storage is used to improve PC performance.

Activate ReadyBoost on this drive (G:)

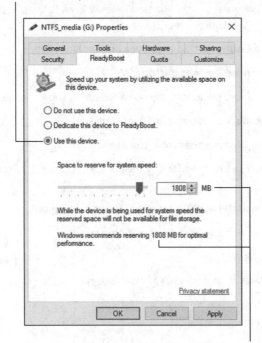

FIGURE 3-1:
ReadyBoost is
ready to boost.

Ensure that these two values match

>> Hybrid drives and SSDs won't benefit from ReadyBoost technology, so these drives either don't show the tab in their Properties dialog boxes or the message on the tab explains that ReadyBoost would be ineffective at improving drive performance.

>> For another performance boost, consider adding a second thumb drive to your PC and dedicating it as well to ReadyBoost.

>> You can use as many as eight thumb drives with ReadyBoost on a single PC.

Setting the number of processors

Your PC most likely sports a processor that has multiple cores. Or, it may have more than a single processor. To confirm that Windows is taking advantage of the extra processing power by setting the number of processors available to Windows, follow these steps:

1. Press the Windows+R keyboard shortcut to conjure the Run dialog box.

2. Type msconfig and press Enter.

The System Configuration tool appears. Refer to Book 3, Chapter 3 for more details on this useful utility.

3. **In the System Configuration window, click the Boot tab.**

4. **Click the Advanced Options button.**

   The BOOT Advanced Options dialog box appears, as shown in Figure 3-2.

5. **Place a check mark by Number of Processors.**

6. **Choose the highest number from the menu button.**

   The highest number is coincidentally the number of processor cores inside your PC.

7. **Click OK to close the BOOT Advanced Options dialog box.**

8. **Click OK to close the System Configuration window.**

9. **Click Restart Now.**

   Windows restarts so that the changes will take effect.

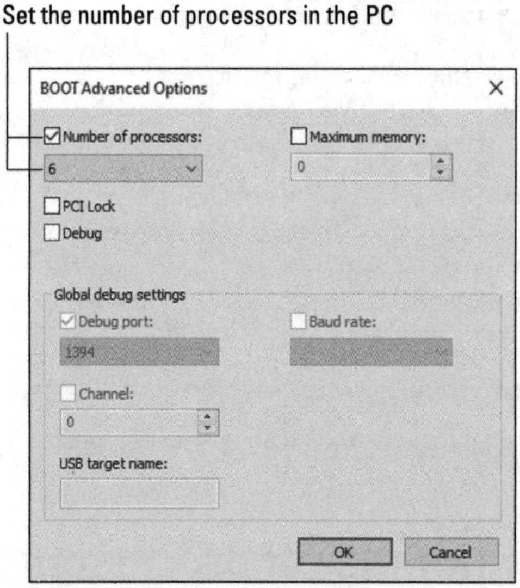

Set the number of processors in the PC

FIGURE 3-2: Set the number of processors here.

The performance boost in your PC from setting the proper number of processors may not be noticeable, at least not dramatically. But at least by following these steps, you ensure that Windows is using the PC's hardware better than it did before.

TIP

» To confirm that the change has taken hold, repeat Steps 1 through 4 in this section. If the number of processors set remains the way you changed it (in Step 7), then it worked.

» This modification doesn't physically alter the number of processors inside the PC. It does, however, direct Windows to use them more effectively.

Disabling background services

TECHNICAL STUFF

A background service runs all the time. It's one of those busy things inside a computer, most of which are necessary but some of which may not be. You can disable these background services to see a slight boost in performance, though the task is a bit technical.

Table 3-1 lists a bunch of services that Windows runs. You might be able to disable some or all of these services to help improve your computer's performance.

TABLE 3-1: **Services You Can Disable**

Service Name	Effect of Disabling
FAX	You can't send faxes, but if you don't send them in the first place, there's no point in wasting resources on this service.
Function Discovery Provider Host	Windows Media Center doesn't function properly.
Internet Connection Sharing (ICS)	You cannot share your computer's Internet access with another computer. If you don't know what I mean, disable this service.
Offline Files	You can't access the offline files if you're using offline files, and you probably aren't.
Remote Access Connection Manager	You cannot use dialup virtual private networking (VPN).
Remote Procedure Call (RPC) Locator	None that I'm aware of.
Remote Registry	You cannot modify your computer's Registry over a network.
Smart Card	You cannot use a smart card to authenticate computer access. This service requires a smart card slot on your computer. (A smart card isn't a memory card.)
Smart Card Removal Policy	You cannot use a smart card for computer access.
TCP/IP NetBIOS Helper	None, unless you're certain that you're using legacy NetBIOS networking programs. (You probably aren't.)

(continued)

TABLE 3-1 *(continued)*

Service Name	Effect of Disabling
Telephony	Your dialup networking may not work.
Themes	You use Windows in a rather plain, old-fashioned view. Fancy desktop features are disabled (transparency and shadows, for example).
WebClient	The FrontPage web design program may not work.

To disable a service, follow these steps:

1. **Tap the Windows key.**

2. **Type** services

3. **Choose the Services App item from the list of search results.**

   The Services console appears.

4. **Locate a service to disable.**

   Use Table 3-1 to help you decide which services to disable.

   Click the Name column heading to ensure that the services are sorted alphabetically.

   TIP

5. **Double-click the service to display its Properties dialog box.**

6. **Choose Disabled as the Startup type.**

   By choosing Disabled, you prevent the service from starting when the computer starts.

   Make a note of the service's original state: Automatic or Manual. Just in case you need to reenable the service, you should know how it was configured before you changed it.

7. **Click OK to confirm your choice and close the dialog box.**

   When you're concerned about compatibility, or that your computer may work improperly after disabling a service, restart Windows. When the system starts up, try it out for a while to ensure that things are working well. Then continue or, if there's a problem, reenable the service to Automatic or Manual or whatever the previous setting was.

8. **Repeat Steps 5 through 7 as necessary.**

9. **Close the Services console when you're done.**

The services shown in Table 3-1 comprise only part of the entire list of services running in your computer. You may be able to safely disable other services that, specifically, would have no negative effect on your PC. It all depends on what you do with your computer and Windows.

Of course, the possibility always exists that disabling a service has no effect on the computer, but when disabled it causes no noticeable improvement in performance. That's the case with many services, which is why you don't see more of them listed in Table 3-1.

WARNING

>> If disabling a service causes your PC to run more slowly or programs to function improperly, reenable the service.

>> Don't randomly disable services. Some are required for your computer to properly function. If you notice anything odd after disabling a service, reenable it.

Index

fragmentation, 62–64
front speaker jacks, 162

G

gaming keyboards, 163
gateways (routers)
  configuring, 203–206
  connecting, 202–203
  defined, 199
  wireless, 200
GB (gigabyte), 402
Gbps (gigabits per second), 201
General tab, System Configuration Utility
   (MSCONFIG), 266–267
GFI (ground fault interrupter) switch, 34
Gibson Research website, 370
gigabyte (GB), 402
glare, 89
Google Chrome, 351
GPS radio, 347
GPT (GUID Partition Table) format, 81
graphics processing unit (GPU), 87, 231
graphics system, 83–88
  connecting, 85–87
  display adapters, 87–88
  overview, 84–85
  terminology, 84
ground fault interrupter (GFI) switch, 34
GUID Partition Table (GPT) format, 81

H

hard disk drives (HDD), 49, 64, 377
  buying, 128
  removing, 125
  upgrading, 418–419
hardware issues
  Device Manager, 257–264
    dealing with errant hardware, 261
    disabling devices, 264
    looking for hardware in Settings
     app vs., 259–261

opening, 257–259
    updating driver software, 261–263
  with making changes, 9
  overview, 12
  random restarting and, 231
  setting permissions, 344–347
  software vs., 11
  wiping out data, 71
hardware troubleshooter, 160
HDD. *see* hard disk drives
HDMI (High-Definition Multimedia Interface)
   port, 86
hibernation
  defined, 129
  issues, 44–45
  network access and, 221
  on Power menu, 229
hiding, file extensions, 185–186
hiding mouse, 171
High-Definition Multimedia Interface (HDMI)
   port, 86
hijacking infections, 364
hives, Registry, 318
hubs (switches), 199
hybrid sleep, 44, 129

I

icons
  for compressed files, 409
  computer location, 348
  for drives, 54
  for Internet connections, 212
  malfunctioning hardware warning, 261
  microphone, 347
  on–off master control, 343
  Padlock icon, 22–23
  Power menu, 228–230
  shortcut, 182
  UAC warnings, 271
  used in this book, 3
improper shutdowns, 227, 236
inbound firewall rules, 373–374

About the Author

Dan Gookin has been writing about technology for nearly three decades. He combines his love of writing with his gizmo fascination to create books that are informative, entertaining, and not boring. Having written over 170 titles, and with 12 million copies in print translated into over 30 languages, Dan can attest that his method of crafting computer tomes seems to work.

Perhaps his most famous title is the original *DOS For Dummies*, published in 1991. It became the world's fastest-selling computer book, at one time moving more copies per week than the *New York Times* number-one bestseller (though, as a reference, it could not be listed on the Times' Best Sellers list). That book spawned the entire line of *For Dummies* books, which remains a publishing phenomenon to this day.

Dan's most popular titles include *PCs For Dummies, Laptops For Dummies,* and *Microsoft Word For Dummies.* He also maintains the vast and helpful website www.wambooli.com.

Dan holds a degree in Communications/Visual Arts from the University of California, San Diego. He lives in the Pacific Northwest, where he spends time annoying people who deserve it.

Publisher's Acknowledgments

Acquisitions Editor: Kelsey Baird
Managing Editor: Michelle Hacker
Senior Project Editor: Paul Levesque
Copy Editor: Becky Whitney

Production Editor: Tamilmani Varadharaj
Cover Image: Maxx-Studio / Shutterstock

Take dummies with you everywhere you go!

Whether you are excited about e-books, want more from the web, must have your mobile apps, or are swept up in social media, dummies makes everything easier.

Find us online!

Leverage the power

Dummies is the global leader in the reference category and one of the most trusted and highly regarded brands in the world. No longer just focused on books, customers now have access to the dummies content they need in the format they want. Together we'll craft a solution that engages your customers, stands out from the competition, and helps you meet your goals.

Advertising & Sponsorships

Connect with an engaged audience on a powerful multimedia site, and position your message alongside expert how-to content. Dummies.com is a one-stop shop for free, online information and know-how curated by a team of experts.

- Targeted ads
- Video
- Email Marketing
- Microsites
- Sweepstakes sponsorship

20 MILLION PAGE VIEWS EVERY SINGLE MONTH

15 MILLION UNIQUE VISITORS PER MONTH

43% OF ALL VISITORS ACCESS THE SITE VIA THEIR MOBILE DEVICES

700,000 NEWSLETTER SUBSCRIPTIONS TO THE INBOXES OF

300,000 UNIQUE INDIVIDUALS EVERY WEEK